Forest Haven Soldiers: The *Civil War* Veterans of Sleeping Bear & Surrounding Leelanau

ISBN 0-9679259-0-8

Library of Congress Control Number: 00-131665

Published by Overmyer Historicals
Grand Rapids, MI USA

Forest Haven Soldiers: The Civil War Veterans of Sleeping Bear & Surrounding Leelanau

Acknowledgments -

The Official Records of the Union and Confederate Armies 1889 Washington Archives, Library of Congress, National Archives & Records Administration, "Michigan in the War" by John Robertson 1882, Elvin L. Sprague's 1903 History of Grand Traverse and Leelanaw Counties, Record of Service of Michigan Volunteers in the Civil War - Michigan Soldiers and Sailors Lansing MI 1915, U.S. Army Military History Institute Carisle Barracks PA, Collections in the Leelanau Historical Museum, Empire Area Museum, Preston M. Smith 1961 Partial Listing Of The Civil War Veterans From Leelanau County, Roy H. Steffens Military Records 1968 Grand Traverse Pioneer & Historical Society, The Historical Collections of the State Library of Michigan, the Grand Rapids Public Library, Detroit Public Library and Western Michigan University. The State Archives in Lansing, and various other State Archives had several references I was able to utilize to compile information on these men. The National Archives & Records Administration in Washington DC, The Traverse Area District Library, the Leland, Northport & Empire Library, Osterlin Library of Northwestern Michigan College, The Clements Library & Bently Historical Library at The University of Michigan, Grand Valley State University Library, Clarke Historical Library of Central Michigan University, Michigan State University Libraries, A History of the Grand Traverse Region by M.L. Leach 1883, The Traverse Region Historical & Descriptive 1884 Chicago H.R. Page & Co., "Remembering Yesterday" collected by Kasson Heritage Group 1976, "Remembering Empire Through Pictures" by Empire Area Heritage Group 1978 D. Taghon, "Beautiful Glen Arbor Township, Facts, Fantasy, & Fotos" 1977 by Robert Dwight Rader, "Some Other Day (Remembering Empire)" by Empire Area Heritage Group, Michigan Cemetery Atlas of the Library of Michigan in Lansing, Michigan Pioneer & Historical Collections 1907, "Michigan Soldiers in the Civil War" by Frederick D. Williams 1960/1994 Bureau of Michigan History - Michigan Department of State, "A Brief History of the Tenth Michigan Cavalry" 1905 by General Luther Trowbridge, Don L. Harvey's "Michigan in the Civil War" WWWeb Page, Kinship Tales: Grand Traverse Area Genealogical Society, Saugatuck Historical Society & Library, History of Solon by Carol Drzewiecki, Grand Traverse Herald, Leelanau Enterprise, Civil War Centennial Observance Commission, "The War, for those in the Traverse area" by Evelyn Tolley Buckingham 1991 Brevard NC, and Frederick Dyer's Compendium of the War of the Rebellion 1908 Torch Press / 1994 Republished Broadfoot Publishing, Morningside Press Wilmington, NC.

Special acknowledgment to the works of Roy H. Steffens 1968 Military Records Project, Preston M. Smith 1961 Civil War Veterans Listing, Bruce Catton, Julia Terry Dickinson, Larry Wakefield, Dr. M.L. Leach, Edmund M. Littell, Al Barnes, Nan Helm, Dave Taghon, and many more listed in the reference index.

Special thanks to my family and to Steve Harold of the Manistee Museum and the Grand Traverse Pioneer & Historical Society, to Laura Quackenbush and Claudia Gaudschaal at the Leelanau Historical Museum, Dave Taghon and the staff at the Empire Area Museum, to U.S. Park Service retiree Earl Plowman, Kim Mann, Bill Herd, Joan DeYoung, Neal Bullington, Betty Welch, and volunteer Bill Valentine of the U.S. Park Service Sleeping Bear Dunes National Lakeshore, in Glen Arbor: Bob Sutherland, Barb Siepker, Bill Thompson, Patricia Hagerman, Ben Whitfield, Norm Wheeler, Elizabeth Edwards, the T.C. County Veterans Office, Old Settlers' Picnic Assoc., Bill O'Brien of the Traverse City Record – Eagle, Deborah D.Cole, Jill Hill, and to Amy Hubble of the Leelanau Enterprise.

My wife and son: Jill & Nathaniel Glen Overmyer for joining me on my research location visits during our D.H. Day camping trips.

My Dad & Mom: Leonard & Betty Overmyer for fostering a commitment to Veterans affairs.

My Dad, (Past American Legion State Commander: Leonard Overmyer II), showed me the Glen Arbor Township Cemetery (graveyard) off Forest Haven Road many years ago during a hunting trip. It was a tradition for us, and sometimes some of the local Glen Lake Students, to pay their respects to this peaceful and undisturbed "Resting Place in the Woods" each Spring. (By bringing in a few flowers & flags for the families & Veterans that were laid to rest there). As a Chaplain in the Sons of the American Legion, & member of the Sons of the Amvets, I often visit the site on Memorial Week-end to place flags on two marked graves belonging to Civil War Veteran's E.W. Trumbull and Dan'l Parker of the 14th & 15th Michigan Infantry. There are also several more unmarked veterans' graves here. The descendents of Edmund Trumbull and Joseph Price also cared for this area.

My Grandparents: Bruce & Lillian Marie Overmyer who encouraged learning about the histories of our family that set a basis for researching about other areas of history. Also my Grandfathers before him: Alfred, Homer, Henry, Hugh, Jacob, Capt. John George, John George, George...

My Brothers & Sisters: Ginger, Sherri, Larry, Jackson, & Leann. For sharing a wonderful childhood in Leelanau County, MI. (In memory of Shannon)

Glen Lake Teacher: Julia Norconk. For spending the summer of 1972 teaching me how to read.

Glen Lake Principal: Dale Sutherland for his encouragement.

The Class of 1982 and all the students of Glen Lake Community Schools, many of whom are descendents of the people in this book. Also my friends and Alumni of Grand Valley State University.

The dedicated Home-room Teachers of my youth: Julia Norconk, Marion Manning, Lorraine Richardson, John Charles Thomas, Harold O'Brien, Ted Sweirad, & Richard Plowman. Also to Bill Bolton, Perry Jones, Jack Radar, Fae Shalda, Lou Alonzi, and Audrey Carmichael for their goodwill toward the students.

Cousin Jack K. Overmyer, Author of "A Stupendous Effort: The 87th Indiana In The War Of The Rebellion" Indiana University Press: for inspiring the idea.

The WWII Veterans and members in the Copemish Read/Osborne American Legion Post 531, Leelanau County American Legion Post 199, Leelanau VFW Post 7731, Eagletown American Legion Post 120, and the Mesick AMVETS Post 120.

G.A.R. Post 168 & 399, and the many Overmyer's who served in the Civil War and inspired my desire to learn more about this era.

Additional thanks to those who helped in the research of more information including: Steve Harold; Laura Quackenbush and the staff at the Leelanau Historical Museum including Claudia Gaudschaal, Mary Wilson, Maria Johnson, and Mark Livengood; Lou & Elizabeth Plummer and Bill Kemperman of the Saugatuck Historical Society as well as Everard Thomas, Kit Lane, and Jan Wolbrink; Gordon Olson and the staff at the Ryerson Historical Room of the Grand Rapids Public Library; David L. Poremba at the Burton Historical Collection of the Detroit Public Library; The Empire Heritage Group & Museum; Ann Swaney at the Osterlin Library of Northwestern Michigan College as well as Prof. James Press and Dr. Steven Siciliano; Curator Michael Winey of the U.S. Army Military History Institute Carisle Barracks, PA; Frank Boles at the Clarke Historical Library of Central Michigan University; Diane L. Hatfield, Marilyn McNitt, Jennifer Jacobs and Kathy Marquis at the Bentley Historical Library of The University of Michigan; Mark Harvey and Charlie Cusack at the State Archives of Michigan as well as Mary Zimmeth and Julie Meyerle; Richard Harrison of the Wisconsin Veteran's Museum; Andy Kraushaar of the State Historical Society of Wisconsin; Also to: Carol Drzewiecki, Donald Pratt, Joseph M. LaVanture, John S. Dorsey, Donald L., Jon F. & Paul C. Dechow, Rose & Fred Dechow, Darlene Sims, Albert K. Spafford, Carol Sanctorum, Bertha Werbinski, Mike Sheridan, Ken Stormer, Paula (Price) Radant, Cici (LaRue) Morse, Marcella Rice (Nemeskel), Mary Ellen Hadjsky, Lt. Col. Ervan L. Amidon, Richard Kulando, Dr. William Anderson, Kim Crawford (16th MI), Mrs. Al Pifer, Dorothy Lanham, Ray and Don Welch, Bob Wilhelm, Bob Wilson, Mrs. Richard Payment, Matt Switlik (Loomis' Battery), Gerome Peebles & Richard Cummings (1st MI/ 102nd Col. Inf.), Mark St.John (20th MI), George Weeks, Grand Traverse Area Genealogical Society, Vicki Wilson's Leelanau County US GenWeb Home Page, Kim Huttonlocher, Brian Russell, Morean Ryan, Western Michigan Genealogical Society, Charles McLaughlin, Bill Parker, Neal Breagh (Sons of the Union Veterans), Ann Bixby, Avis D. Wolfe, Elaine Burgin-Orvis, Christine Byron, Bill Wilcox (U.S. Nat. Guard), The Historical Society of Pennsylvania, The Camera Shop of Traverse City, Anthony Casciani of Traverse City Print & Copy, all of the wonderful people who sent letters and provided family histories, (.....& The Doobie Brothers: For the traveling music).

Historical Re-enactors
Civil War Muster, Jackson MI
(Leonard G. Overmyer III)

Forest Haven Soldiers: The Civil War Veterans of Sleeping Bear & Surrounding Leelanau

Sections:

Civil War Veterans of the Sleeping Bear Dunes National Lakeshore
(Courtesy Leelanau Historical Museum)

Forest Haven Soldiers: The Civil War Veterans of Sleeping Bear & Surrounding Leelanau

Introduction -

"Forest Haven Soldiers" is the result of a special desire to record information about the very brave souls who lived in our communities and served in the U.S. Civil War. These early settlers were likely as appreciative of the beauty of Leelanau County then, as we are now. They no doubt shared stories of this tranquil area with their comrades as we see many men from the same units, and others who served in the same locations, traveling up to the Leelanau area after the Civil War. It was a time where they could live off the land and were beholden to none; a chance to live on a harbor that was always home.

While my focus began in the Glen Lake area of the Sleeping Bear Dunes National Lakeshore, it also expanded into the rest of Leelanau County and surrounding Grand Traverse Region. Most of the Glen Arbor area soldiers served in the 10th MI Cavalry and in the 15th MI Infantry. Other Glen Lake soldiers had joined numerous units back in their original home state or throughout Michigan. Numerous men served together from Northern Leelanau County & other surrounding areas that are certainly worth mentioning. Many in the Northport area served in the 1st MI Sharpshooters and the 26th MI Infantry with others from Traverse City. Their unit's Civil War Flags are held in reserve in Lansing, MI and replicas are on display at the Capital.

Many men enlisted singly or with a companion, walking to Grand Rapids or Chicago where regiments were forming.[1] For instance, at the start of the war, a group of 30 men from Manistee enlisted with Co. D. of the 37th Illinois.[2] Transportation by boat was also a more able means in that day. Men sailed over in groups to Wisconsin to join the Union Army. Several others joined in the 1st New York Light Artillery / Chicago Light Infantry.

The two main G.A.R. (Grand Army of the Republic) Veteran Posts in our area were the Murray Post # 168 of Glen Lake, active from 1883-1913, and the Woolsey Post # 399 of Northport, active from 1884*-1921, (*though records show Northport's G.A.R. didn't formally organize until 1889, they were active since ~ 1884). Other Regional Posts included: Four in Grand Traverse especially Traverse City McPherson Post # 18, Andrew Clark Post # 423 in Lake Ann, E.P. Case Post # 372 in Benzonia (to which the book "Never Call Retreat" by Bruce Catton was dedicated to), Carver Post # 123 in Frankfort, there were four Posts in Manistee and seven in Wexford Counties. (A few of the Michigan G.A.R. Post buildings still standing as of 1999 include Detroit, the Colgrove Post in Marshall, the Dewey Post 60 in Leslie, & the Sunfield Post.)

Benzonia local author Bruce Catton in his book, *Waiting for the Morning Train*, described many of these men. "The Civil War veterans were men set apart. On formal occasions they wore blue uniforms with brass buttons and black campaign hats... whatever they may have been as young men they had unassuming natural dignity in old age. They were pillars, not so much of the church (although most of them were devout communicants) as of the community; keepers of its patriotic traditions, the living embodiment, so to speak, of what it most deeply believed about the nation's greatness and high destiny."[5] Catton also points out the use of Lilac blossoms in Memorial Day (Decoration Day) observances.

In 1998, while doing volunteer activities on behalf of the Sons of the American Legion & AMVETS, I was invited by John E. Obermeyer, Department of Michigan Graves Registration Officer for the Sons of Union Veterans of the Civil War, to help record some of these brave souls into the National Register. While researching the histories of these men, I found so much lost memoirs that I felt compelled to tell their stories.

I hold a special appreciation to the Military Record compilation done by Roy H. Steffens back in 1968 and 1973 that is in the holdings of the Grand Traverse Pioneer & Historical Society headed by Steve Harold. This compilation was an excellent reference point even though it contained some errors, which this book has helped correct and update. Many Civil War records are incomplete and inaccurate in part due to the lack of educational opportunities that existed during that period. There is often confusion on many of the home area listings because many township names are used more than once in Michigan (i.e. Bingham is not only repeated, but was in the process of being formally organized during this period). It also gets difficult when the soldiers left "Centerville" Township in Leelanau County to travel down state and enlist with others from "Centreville," MI or enlisted at Solon in Kent County and later lived in Solon, Leelanau Co. Some of these names may have then become intermittently used in past records and are unintentionally credited here. During this long research, many additional area veterans that had been unknown were discovered. There are also numerous soldiers buried in unmarked graves in Leelanau County, including Northport and the Glen Arbor Township Cemetery that is within the Sleeping Bear Dunes National Lakeshore.

As mentioned, several men who had served in the same locations during the Civil War traveled up to Leelanau after the war, no doubt, in part, due to family ties and the stories of the beauty of our area told to them by our local soldiers. These later residents are listed further in the text. The actions of our local soldiers are listed based on their unit histories during their time of service. Where the time of service was not specified, a general unit history is given. It should be understood in those instances that the soldier may have served in all, or just part of, the unit's time of service.

The following pages primarily list those veterans that have been identified with the Sleeping Bear / Glen Lake area and may include parts of Centerville and Leland Townships, (though many of those area men are listed with Northport). Most of the Glen Lake area is focused around the Townships of Cleveland, Empire, Glen Arbor, Kasson and Solon. The remaining being listed with Northport or under Miscellaneous Leelanau County, which may also include some men from Glen Lake. Whenever more than four Glen Lake soldiers served in the same Regiment, a general Unit service history is listed.

The Civil War histories begin with the two main units from the Sleeping Bear / Glen Lake area: The 10th MI Cavalry and the 15th MI Infantry, followed by the 26th MI Infantry and 1st MI Sharpshooters The remaining Michigan soldiers are listed by numerical order, while soldiers who served in other States are listed alphabetically by Township. A Reference Index is also included at the end of the book. Wherever possible, the final resting-place of these brave soldiers have been listed. Several of the named Cemeteries have long been abandoned and unfortunately, some are with little trace that they once existed.

8

President Abraham Lincoln   U.S. Civil War
Photo from the National Archives & Records Administration, Washington D.C.

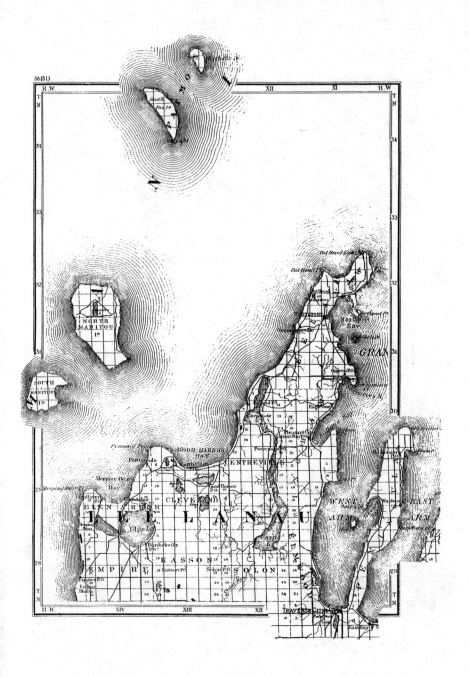

Forest Haven Soldiers: The Civil War Veterans of Sleeping Bear & Surrounding Leelanau

We begin in a peaceful place in the woods among the tall timber and wildflowers of Leelanau County. A site, by Forest Haven Road and M-22, where lies the old Glen Arbor Township Cemetery. It was used primarily in the 1800's and beginning of the 1900's for the early pioneers of the area. This quiet location holds the final resting-place of several Civil War soldiers. Apart from the Revolutionary War, these men served in perhaps the most important conflict in our Nation's history. This cemetery was once described (by historical writer Al Barnes) in this manner:

> "At the edge of the village of Glen Arbor is an abandoned and overgrown cemetery. Only a few graves can be identified. Trees have grown about them and a tangle of underbrush makes walking difficult. A patch of myrtle, once a decoration for someone's grave, has spread across the cemetery roadway. Here and there a rusted G.A.R. sign can be seen. Memory of many people who lie there is gone. The cemetery tells a part of the history of the village, which should be salvaged and, in some way, somehow, made to live again in the minds of the present residents."[4]

There are no monuments here that stand to honor their accomplishments. No flags that fly in remembrance of their sacrifices. No care given to their final resting place. Yet these and other area men faced the most deadly and challenging events in our Nation's history. "One of every six Michigan soldiers would die as a result of war service."[5] Of our area men in the 26th MI Infantry, this number would be one of every three. The service of these brave souls are listed within the pages of this book along with other local comrades.

Before we go further into the lives of these men, let us digress a moment to tell about the pre-Civil War years in our area of Leelanau County in order to give an idea of the beauty these early pioneers were experiencing before they went off to serve their country.

Until the mid 1800's the beautiful peninsula now known as Leelanau County was a forest-covered wilderness blend of foliage, lakes, sand bluffs, and streams. Each spring, great flocks of pigeons would frequent the region. Along the shores were nestled a few Ottawa and Ojibway Indian villages, whose peaceful inhabitants hunted and fished, and planted their small clearings during the summer. Later they would travel south to the Kalamazoo River to pass the winter months.[6] Many years before white men came to live in the great forests of northern Michigan, the beautiful areas around Grand Traverse were often referred to as the land of Muh-quh Se-bing (The Bear Walk) by the Indians who hunted for game in the forests.[7]

Travel by white frontiersmen (Che-mo-ka-mon) was done mostly by boat on the Great Lakes and the Manitou (the Great Spirit) Islands served as a resting-place. In 1773 the trader St. Pierre wrote about the Manitou Islands in a report:

> "We came too anchor under the lea of the Northmost of these islands it looking blak to North I did not think it prudent to proceed farther, for there is severall shoals off from Wabashana points which would be impossible to avoid in a dark night, at 12 this night the wind more moderate we weighed anchor and kept under Easy sail all this night."[8]

There is an Indian burial ground by Good Harbor Creek east from North Unity and a trail ran along the south shore of the western lobe of Glen Lake that was yet still distinctly discernible in 1856. Along this trail was an Indian Village a few rods west of the south end of the bridge which now spans the narrows. Pottery was once recovered over a 1/2 acre area at that point. A similar find was made across the bridge about sixty rods northeast of the north end of the bridge. There were at least 5 Indian Villages identified in Leelanau County and 3 burial grounds (including Shabasson's Chippewa). One village was at the site of the D.H. Day Campground. As late as the early 1900's, Indians remained in the Empire area. They made camps just north of the South Bar Lake outlet and traveled to Pearl Lake for the winter.[9] Others traveled to the shores each summer by canoe to sell goods. Near Burdickville, on the road to Maple City, was a large rock with a worn center that is said to have been used by the Indians for grinding their corn.[10]

Sleeping Bear Point, upon which is an immense sand dune, derived its name from a clump of trees that appeared as a Sleeping Bear when viewed from the Lake, serving as a widely recognized land mark for early navigators.[11] It also has many traditions. One of which was that the "Bear" was a scene of a terrific battle "in the long ago." There is reference to a battle on the dunes at Sleeping Bear Point between the Ottawa's and Prairies in past folklore.[12] Another is the Legend of Sleeping Bear: Across the great waters, in the land now called Wisconsin, there was a great fire. A mother bear and her two cubs took to the water to escape. The swim across to Michigan became too much for the little cubs and they sank to become the location of the Manitou Islands before they could reach the shore. The exhausted mother bear reached the shore but was so saddened at the loss of her cubs that she lay on the shore in grief and became covered in sand while keeping vigil for her two lost cubs, becoming the "Sleeping Bear."

D.H. Day Cabin in Glen Haven, MI
(Courtesy U.S. Park Service, Sleeping Bear Dunes
National Lakeshore)

12

In the way this shining dune looks west toward the storms and the sunsets there is a profound serenity, an unworried affirmation that comes from seeing beyond time and mischance.

– Bruce Catton, *Waiting for the Morning Train.*[13]

Early photograph at Aral (Otter Creek), MI
(Courtesy U.S. Park Service, Sleeping Bear Dunes
National Lakeshore)

The Glen Lake region owes its first developments to the wealth of timber that abounded and its excellent situation as a summer resort as well as a winter beauty spot. As the early settlers arrived they saw sites such as the Sleeping Bear and the vast forests. They saw an open clearing which, completely surrounded by trees, they found to be the council grounds of the Indians - a veritable glen in the dense verdure. The word "glen" therefore became important in the minds of the early settlers. (It is of interest here to note that many bears prowled the heavy forest and created several incidents, with the results that it was first called Bear Lake. Its' name was soon changed, however, to Glen Lake.)[14] In the 1830's a survey crew led by Sylvester Sibley documented the northern area of Glen Lake.[15] In the Otter Creek (Aral) area, Orange Risdon and L.S. Scranton were early surveyors.[16]

Then, as now, they heard the morning songs of the **Whippoorwills** among the forests of Sleeping Bear Bay; Loons echoed from the secluded beaches of Port Oneida, to the inland lakes of Otter Creek; and at sunset, the cry of the Bald Eagle filled the North Manitou skies.

In 1839 Princeton graduate, Reverend Peter Dougherty, established Old Mission among the Indians, including "Medicine Man" Manitowaba. (This was later removed to New Mission - Omena in 1853 where,[17] according to the early settlers, Rev. Dougherty was responsible for the present name of the village. It was his custom, when approached by the Indians with information or a question, to reply in Indian tongue, "O-me-nah?" which meant "Is it so?" This amused the Indians, who suggested the given name).[18] Reverend Dougharty also translated several prayers in native Ojibway.

These included a hymnal published by The American Tract Society about 1845 and prayers from the "Easy Lessons on Scriptural History" by Reverend Peter Dougherty in 1847, (John Westfall and Co. for Presbyterian Board of Foreign Missions).[19]

HYMN: 1 From all that dwell below the skies, Let the Creator's praise arise; Let the Redeemer's name be sung Through every land, by every tongue. 2 Eternal are thy mercies, Lord, Eternal truth attends thy word; Thy praise shall sound from shore to shore Till suns shall rise and set no more. 3 Praise God, from whom all blessings flow; Praise him, all creatures here below; Praise him above, ye heavenly hoist; Praise Father, Son, and Holy Ghost.
Nugumowin: 1 Ku-ken-u a-king a-a-jig, Tu-ma-mo-yu-wu-gan-dum-og, She-nu-nu-gum-o-tou-a-wat, Ga-ge-zhe-kum-ag-o-wa-jin. 2 Ka-ge-nik tab-wa-mu-gut-on, E-neu ke-dik-e-to-win-un, Tu-mud-wa-non-da-goz-e-wug, Miz-e ga-ma-mo-yu-wa-jig. 3 Ma-mo-yu-wum-a-ta, ma-bum, Wan-je-sha-wan-da-goz-e-yung, Wa-os-e-mint, wa-gwis-e-mint, Gia Pa-niz-it, O-je-shag.

THE LORD'S PRAYER: Our Father, who art in Heaven, hallowed be thy Name; Thy kingdom come; Thy will be done on earth as it is in Heaven; Give us this day our daily bread; and forgive us our trespasses, as we forgive those who trespass against us; and lead us not into temptation; but deliver us from evil, for Thine is the Kingdom, and the Power, and the Glory, forever and ever. Amen.
Ojibway: No-sa-non ish-pe-ming a-yah-yun gwa-tah-me-quan-dah-gwuk ke-de-zhe-ne-kah-zo-win; Ke-do-ge-mah-we-win tuh-pe-ah-yah-muh-gud a-zhe-min-wan-duh-mun; mah-no tuh-e-zhe-wa-bud o-mah ah-keng, ish-pe-ming gi-ya; me-zhe-she-nom suh non-goom ke-zhe-guk kuh-ba ge-zhik kah-o-buh-(q)ua-zhe-guh-ne-me-yong, gi-ya wa-be-nah-mah we-she-non eu nim-bah-tah-e-zhe-wa-be-ze-ne-nah-nin, e-zhe-wa-be-nah-mah-wung-e-dwah e-gu ma-je-do-duh-we yuh-man-ge-jig; ka-go guh-gwa-de-ba-ne-me-she-kong-in ning-uh-je zhe-sho-be-ze-yong; gi-ya me-tah-gwa-ne-mah-we-she-nom muh-je ah-ye-we-shun; ken suh ke-te-ban-don eu o-ge-mah-we-win, gi-ya eu kush-ke-a-we-ze-win, gi-ya eu be-she-gan-dah-go-ze-win, kah-ge-nig gi-ya kah-ge-nig. Ah-men.

It is said that when Reverend Dougherty first came to New Mission (Omena) that he found Apple trees great in girth, indicating that they had been grown from seeds brought by the early Frenchmen who likely stopped on the shores of Leelanau.[20]

NEAR GLEN ARBOR, SHORES OF GLEN LAKE

In the year of 1840, Walter W. Barton erected a dock on South Manitou Island followed in 1846 by his brother-in-laws, Nicholas and Simeon Pickard, and a fisherman named Carson Burfiend came from Germany who would eventually settle at Port Oneida. That year, Indian Agent Henry R. Schoolcraft designated the name of Leelanau County to the peninsula. This was a name he used for an Indian girl in one of his books, Leelinau or The Lost Daughter.[21] Many also attribute it to an Indian name meaning "Land of Delight." This can also be ascribed to the French words meaning land in the lee of the prevailing winds over Lake Michigan: Lee-lan-eau.[22] The name also appears in Longfellow's "Hiawatha," who got his Indian lore from Schoolcraft.[23]

In 1847 John LaRue/Larue (Dec. 6, 1814 - Dec. 21, 1897) came from Chicago to the Manitou Islands in search of better health. As mentioned, the Islands had Pier's owned by Pickard & Barton. The lighthouse was kept by a man named Clark and there were a few fishermen on the North Manitou Island.[24] A trapper named Nazaros Dona camped near Carp River (Leland).[25] The next year (1848) LaRue moved his establishment over to the mainland, locating at Glen Arbor, what was then called Sleeping Bear Bay.[26] He built a log cabin near where the Crystal River empties into Lake Michigan, on land now occupied by the Leelanau Schools.[27]

In 1848 Rev. George N. Smith traveled with Indians in a birch bark canoe from Kalamazoo to Mackinaw. The next year (1849) Rev. Smith, Teacher James McLaughlin, Blacksmith William H. Case (McLaughlin's brother-in-law), Farmer's Assistant George Pierson (A veteran of the War of 1812), and their families traveled by schooner to Grand Traverse Bay and landed in Northport to establish the second Indian Mission in the region. The Indians would also know this area as Waukazooville. That first year they decided that it was proper to celebrate Independence Day. Unfortunately, they had no flag so George Pierson gave up his red flannel shirt for the stripes, Mrs. McLaughlin gave cloth for the white, and the *boys used a pot of lead colored paint & laundry indigo bluing for the rest![28]

* Several of the McLaughlin's, and their distant Cousins, went on to serve their Country in the Civil War and a few are listed throughout this book including: David McLaughlin who later served in the 1st MI Eng. & Mech., James McLaughlin in the 10th MI Cav., Rob & Thomas McLaughlin in the 1st MI Sharpshooters, also John McLaughlin served in the 26th MI Inf. and Patrick McLaughlin would become Captain of the 16th MI Inf. and later took a commission as 1st Lt. for the 1st / 102nd Colored Infantry where he was killed in action at South Carolina in the final year of the war.

In the summer of 1850 two sisters on their way from the Manitou Islands to Traverse City (Mrs. H.D. Campbell & Mrs. Hillery) stopped at the little settlement. They were the first other white woman they had seen in sixteen months. They also received mail about twice a year.[29]

In April of 1851 the steamboat "Michigan" arrived with provisions at Northport. That summer, John Dorsey (who later served in the 15th MI Inf.) located at Glen Arbor, (his wife was Elizabeth.).[30] Alonzo Slyfield purchased land past North Bar (Perry) Lake near Sleeping Bear Dunes and settled there a few years later. He would eventually sell some land to Joe Perry during the first year of the Civil War.[31] Also that fall (1851), John LaRue brought in a cargo of goods to trade with the Indians. LaRue would later settle near Otter (Early) Creek and then in Empire with others such as H. Marvin La Core (7th MI Inf. & Navy) Mr. Aylesworth, Richard Tobin, Robert Green, the Stormers, and J.R. Perry. (LaRue had married Sophia LaCore.) In December of that year, Abraham Wadsworth began his new survey of the Leelanau peninsula.[32] The year 1852 would see the arrival of Joseph Dame from Old Mission to Northport. Dame would later write a letter to the New York Tribune in which he described the area as ideal for agriculture. Interest from the letter led to more white settlers to the region.

In 1853 Rev. Smith traveled by boat with his family to get two of his children to Olivet College. They became stranded for a time at Sleeping Bear Point and stayed with the John LaRue family.[33] That year, both Smith & Mason served as Justice of the Peace. Antoine Manseau settled at Carp Lake from North Manitou Island and was soon followed by others including John Bryant, John Porter, Simon & Jacob Schaub, and John I. Miller (15th MI Inf.). A Catholic Indian Mission was also formed about 4 miles south of Omena under a French Priest, Father Ignatious Mrack. This was later moved to Peshawbestown (formerly Eagletown with Father Angelus Van Paemel) in 1855. That year, Father Mrack traveled from Peshawbestown to the home of Richard Tobin just South of the Glen Lake narrows to celebrate Mass with the area settlers.[34] A church and cemetery would later be established nearby.[35] Father Mrack also attended to the Chippeway and Ottawa (Odawa) Indians at Manistee and went as far north as Petoskey. He later became Bishop of Marquette in 1869 and would later return to Peshawbestown in 1878 to spend the remainder of his life (1891).[36]

Meanwhile, over in the lower Traverse Region by Silver Lake, Lyman Smith settled (1853) over in where his three year old son, Albert, would later be stolen by Indian Chief Whitefoot on July 22, 1861. Albert lived many years with the Indians and later a Cowboy's life out West before learning of his abduction from an old Indian squaw. A letter written to the Governor of Michigan would eventually lead to an incredible family reunion thirty-five years later![37]

Back in Leelanau County, more white settlers gradually began to arrive. In 1854 O.L. White and J.M. Burbeck established a general store and the next year a dock was built by H.O. Rose and Amos Fox. Township supervisors included Samuel G. Voice (Boice), Joseph Dame, and Lansing Marble. Also in the year 1854, H.C. Sutton started a community called Suttonburg while Army Veteran John E. Fisher (8th Inf.) and Dr. William H. Walker (14th WS Inf.) established settlements in Glen Arbor followed by his brother-in-law George Ray, Erastus Nutt, & William D. Burdick (4th MI Cav. & 15th Res.).[38] John Fisher gave the Crystal River its name for the clarity of the water and Mrs. Harriet Fisher named Glen Arbor. She was inspired by observing a dense mass of wild grapes entwined in the treetops and said it was a glen arbor created by nature.[39] The town once used a large hollow tree for a post office.[40] The tree was located near the center of the present village and near an old Indian council ground. It was the custom for persons wishing to post letters, to place them in this hollow tree, and the (Indian) runner, when the spirit moved him, would collect them and take them to the nearest post office, usually Traverse City.[41] The main Council tree was a large hollow oak which stood in front of the present (1999) Fire Department and was removed in the mid 1970's when Lake Street was renovated. The hole was about three feet from the ground and a leather pouch was used to hold the mail.[42]

16

Early photograph of Glen Arbor, MI
(Courtesy Leelanau Historical Museum)

The steamer "Michigan" painted by Charles Robert Patterson
(Dossin Great Lakes Museum)

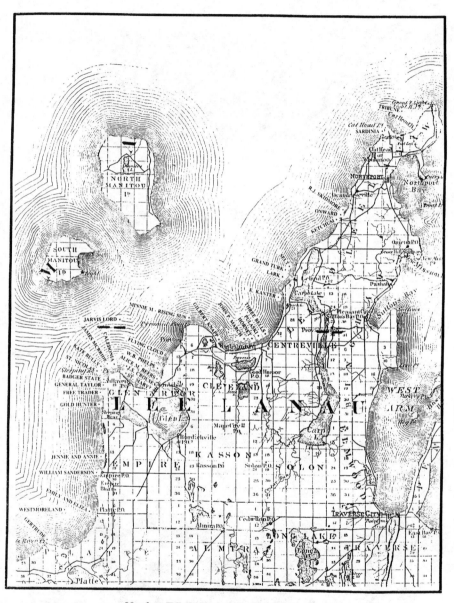

Map from H.F. Walling's 1873 *Atlas of Michigan*
featured in "Shipwrecks Of The Sleeping Bear" by Steve Harold

In the fall of 1854 occurred the wreck of the Westmoreland near Sleepy Bear Point. According to Frank E. Fisher, the propeller Westmoreland, Capt. Clark, plying between Chicago and Buffalo, was loaded with barrels of pork, high-wines and oats. She sprang a leak off Little Point Sable, wind northwest and a heavy sea running. She tried to make South Manitou harbor and when opposite Platte River bay, the water in the hold put out the fire so they headed for shore before the wind. There were 34 people on board including the crew. The captain ordered everyone to boats as the ship was sinking. Part of the crew did not respond to the captain's orders, having made too free use of the high-wines, and only 17 were saved including Captain Clark, First Mate Paul Pelky, and two cabin girls, Kate and Anna. The lifeboat struck shore in Platte River bay on November 11th with some snow on the ground. They built a fire and remained until morning. Capt. Clark detailed parties to go both ways on the beach to hunt civilization. A party of two came to Sleeping Bear Point and there discovered cattle and mule tracks, which they followed to Glen Arbor Bay and came to the house of John E. Fisher and family. John Fisher and others went to their rescue and kept them in the Fisher home for three weeks since some had frozen feet and hands. The men would later follow the beach to Northport thence to Traverse City and to their homes while the two girls stayed with John E. Fisher and his wife.[43]

In 1855 Philander P. Smith (24th WS Inf.) came to Sleeping Bear Bay and a number of Czechoslovakian families settled in North Unity, Port Oneida areas. Many would later serve in the 15th MI Inf. during the Civil War, including Anton Kucera, Vaclav Hajek, Jan/Lohn Cizkovsky, Joseph Masopust, and Mathias/Metj Nemeskal.[44] (An old Bohemian cemetery over at Bowers Harbor holds the final resting-place of early pioneers Leopold and Petronilla Kroupa in an unmarked grave.)[45]

One interesting story tells of sometime around 1858 that Anton Kucera was on his way back from Mackinaw with several friends who had been trying to transport a stove back to their settlement. After being lost several days they left the stove and eventually found an Indian's hut. They soon picked up a trail along Lake Michigan and found their way home.

In 1856 Frederick F. Cook (Sgt. in the 26th MI) arrived at North Manitou Island. On one winter occasion, Mr. Timblin made a deal to have Mr. Cook use his Oxen to take his corn into Traverse City to be ground and invest in groceries for the two families.

Traveling to Peshawbestown, he procured a Pony & Sled while leaving the Ox in the care of the Indian Village. He proceeded up the bay on the ice to Traverse City where he got the corn ground and supplies of groceries before he started his homeward journey. Before he reached Peshawbestown, a snowstorm came on, which completely hid the shores of the bay from view. In an attempt to gain ground by crossing a wide crack in the ᵕ, the Pony jumped and slipped into the water. Mr. Cook seized him by the ears to prevent him from sinking and in the process became thoroughly chilled as to be almost helpless. Fortunately, several Indians heard his callings for help and promptly came to his assistance. Some of the Indians drew him on a hand-sled to Peshawbestown, while others cared for the half dead Pony. The meal and the groceries had gone to the bottom of the bay. There was a scene of sorrow when Mr. Cook reached home. Mrs. Cook wept freely for the loss of the little supplies that had seemed to promise a short respite from starvation.[46]

In Glen Arbor, Rev. Charles E. Bailey assisted in the first religious meeting in 1856. (Years later, Enos B. Bailey would Captain Co. B. of the 10th MI Cavalry and Levi Bailey served in the 26th MI Inf.) Captain A.W. Rossman and M.D. Todd purchased George Ray's Central Dock in 1860 while Thomas Kelderhouse built another.[47] Additional early Pioneers are said to have included:

Joseph Oliver, Peter Gravel, William Coggshall, Seth Norris, Lockland Campbell, Thomas Deering, The Ericksons, William H. Case, Charles C. McCarthy, Henry A. Merrill, John Porter, H.S. Buckman, Henry Decker (Civil War Veteran), Mr. Dorr, L.F. Sheridan, Ebenezer Cobb, Ordeliai Goff, Thomas Wickham, Kasson Freeman (Maple City), Elie Dunning, John W. Van Nostrand (15th MI Inf.), Charles Dumbrill, Trumbull, Pratt, Brissey, Hutzler & Haas families, Rev. Daniel & Wells B. Miller, John Bryant, and the many Civil War soldiers listed in this book.[48] Other early families included Brotherton, Harwood, St. Peter, Nathan Carrol, John Brooke, Hiltons, John Dunn from Canada, Westman & Jacksons (Indians), Leonard Rohr, Wyse family, Slyfields, Charlie Plowman[49] and the many families listed further in the early census records.

D.H. (David Henry) Day would later established operations in Glen Haven and the area continued to grow. In 1860 there were 17 dwellings on South Manitou Island with approximately 73 people. The ramshackle town hall of Glen Arbor would be the place of the fiddle and harmonica booming out square dances such as "Turkey in the Straw."[50]

Early Census records were gathered by Philo Beers June 21, 1860 for the Township of Glen Arbor, the following are listed by number, generally head of the household, and does not list some of the younger men who were still living at home. Several of the family's spellings are likely from a soundex listing since many did not know English yet:

Listed as Farmers unless otherwise specified - Thomas Wickham, Henry D. Oliver, William Wishvelle?, Henry Decker, Daniel Moore, Warren Akin, Bishop Drecker/Tucker?, John Boizard, John Dorsey (Cooper), Charles McCarty (Miller), John Fisher, George Ray (Merchant), Kehimiak Roberson (Day Laborer), Charles Barrett, Alexis Goffrost?(son was a Shoemaker), Norman Doring, Austin Burdick, William Burdick, George Stetson (Hunter & Trapper), Laughlin Campbell, Frederick Warner, Carl Burfiend, Frederick Drekow?(Dechow), John Bates, George Hessal?, Henry Ekhart, Joseph Browser?, Julius Browser, Orens Bartling, Jacob Munce, William Harisoling? (Merchant), John Bribenstein, August Kenner, Joseph Pluffer (Cooper), Kirk Leilsaner (Shoe Maker), Charles Gruber (Wagon-maker), Bristace Goets?(Day Laborer), William Kechnrelf? (Sawyer), John Harting (Carpenter), Gustac Peltzer (School Teacher from Prussia), Kirk Logermann, Jacob Reid, Frank Riegel, John Kolando, William Vrasel?, Vensel Janttus?, Michael Phason, Charles Wishoshil?, Joseph Schrelda?/(Shalda), Frank Koritz, John Otts, Casper Kepel, Jones Grupner?, Alson Shephancek?, William Ziegler (Fisherman), Jacob Kelsog (Jr.), (Kellogg), Auton Kulzer, Joseph Bergmaun, Jacob Kelcog, Catherine Wagner & Catherine Kalzian (Widows), Joseph Bronson (Farmer), Henry Fisher (Merchant), Lewis Veckler (Carpenter). Ironically, John LaRue (Larue) was already settling areas by Empire at this time.

Early Census records were also gathered by Philo Beers on North Manitou Island July 26, 1860 and at South Manitou Island July 30, 1860. (The Author has given a copy of these records to the Empire Museum.)

By 1862 there were 2,157 inhabitants in Leelanau County of which 1,603 were Whites and 554 were Indians. The county was then described as: embracing the entire peninsula formed by Lake Michigan and Grand Traverse Bay. It extends south seven miles below the mouth of the Betsie River (at that time). It is bounded on the east by Grand Traverse

Bay, on the west by Lake Michigan, and on the south by Manistee. It has (in 1862) eighty-six miles of lake and forty miles of bay coast.[51]

During these years the farmers of the county found that their principal cash crop was potatoes.[52] Fruit growing also became a major activity. An 1862 letter by Rev. George N. Smith of Northport gave the results of his experience in fruit growing, and expressed firm belief that this region was unsurpassed for that purpose.[53]

Another account given in 1862 mentions that generous hospitality is, and always has been, a prominent characteristic of the people of this county. In 1862 the first road from Northport to Traverse City was built in the county. The route had formerly been an Indian trail. In the years that followed, other roads were constructed, most of them following trails created by the Indians.[54]

The wealth of timber in the area would entice even more settlers to this beautiful region. It was said that one Hemlock tree cut down in the Glen Lake area measured six feet in diameter. It took two men half a day to saw through it and growth rings indicated that it was 624 years old.[55]

It is no wonder then, that at the time the men of our communities went off to serve their country in the Civil War, stories[56] of this serene beauty would entice other soldiers to travel to Leelanau after the War.

D.H. Day Store in Glen Haven, MI
(Courtesy U.S. Park Service, Sleeping Bear Dunes
National Lakeshore)

First Old Settlers' Picnic 1893
(Courtesy Leelanau Historical Museum)

Old Settlers Picnic (~1897)
Believed to be identified as: Top row L-R – Judge Gilbert, T. Herbert, William Beeman, Geo. Axtel, Harp Kellogg, John Ruegsegger, John Burfiend, Ed Cluff, S.B. Cate, Carles Miller, Charles Fritz, 2nd row – John Nash, Frank Fisher, Geo. Lourie, Lime Sheridan, Joe Tremaine, Marshal Miller, Josiah White, John Trumbull, Asher Atkinson, John Dorsey, Bottom row – Geo. Ziegler, Dave McQueer, Elmer Atkinson, John Ehle, George Kellogg, B.J. Decker & Dr. Payne of Suttons Bay. (Courtesy Grand Traverse Pioneer & Historical Society)

Early photographs from the late 1800's include
Good Harbor, Glen Lake Picnic, & Narrows.
(Courtesy U.S. Park Service, Sleeping Bear Dunes
National Lakeshore)

Alexander Hessler

ABRAHAM LINCOLN

The Boys in Blue

The Civil War officially began on April 12, 1861. This was when the United States garrison at Fort Sumter, South Carolina under the command of Major Robert Anderson was bombarded from Confederate posts led by Brigadier General Pierre G.T. Beauregard, a former colleague. There were earlier tensions between the North & South with the happenings of John Brown; the publishing of Uncle Tom's Cabin, and the election of United States President Abraham Lincoln.

It was once reported that the Grand Traverse region held approximately 600 eligible men at the start of the conflict and eventually more than 200 served in the Civil War.[57] This now appears to be a very conservative estimate as these numbers were likely much, much higher. Those numbers also do not appear to take into consideration the large number of men who had recently traveled to the region and then went back to their home state to join in the war or the many who died in action.

At the outbreak, the Union military commander was Mexican War hero Gen. Winfield Scott. By this time the commander was of an advanced age so the command was offered to Col. Robert E. Lee. Unfortunately for the North, Col. Lee chose to followed his native state (Virginia) into the Confederacy and became its' most famous General. The Southern states that made up the Confederate States of America under President Jefferson Davis were: Alabama, Arkansas, Florida, Georgia, Louisiana, Mississippi, North & South Carolina, Tennessee, Texas, and Virginia.

The first major conflict of the war was the Battle of Bull Run (Manassas) in July of 1861. Union Federal forces led by Gen. Irwin McDowell crossed the Potomac River in an effort to disrupt rail lines at Manassas Junction. The Rebels led in part by Gen. Thomas J. "Stonewall" Jackson repulsed them.

An ever-cautious Major General named George B. McClellan was made head of the Union armies who drilled the army into an organized force. Following the February 1862 Battles of Ft. Henry & Donelson, the Battle of Pea Ridge was fought in Arkansas. In April the Union took Fort Pulaski. McClellan launched the Peninsular Campaign of 1862 into what was known as the Seven Days' Battles. That summer the armies were involved in the Valley Campaigns & Second Manassas in August, (where Francis Z. Fowler of the 1st MI Infantry would become known as one of the first Grand Traverse region men killed in battle, buried in Ogdensburg Cemetery.[58] In later folklore, Fowler Road in northern Benzie County was considered "haunted"). Fighting continued at the Battle of Cedar Mountain. Later on September 17, the two armies fought to a draw along a Maryland creek called Antietam in the bloodiest single day of the war. (This Battle featured service by Gen. Alpheus S. Williams "Old Pap" of Michigan.) The up-coming winter would bring the battles of Fredericksburg, VA. and Stones River at Murfreesboro, TN.

In the West, troops under General Ulysses S. Grant & Gen. Buel had been involved in the bloody Battle of Shiloh, TN on April 6th & 7th, 1862. Of this battle Grant wrote, "Shiloh was the severest battle fought at the West during the War, and but few in the East equaled it for hard, determined fighting."[59] On April 25, 1862 Admiral David Farragaut led the Federal Navy up the Mississippi and captured New Orleans. This campaign included Corinth, Arkansas Post, and various Mississippi River Battles that culminated in the Siege of Vicksburg, MS which surrendered on July 4, 1863. The same victory day as the Battle of Gettysburg, Pennsylvania.

General U.S. Grant
(State Archives of Michigan)

Confederate General Robert E. Lee
(Library of Congress)

Shiloh April 6-7, 1862
(Library of Congress)

Union Cavalry General Phillip Sheridan (who once commanded the 2nd MI Cavalry) was also active in leading campaigns such as in the Shenandoah Valley while the clash of the Monitor & Merrimac became a well known Naval conflict.

President Lincoln appointed several men to command the Northern Armies: McClellan was replaced by John Pope who was defeated at the Second Battle of Bull Run (Manassas) in the late Summer of 1862, McClellan again took command only to be replaced by Ambrose Burnside after Antietam. Joseph Hooker replaced Burnside after the 1862 Winter Battle of Fredericksburg. After Murfreesborough he lost to General Lee at Chancellorsville in the spring of 1863. Then command fell to Gen. George Meade who led a successful defense at the Battle of Gettysburg, which took place July 1 to July 3, 1863. "All that month there is heat and wild rain. Cherries are ripening over all Pennsylvania, and the men gorge as they march..."[60] (It has been claimed in some of our local folklore, and from diaries of several soldiers, that some of these same cherry pits were saved and brought back to the Grand Traverse region for planting later on. This could very well be true, as soldiers of that day were often farmers by up bringing; used to living off the land and being resourceful with what little agricultural opportunity they chanced upon). This famous battle began with skirmishes against Gen. Harry Heath by Union Cavalry led by Gen. John Buford and George Custer while Federal troops led by Gen. John Reynolds arrived, then heavy fighting at: Culp's Hill, against Confederate Gen. Sam Hood, and Little Round Top (Joshua L.Chamberlain). On the third day there was an unsuccessful Confederate attack led by Generals George Pickett (Pickett's Charge) and Louis Armisted under the command of James Longstreet against Gen. Winfield Hancock. Of the almost 5000 Michigan men who were engaged at Gettysburg, an estimated 1131 were killed, wounded or missing.[61] With General Meade too weakened from the battle to give chase, overall command was turned over to Western Commander Gen. Ulysses S. Grant while Meade remained at the head of the Army of the Potomac. Two months later, after battles at Jackson, MS and Snickers Gap, VA was the Battle of Chickamauga, GA. That same fall would also see battles at Brandy Station, Lookout Mountain, Campbell Station, Knoxville, and Mine Run.

The Western Union Armies were turned over to General William T. Sherman. With the help of General George H. Thomas, Sherman led victories at Missionary Ridge in Chattanooga, TN on Nov. 25, 1863 and in the following spring the armies fought the battles of the Wilderness, Spotsylvania, Resaca, North Anna, Totopotomoy, & Cold Harbor. This series of battles had cost more lives lost from Leelanau County Michigan than any other in the Civil War. General Grant wrote of these Battles in his *Personal Memoirs*, "...bloody and terrible as they were on our side, (they) were even more damaging to the enemy, and so crippled him as to make him wary ever after of taking the offensive."[62] More conflicts occurred at Pumpkin Vine Creek, Dallas, and New Hope Church. In June of 1864, General Sherman fought Confederate Generals Nathan Bedford Forrest at Brice's Cross Roads and Joseph Johnston at Kenesaw Mountain. They would again clash at Tupelo, MS in July. The Federal Army eventually captured Atlanta, GA Sept. 2, 1864. The Union then made their famous march from Atlanta to the Sea. They destroyed everything in their path and captured Savannah in December and then turned North to invade the Carolinas.[63]

WILLIAM T. SHERMAN

The countryside in between Savannah and Goldsboro, N.C. was daunting. The winter season made foraging difficult and constant rains filled the many rivers, leaving miles of swampy ground to traverse. Fortunately, this was the Army of the West, filled with lumberman from Michigan and rail-splitters from Indiana and Illinois. These resourceful men from the American backwoods formed Sherman's Pioneer Corps, whose axes and improvisational skills corduroyed the roads, built the bridges and forded the rivers at an astonishing rate of 12 miles a day.[64]

Major campaigns beginning in the winter of 1864 included the battles of Franklin, Gun Town, Nashville, and Cedar Creek. Many captured soldiers were held in various Civil War prisons. In Andersonville, GA almost 13,000 soldiers perished.

Grant & Lee had attacked each other ruthlessly in numerous battles including Jonesboro and Winchester, culminating in the Siege of Petersburg, which ended April 2, 1865. After the battles at Hatcher's Run & Five Forks, Confederate General Robert E. Lee withdrew his troops and surrendered on Palm Sunday, April 9, 1865 at Appomattox Court House. Five days later in Washington D.C., a young Southern actor named John Wilkes Booth assassinated President Lincoln. Later, the Union Troops Victory Parade "Grand Review" was held in May of 1865 in Washington D.C. (Our Memorial Weekend). General Grant would eventually serve as President of the United States and, with the help of Author Mark Twain, completed his personal memoirs before his death in 1885.[65]

Federal Soldiers before Petersburg, U.S. Civil War 1865.
Photo from the National Archives & Records Administration, Washington D.C.

29

Murray G.A.R. Post 168 of Glen Lake
Circa 1890 (Courtesy Empire Area Museum)

Woolsey G.A.R. Post 399 of Northport
(Courtesy Leelanau Historical Museum)

In comparison to the <u>approximate</u> deaths in other U.S. Wars, the Civil War was the most devastating. Approximate American casualties:[66]

American deaths in **French & Indian War** were ~ 3000 +
American deaths in **Revolutionary War** were ~ 4500 +
American deaths in **War of 1812** were ~ 2500
American deaths in **Mexican War** were ~ 13,300
American deaths in the **U.S. Civil War** were ~ 624,500.
American deaths in **Spanish/American War** were ~ 2450
American deaths in **WWI** were ~ 116,700
American deaths in **WWII** were ~ 407,300
American deaths in **Korea** were ~ 43,700
American deaths in **Vietnam** were ~ 58,200
American deaths in **Persian Gulf (Desert Storm)** were ~ 293

It should be noted that this was a time in history where disease ran rampant, both in the Service and at home. It was also a time where records were not always accurate and many people could not read or spell. As a result, many names are from a soundex listing and many men who were listed as deserted were actually captured, dead, or their terms expired and they went home before the official orders came through. We were also a very agricultural country, so if an accident or illness happened back home, sometimes men <u>had</u> to leave, whether the official paperwork was completed or not. This was likely considered understandable as many men who volunteered and were later listed deserted, still took an active and proud part in their G.A.R. membership. As mentioned in the introduction, most men from the Glen Lake area at the time of the war served in the 10th MI Cavalry or the 15th MI Infantry. At times, bonuses were offered for volunteers to fill the required county quotas. This could reach as high as $600. This was a very enticing amount, especially for new immigrants to the area. Enough to pay for a 40-acre homestead and care for families while men went off to war.[67]

The main G.A.R. (Grand Army of the Republic) Veteran Post in our area was the Murray Post # 168 of Maple City Glen Lake. This was originally formed at Empire, MI in 1883. Meetings were also held in Oviatt, Burdickville and Solon, though most were eventually at Maple City. The first Post Commander was John Dorsey of the 15th MI Infantry, (far right end of second row in photograph). Other Charter members were: Samuel Berry, George Cook, Robert Day, William Houghton, Nathaniel C. King, David Knox, H. Marvin LaCore, James McCormick, David McLaughlin, Robert H. Monroe, Daniel Parker, Joseph Price, William E. Sheridan, & George W. Stetson. In addition, George W. Slater was a Charter Petitioner. Post met "on or before the full moon of each month." The other G.A.R. Post in the county was the Woolsey Post # 399 of Northport.

The last Civil War veteran that was alive in Michigan was Joseph Clovese in Pontiac who lived to be over 106 years old and was a Drummer Boy during the Vicksburg campaign. He then later enlisted in a "colored regiment."[68]

31

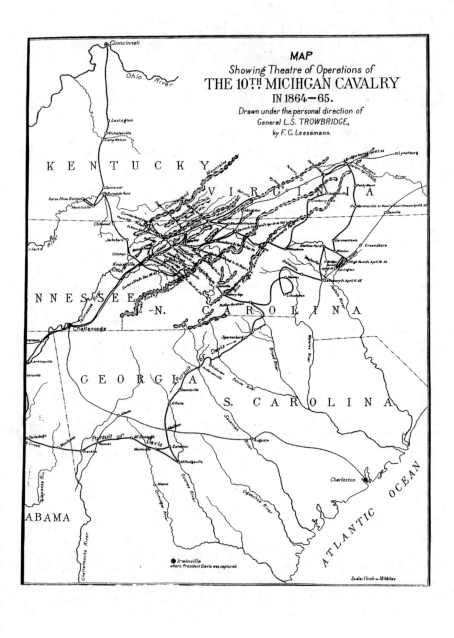

MAP
Showing Theatre of Operations of
THE 10TH MICHGAN CAVALRY
IN 1864—65.
Drawn under the personal direction of
General L.S. TROWBRIDGE,
by F. C. Leesemann.

Scale: 1 Inch ~ 18 Miles

Forest Haven Soldiers: The Civil War Veterans of Sleeping Bear & Surrounding Leelanau

Many men from Grand Traverse quickly volunteered at the start of the Civil War and are listed further on in this book.[69] However, since the Sleeping Bear Lakeshore area was such a vast wilderness at the time, the first main organization for recruitment didn't happen until later in the middle of the war. Part of this enlistment was at Glen Arbor, then the most developed of the early settlements of Glen Lake.

10th MI Cavalry The "Plucky Boys" of Co. E.

Most of the area soldiers who served in the 10th Cavalry enlisted in the summer of 1863. Unit history includes: Stationed at Camp Lee, Grand Rapids, MI Oct. 22, 1863. Captain Harvey E. Light's Company E. with 1st Lt. Edwin J. Brooks of Northport, age 28, commanded by Colonel Thaddeus Foote (of Gen. Custer's 6th MI Cavalry) and Lt. Colonel Luther S. Trowbridge (of Custer's 5th Cavalry).[70] Unit's Reverend was Henry Cherry. Called into service of the United States by President Abraham Lincoln for the term of three years, unless sooner discharged. Attached to District of North Central Kentucky, 1st Division, 23rd Corps, Dept. of the Ohio

Duty at Camp Nelson, KY Nov-Dec 1863. The stay at Camp Nelson was exceedingly unpleasant with cold weather and much sickness in camp. At Lexington, KY until Jan. 25, 1864.

Moved to Burnside Point (until Feb. 25) having engaged the enemy at House Mountain. Marched to Knoxville, East TN. The march across the mountains was very difficult for both man and horses due to rain, snow, sleet, and ice. Heavy branches overloaded with snow were breaking on all sides. One man of Co. E. was seriously injured, and had to be left behind at the first available stopping place, while the Colonel narrowly escaped injury from a large branch, which struck his horse. As the regiment wound down the side of the Cumberland Mountains the view from the top was one of rare beauty. Action at Flat Creek Valley March 15. Moved to Morristown on the 16th via Strawberry Plains and two companies under Captain Light were detached for service at Knoxville during March.

Expedition to Carter's Station April 24-28 via Rheatown, Jonesboro where the enemy in force held the bridge, occupying a strong redoubt and rifle-pits. About one-third of the regiment was dismounted and charged on the double-quick, carrying the works and driving the enemy into a large mill near by, a gallant affair with an inferior force. Then Johnsonville, Bull's Gap, & Watauga River under Lt. Colonel Trowbridge.

On April 25 - Reached Carter's Station and, after severe engagement by a well-executed assault, drove the enemy in strong force behind works on the opposite side of the river. In command of Lt. Colonel Trowbridge, together with the 3rd Indiana Cavalry, this assault was commenced against rebel General A. E. "Stonewall" Jackson. The Union force had one mountain Howitzer, commanded by Edwin J. Brooks (of Northport, MI), but owing to a very limited amount of ammunition he was unable to accomplish much, yet made some remarkably telling shots. (Brooks had previously served in the 1st NY Light Artillery.) It was soon ascertained that there was no possible way of reaching the bridge without first dislodging the enemy from their strong position. Using dismounted Cavalry, the first gallant men to advance into the enemy's position were Major Israel C. Smith and Captain Benjamin K. Weatherwax who was shot through the heart. In addition, the whole command lost over seventeen men killed or wounded. They were unable to destroy the Railroad Bridge over Watauga River at Carter's Station. Brigadier General Mahlon Dickerson Manson ordered infantry to retire since the destruction of the bridge was not sufficient in importance to warrant the loss of life that would necessarily follow and the fight was already a brilliant success. For the gallant charge on the enemy's works, the 10th was highly complimented by General Schofield. Lt. Edwin J. Brooks of Co. E. became Captain of Co. M. and Lt. William H. Dunn (from Saugatuck) of Co. D. became first Lt. of Co. E. The Cavalry went on to be engaged at Powder Springs Gap April 29. Unit attached to 2nd Brigade, 4th Div., 23rd Corps.

May, 1864 activities - Newport, Dandrige, Reconnaissance from Strawberry Plains to Bull's Gap and Greenville under Col. Foote. Detachments of the regiment have been in repeated skirmishes with the enemy and always successful, having killed around thirty Rebels and capturing forty. Sgt. Clark of Co. A. was wounded in the knee and the Colonel slightly in the foot. They have scouted continually in small parties over the valley.

Skirmishes at Morristown June 2nd, Bean's Station on the 16th: where Col. Trowbridge had been ordered to go up the Virginia line to capture a large number of horses that were said to be in pasture. They were not expected to meet the enemy before Kingsport but unfortunately met them at Bean's Station. Col. Trowbridge ordered Captain James B. Roberts (Co. G.), with two companies, to charge them. One of these companies was commanded by Captain Edwin J. Brooks (formally of Co. E., now Co. M.). Brooks was smarting under some ill treatment from a superior officer, and immediately dashed forward with his company. After routing the Rebels handsomely and charging them for a couple of miles, Captain Roberts wisely ordered a halt; but Brooks had gone ahead with a few of his men, and actually kept up that charge, with only three men with him, for a distance of 10 1/2 miles! Brooks would later be rewarded for his gallantry by the brevets of Major and Lieutenant Colonel.

Other June skirmishes included a brisk fight at Rogersville on the 17th and Kingsport 18th. The next morning, while giving the horses a much-needed feed in a meadow near Blountsville, the enemy made a sudden dash on our pickets, but was promptly driven back. One man of Co. M., coming in from picket when the attack was made, was mistaken for one of the enemy and lost an arm shot from one of our own men. More June action at Cany Branch 20th, New Market 21st, Mooresburg 23rd, William's Ford 25th, and Dutch Bottom on the 28th. An affair occurred at Wilsonville where Lt. Dunn made an attempt to rescue Col. Fry of East TN who had been captured by a roving band of guerrillas. They eventually skirmished with the enemy who killed a picket (David A. Crammer of Ottawa Co. MI) and drove them back by sharp fire from their Spencer rifles.

Engaged at Sevierville July 5th and Newport July 8th. July / August 1864 - Strawberry Plains to Greenville, Morristown, several companies remained in Knoxville during Brigadier General Alven Cullem Gillem's August expeditions under Lt. Col. Trowbridge and Major Smith from Knoxville. At Morristown they met and drove back Confederate

Head Quarter 10th Mich Cav
Straw berry plain Tennessee
June 10th 1864,

General,

During the month of Feb last I received notice from Lieut Adair, Mustering & Disbursing Officer at Detroit, Mich, that the Muster of the Rev Henry Cherry as Chaplain to the Regiment was not recognized by the War Department, owing to some supposed irregularity in the form of appointment, accordingly the Chaplain has received no pay since Dec 31st 1863. He has been informed by Capt Knight, Mustering & Disbursing Officer at Detroit, to whom he returned his certificate of Muster, that his Muster as Chaplain

Henry Cherry
June 10 1864   4

had subsequently been treated by the War Department as valid & his original Certificate of Muster was therefore returned to Mr Cherry.

I have the honor to request an official notification of the validity of the appointment & muster of the Rev Henry Cherry as Chaplain to the Regiment in order that I may incur no censure in treating as such and that he may receive his monthly pay of which he stands in distressing need

Brig Genl Thomas
Adj't Genl
Washington DC

{ I have the honor to be
General, very respectfully
Your Obt Servt
Thaddeus Foote
Col 10th Mich Cav
Comdg

Rev. Henry Cherry

Letter written by Col. Foote on behalf of
Rev. Henry Cherry
(Courtesy Western Michigan Historical Collections
Photograph from Michigan Archives)

OFFICERS OF THE TENTH MICHIGAN CAVALRY

Col.
Thaddeus Foote

Col. and Bvt. Maj.
Gen.
Luther S. Trowbridge

Col. and Bvt. Brig. Gen.
Israel C. Smith

Major
Cicero Newell

Lt. Col. and Bvt. Col.
John H. Standish

Capt. John Standish
(Michigan Archives)

MAJ. HARVEY K. LIGHT

Major Arnold's battalion of rebel cavalry. In the beginning of August Colonel Thaddeus Foote went home on leave of absence and resigned his position on account of disability. Lt. Col. Trowbridge assumed command. Other soldiers from Leelanau County in the 26th MI Infantry were here for a brief time. Skirmishes with the enemy occurred at Mossy Creek on Aug. 18th and Bull's Gap on the 21st. Met Confederate Harry Liter Giltner's Brigade at Blue Springs on the 23rd and had a sharp fight for a time, drove the enemy from a strong position seven miles through Greenville.

On Aug. 24, Back at Strawberry Plains Captain John H. Standish (Co. A.), with about 60 men of his regiment, many of whom were sick, and about 150 men from other commands, with a section of John H. Colvin's Illinois Battery, successfully repulsed an attack from Confederate Wheeler's whole Cavalry Corps, numbering several thousand men with 9 pcs. of artillery. Standish played a splendid game of bluff, blazing away with his two pieces of artillery as if he had a great number of men stowed away somewhere. (When Colonel Trowbridge reported to General Gillem for duty, he had taken with him every man that was fit for duty, leaving behind only the sick, some blacksmiths, horse farriers, and other special duty men to remain under Captain Standish). Eight men held the ford and prevented an entire brigade from crossing for 3 hours until they were completely surrounded. The Rebels, by swimming the river above and below the ford, succeeded in capturing the whole party. A large, powerful farrier in Co. B by the name of Alexander H. Grigg, (Greenfield, Wayne Co.), was badly wounded in the shoulder. Confederate General Wheeler was much astonished at the valor of these men, and at once paroled a man to stay and take care of this wounded man. Approaching the wounded farrier, the following dialogue is said to have taken place:

"Well, my man, how many men had you at the Ford?" asked General Wheeler. "Seven, sir" said Griggs. (The eighth man had gone off on his own hook before the capture). "My poor fellow," said Wheeler, "don't you know that you are badly wounded? You might as well tell me the truth; you may not live long." "I am telling the truth, sir. We had only seven men," said Griggs indignantly. "Well, what did you expect to do?" laughed Wheeler. "To keep you from crossing, sir," said Griggs. "Well, why didn't you do it"? laughed Wheeler who was greatly amused. "Why, you see," said Griggs, "we did until you hit me, and that weakened our forces so much that you were too much for us." General Wheeler was greatly amused and inquired of another horse farrier prisoner, "Are all the 10th Michigan (Cavalry) like you fellows?" "Oh, no!" said John Dunn of Co. I., "we are the poorest of the lot. We are mostly Horse Farriers and Blacksmiths, and not much accustomed to fighting." "Well," said General Wheeler, "If I had 300 such men as you I could march straight through Hell." The heroic defense of this post with the large Railroad Bridge against fearful odds forms a bright page in the history of the conduct of Michigan troops.

On this same day near Flat Creek Bridge, Major Israel Canton Smith of the 10th MI Cavalry, with the detachments left at Knoxville, (73 men), charged into the 8th & 11th Texas Cavalry, about 400 strong, totally routing them and capturing their Colonel and others. Then suddenly came upon William Young Conn Humes' Division at Flat Creek bridge, were drawn up in the line of battle and were obliged to retire. The enemy immediately pursued and recaptured the prisoners and several officers & men, whom they first robbed of everything and then paroled. The gallant charge of Major Smith ranks among the most daring and brilliant exploits of the war. (Smith had previously served with distinction as a 23 year old Captain in the 3rd MI Inf. Service in the Battles of Fair Oaks, wounded at Groveton, 2nd Bull Run, Chancellorsville, & wounded in action in the Battle of Gettysburg.).

In September, this regiment, under the command of Colonel Trowbridge, was stationed at Strawberry Plains and involved in various scouting. On the 4th it participated in surprising and routing Confederate General John Hunt Morgan who was killed in the Greenville battle by forces led by Major Cicero Newell (of Ypsilanti, MI). Confederate General Morgan; with a force of about 7000 men were encamped along the Greenville road, in East Tennessee. The 10th Michigan Cavalry, then in command of Major Newel, encamped near Bull's Gap and was ordered by General Gillam to attack the enemy. Marching all night, Newel dismounts his men at daylight and charges into Morgan's first camp, driving the enemy in hot haste, leaving their breakfast half cooked, and their dead and wounded. Reaching the second camp, the enemy is found in better condition. General Gillam then came up with Colonel Brownlow's 9th Tennessee Cavalry and charged in with sabers, but a sharp fire from the enemy drove the regiment back. Then Colonel Miller's 13th Tennessee Cavalry came up and engaged the 1000 Rebels that had been driving back the 9th TN as the 10th MI Cavalry opens fire at about half pistol range with carbines, and soon the road is blocked with dead and wounded men and horses. The Confederates hastily fall back to the woods and the Artillery shells them out to Greenville. General Morgan was shot by Sergeant Cambell & the 13th TN Cavalry while rushing for his horse. Captain Blackburn had shouted for him to Surrender and Morgan throwing a coat retorted, "Not while I live!" Both drew revolvers and fired at each other in warning but missed (they had been schoolmates together). Morgan yelled out, "Blackburn!" and was shot through the heart by Sgt. Campbell. He fell at the feet of Darius H. Grow of Co. H. 10th MI Cav. (who was buried in Adrian, MI in 1916). A woman named Williams had notified General Gillem of Morgan's location. Morgan's staff (among whom was a grandson of Henry Clay), 100 men, and six pieces of artillery were taken.

During Sept.-Oct there were expeditions from East TN toward SW Virginia. Skirmishes on Sept. 10th at Sweet Water and Thorn Hill, at Sevierville on the 18th, and Carter's Station on the 30th. They encountered the enemy at Johnson's Station and Watauga Bridge on Oct. 1 & 2nd, Chucky Bend on the 10th, then Colonel Trowbridge went to Michigan to help with new enlisted men. Major Newell took over. Skirmishes at Newport on the 18th, Irish Bottoms on the 25th, and Madisonville on the 30th.

Russelville, Flat Creek & Stoneman's raid Nov.- Dec.1864. During Nov. 16-17 a large force of the enemy under John Cabell Breckenridge appeared in front of the post at Strawberry Plains and on Nov. 17 commenced a vigorous attack with artillery from the south side of the river, sending a large force of cavalry to the rear on the north side. There was constant skirmishing with occasional artillery firing for four days but the enemy was repulsed at every point. Confederate General Breckenridge, under orders from General Sam Hood, was attempting a counter movement to General Sherman's March to the Sea.

Proceeding this activity, back on Nov. 13th about 100 men of the 10th MI Cavalry under Major Israel C. Smith and the same number of the 1st Ohio Artillery were headed out to assist a brigade under General Gillem retreating from Bull's Gap, about 40 miles above Strawberry Plains. The retreating troops were panicked and confused with one

Bridge at Strawberry Plains, 20 miles NE of Knoxville, TN. U.S. Civil War 1864.
Photo: George N. Barnard - Library of Congress

The Grand Traverse Herald.

MORGAN BATES, Editor and Proprietor

TRAVERSE CITY:
FRIDAY MORNING, DECEMBER 16, 1864.

Close of Volume Six—A Brief Retrospect.

This number closes the Sixth Volume of the GRAND TRAVERSE HERALD. It is a source of gratification that six years of labor is what was deemed, by many of our friends, a visionary backwoods enterprise, has not proved altogether unprofitable to this community and to ourselves. A brief retrospect may not be inappropriate.

The first No. of the HERALD was issued in November, 1856. At that time the whole mercantile business of the County was transacted by Hannah, Lay & Co., in the lower part of a building 20 by 30 feet in size, and the gross sales did not exceed twelve or fifteen thousand dollars per annum. Now the same firm have a store 90 by 120 feet, divided into four compartments, each 30 by 90 feet, one of which is devoted exclusively to Hardware, Iron, Steel, Nails, Crockery, &c. Agricultural implements, Saddles, Harness, &c., &c. Another to Dry Goods of every description, both wholesale and retail. A third to Groceries at wholesale and retail, and a fourth to Provisions, Cabinet Furniture, &c., &c. Their annual sales amount, probably, to one hundred and seventy-five thousand dollars.

GREAT INDUSTRIAL TRIUMPH.

Another and Most Important Branch of Enterprise in Michigan—Manufacture of Steel at Wyandotte upon an Improved Plan—Its Complete and Signal Success—Prospect of a Revolution in Steel Making—Great Results Likely to Flow Therefrom.

News from the Grand Traverse Boys.

The Battle at Franklin, Tenn.

When Mr. Lincoln's Majorities Came From.

The Devoted Band.

notable exception, brave and gallant Colonel Miller, with his sturdy regiment, the 13th TN. The veterans of the 10th MI Cavalry were at a rise of ground a little out of Morristown, silently waiting behind a fence on a clear, moonlight night. As the troops of General Gillem passed, on came the exulting enemy in pursuit. When the Rebels were a few rods from the fence there rang out from that dark line. "Halt! who comes there?" "Johnny Rebs!" was the quick response. Then came the sharp, quick tones of Major Smith's voice, "Ready, Aim, Fire!" and from the line leaped forth a blinding sheet of flame, carrying with it death and destruction to many brave men. Major Smith then made their way back to Strawberry Plains to ready for the on-coming battle.

There was at Strawberry Plains an entrenched camp, the defenses of which had been constructed by the 10th MI Cavalry. The position was an admirable one, and the defenses well made. About midnight of the 14th the enemy was reported crossing the river at McKinney's Ford. The next morning Major I.C. Smith arrived back while Colonel Trowbridge, who had arrived back from Michigan to find Major Cicero Newell calmly awaiting Breckenridge's approach, telegraphed General Tillson for reinforcements. The next day before the battle began, 350 men from the 2nd Ohio Artillery arrived at Strawberry Plains to join a group that also included a small battalion of Kentucky Cavalry that had happened to stop by, several scouts, and Captain Wood's Illinois field battery. That evening Major Newell reported rumbling of the Rebel artillery being positioned in the night.

On the morning of the 17th, as day was breaking, the enemy opened with artillery from College Hill. Captain Wood, at the Fort, followed with an exciting artillery duel for some time. At the same time a strong skirmish line was thrown out at the rear. The fighting became sharp and constant through the 21st until the Confederates began falling back and Major Newell with men of the 10th Cavalry crossed the river and drove the last of the Rebels from College Hill. General Breckenridge had been stopped at Strawberry Plains by a force less than one sixth his own number. He came no nearer to Knoxville, TN than that, about twenty miles. Colonel Trowbridge would be later surprised to see in official reports that General Ammon was falsely given credit for the repulse at Strawberry Plains and Breckenridge was recorded as making it to the vicinity of Knoxville. (Though Generals Tillson and Ammon had their headquarters in Knoxville and were being kept informed, Gen. Ammon had no communications with Colonel Trowbridge at that time).

Then the 10th MI Cavalry was involved in an expedition from Strawberry Plains to Clinch Mt. and in December they marched to Knoxville, TN and a detachment under command of Captain James B. Roberts of Ionia, MI (Co.G.) helped destroy the salt works and engaged the enemy at Kingsport on the 12th, at Bristol and Saltville on the 20th.

Attached to 2nd Brig., 4th Div., Dist. of East TN Dept. of Cumberland under command of Brevet Brigadier General John Palmer. Captain Harvey E. Light of Co. E. had been commissioned Major and sent out to recruit 600 men. Lt. William H. Dunn then became Captain of Co. E. on Jan. 6, 1865. The 10th Cavalry skirmished at Chucky Bend on Jan. 10, Brabson's Mills, Boonesville, and Duty at Knoxville until March 21. (In February, Captain Brooks and Lt. Barr took part in a celebration of the MI Battery for Lt. Carlton Neal who was promoted to Captain of Bat. L. that contained James U. Auton of Glen Lake).[71] During their stay at Knoxville, they had to be on the guard for poisoned pies by food peddlers.[72]

Joining General George Stoneman's expeditions to VA & NC. The regiment, in command of Colonel Trowbridge of the 10th MI Cavalry, who had resigned his appointment of Provost Marshal General of East Tennessee in order to take command of the regiment, entered upon that campaign. There were so many other great things transpiring at that time of the war that the Stoneman expeditions were given little attention, but they were of great magnitude and accomplishment.

In the spring of 1865 Union General Ulysses S. Grant, anticipating that if Confederate General Robert E. Lee should be forced out of Richmond he might undertake to move through southwestern Virginia, and, driving our forces out of East Tennessee, strive to establish himself in some of the many strong positions which the mountainous country afforded. He ordered General Henry Thomas to send a force to destroy the railways, so far as possible, towards Lynchburg, thus putting a great obstacle in the way of possible movements.

The expedition, consisting of three brigades of cavalry, under the command of General Stoneman, was concentrated at Mossy Creek, March 22nd. On the 25th of March, ten miles west of Jonesboro, everything that could retard a rapid march was left behind. This was followed by deceptive movements of the Horse Soldiers to deceive the enemy as to the point of attacks. On the 27th they reached a little town far up in the mountains of North Carolina called Boone. At this place Major Keogh, of General Stoneman's staff, (whom afterwards was slain by the Indians in the Custer Massacre), with a detachment of the 12th Kentucky Cavalry, routed a company of Rebels. Here the brigades separated, General Stoneman, with Palmer's brigade, moving on to Wilkesboro by Deep Gap, while the other two brigades, with the artillery, moved to the same point by the Flat Gap Road. Upon moving north, General Stoneman found the railways running from Lynchburg to East TN entirely at his mercy. This group also contained men of the TN brigade under Colonel Miller. Then at Jacksonville Major Wagner, of the 15th PA Cavalry, was dispatched to Salem, where he began the work of great destruction.

The balance of the command moved on to Christiansburg, where it arrived about midnight April 4, 1865. The 10th Michigan Cavalry was at once sent to the east to destroy bridges (six) over the Roanike River, and the 11th Michigan Cavalry went to the west to destroy the great bridge over New River. The next morning those bridges were effectively destroyed. This destruction would have been avoided could the events of the next few days have been foreseen. (Lee's Surrender). The main objective of the expedition was accomplished. The main railways that would have been needed by Lee for an escape from Grant had been totally disabled.

The 10th moved on towards Martinsville, Henry Ct. House where they attacked the enemy under the command of Colonel Wheeler. Captain James H. Cummins led this charge and the 10th MI attacked with vigor driving the enemy back and out of the woods. As the Rebels took refuge in a deep depression, they became targets for the Spencer carbines of Captain Dunn and his "Plucky Boys." The Rebels lost at least 27 men while the Union lost four men including Lt. Kenyon. Lt. Field was also wounded in this battle. (This action made the enemy believe that the Union's target would be Greensboro, so the Rebels moved troops from Salisbury to Greensboro only to later find Union General Stoneman appear before Salisbury). The brigade reunited at Martinsville and moved to Danbury and Germantown. Then Palmer broke off towards Salem and Stoneman's

You will have discovered that my paper is poor, my pen is poor, & my ink will hardly flow; but at present, it is the best we can do & we must use this or none. My best regards to your own family, to the Colonels, & to David's, & to Mr Grahams.

As ever
Most truly
Yours
Henry Cherry.

Head Quarters 10th Mich Cav
The U. S. CHRISTIAN COMMISSION sends this sheet as a messenger between the soldier and his home. Let it hasten to those who wait for tidings.
Knoxville Tenn
March 27th 1865

Hon Amos Gould,
Dear Sir,
Since Dec 7th we have been located on the opposite side of the Holstein river from Knoxville. We are so high up the hill that we have a fair & beautiful view of the city & the river between us which is somewhat over 1000 feet wide & in low water from 8 to 12 feet deep in the channel. Directly back of our camp & about 200 feet higher than we are, is a strong fort with 8 cannon & to the south of us a quarter of a mile distant & about as high as the fort back of us is another larger & stronger fort with 12 Guns. Fort Sanders is in full view from where we are, on the Knoxville side of the river & that

the fort which the Rebels attempted to take by storm, & into the ditch of which were piled 537 men in a few minutes, by being tript up with a telegraph wire which was wound from stump to stump near the edge of the ditch, while it is said 1000nd lay in a hollow beyond having their charge impeded by wires fastened near the ground & by this strategy the Rebels under Longstreet were defeated & Burnside held the city, driving Longstreet's forces beyond Straw berry plains & afterward to near the Virginia line. For the last three weeks there has been quite a stir in these parts. Over 70,000 troops are said to have passed through Knoxville to operate somewhere around Lynchburg. Genl Stoneman has command of the Cavalry 12,000 strong & if Thomas does not go up he will probably

command the whole. It is said Genl T will go. The road is finished 67 miles & the construction train are moving on. — Our Regiment now number over 1200 but we lack horses. Only 700 could be mounted for the raid. They are in the post of honor, that is, they are in advance of all the forces, & it is just what they were wishing for, for they know the country, having raided through it many times during the past year. We are all hopeful & joyous over an anticipated speedy peace. But we are (I mean we who have families at home) all sorrowful & downcast at the fact that no pay master yet comes, though in another 5 days it will be 7 month that our pay is due, & we want it for ourselves & our families. It is hard to be thus treated & bear it patiently. But we must bear it.

it is said over 100,000 have passed toward
Virginia. The last we have heard from
them was that at Jonesboro Gen'l Stoneman
sent the 10th Mich in advance toward Boone
& all the Cavalry march'd for Salisbury.
Yesterday we had news of the surrender of
Lee's Army, & from every Fort around Knoxville
demonstrations of joy were given in the fire
of Cannon. If I understand the conditions
surrender, (at an hour when necessity would
have compelled it) I regret that Grant should
have offered any other than Unconditional
surrender, & then let Government show such
mercy & leniency as might be wise & proper.
Johnson may assume command and ask for
the same terms. He has the same right, for
he is no more in rebellion than Davis & Lee.
But perhaps all is right & we do not
hold of the right end of the reports.
Peaches, Plumbs, & apples have been in blossom some
time. The weather is charming. My best regards
to each & all of your family.
                            Most truly Yours
                            Henry Cherry.

Captain Harvey E. Light was promoted
Major of the 10th MI Cavalry
(State Archives of Michigan)

Michigan Cavalry with their Spencer carbines.
(State Archives of Michigan)

Brigade headed for Salisbury, as mentioned. At Salem General Palmer sent the 15th PA Cavalry to strike railways while Captain Roberts and the 10th MI Cavalry destroyed bridges over Abbott's Creek, NC where they were furiously attacked by Samuel Wragg Ferguson's Brigade of about 1200 Rebel Cavalry at High Point. Captain Dunn with his reliable and plucky company had just been placed behind a barricade across the road. The meeting was a mutual surprise. The 300 men of the 10th MI Cavalry fell back by alternate squadrons, constantly presenting an unbroken front to the enemy, while wheeling out of column into line and steadily delivering their volleys from their Spencer carbines until they could see another squadron formed to receive the shock of the enemy, then wheeling into column and falling back to a new position. This daring fight was constant and fierce, without a moment's interruption for nearly three hours, and extending over a space of about six miles, when the enemy became discouraged at his failure to surround the handful of Cavalry and ceased pursuit. William H. Dunn (formerly 2nd Lt. of Co. D. & 1st Lt. Co. E.), then Captain of Co. E. in this action bore a most conspicuous and gallant part at Abbott's Creek for which he received the commission of Major by brevet from the Secretary of War. Worthy of special mention in this action was the brave Leelanau Co. soldiers as well as Mjr. Standish, Cpt. Roberts, Minihan, Lt. Beech, and Sgt. Dumont.

When General Stoneman went to capture Salisbury, N.C. he met the enemy at a stream a few miles from town and ordered Major Israel Smith to take twenty men and flank the enemy. There surprise attack caused the Confederates to break and resulted in over 1100 Rebels being captured.

A few days later they learned of the surrender of Lee's army and moved toward South Carolina until the surrender of Johnston's army. Then they were ordered to pursue Confederate President Jeff Davis. They were through Statesville, * **Catawba River**, Howard's Gap, Blue Ridge Mts., & Asheville through April 26. Having already learned that they had help drive President Davis into the hands of General Pritchard and the Michigan men of the 4th MI Cavalry, they returned towards Knoxville, TN and on May 25th reached a base of supplies at Guntersville, on the Tennessee River. From March 25th to May 25th they had been living in the enemy's country, cut off from all bases of supplies, with no opportunity to hear from the loved ones at home.

* It was during this time that an event took place that seemed to have been made just for the men of Company E. from Leelanau County, Michigan. At the time of Lee's surrender, a Major from a Georgia regiment in the Artillery took a foolish notion that he and men of his old battery could steal away without being paroled to Mississippi. They went along the base of the mountains for a few days until they reached the **Catawba River** at a ford a few miles from Newton, in Western North Carolina. The river at that point was very wide, and the ford led across to an Island in the middle of the river. The Rebels approached very cautiously, keeping a sharp lookout for blue coats, but none were visible, and they all got safely across to the Island without seeing a sign of the Union.

Meanwhile, several men from Co. E. 10th MI Cavalry saw what was happening and decided to fix a clever trap. They knew that these Confederate fellows would likely send forward scouts to signal the rest of the Rebels back on the Island and the Union soldiers from Grand Traverse, having grown up around sand dunes and the Manitou Islands, were well adapt to hiding among the dunes over looking the island. (If only the Rebels knew just who they had run into!)

From the Island the Rebels scanned the bank of the river but could see nothing, especially over the reflection of the waters. (Something their opponents did all their lives). At last the Major sent out two men with instructions to signal if they found everything all right. They went, and the Rebels back on the Island saw them go up out of the water, up the bank, and disappear without giving a signal. The Rebels waited and waited and finally concluded that they must have spotted or gone in search of food, for they were nearly starved. They thought it a mean trick, anyway. After waiting a long time in suspense, and expressing hearty indignation at the greedy trick of those fellows, the Major decided to go across and pledged to his comrades that he would not leave them as the others had done. Upon reaching the bank of the river the Rebel Major noticed that the road had been cut down through the bank, making quite a deep cut, and directly across the road at the top of the hill someone, at some stage of the war, had dug a rifle pit in the dune. Suddenly a low voice, nearly overhead, sounded out. "Halt!" He looked up and saw lying on the top of the sandbank along the cut, a Sergeant (Enslee B. Larue of Glen Arbor & Empire, MI) with about a half dozen men, all covering him with their carbines. "All right, Johnny. Come in out of the wet. You may just throw down what arms you have, and then ride up right over the hill and you will be cared for. If you do as I say, you will be all right, but if you turn around or make any sign to those fellows over on the Island, you will be in a bad fix. Don't make any noise, Johnny. We will treat you well, only do as I say." Of course there was nothing else for the Major to do so he rode over the hill as the other two men had done before, without making a sign to his anxious comrades on the Island. He at once found himself in the camp of Co. E. 10th MI Cavalry, under the command of a very clever young Captain named William H. Dunn of Saugatuck, MI (then about 21 years old), and was treated with great kindness and hospitality. Unfortunately he had the mortification of seeing his whole battery, about eighty in number, taken in the same way. It was one of the cleverest bits of strategy that he ever saw; all taken in like a lot of Turkeys walking into a pen. With no one being unnecessarily hurt.

In the afternoon, Captain Dunn and Co. E. were relieved (by the 11th MI Cavalry that had also included 4 men from Glen Lake), and went to headquarters at Newton taking the Confederates along with them. The Rebel Major rode with Captain Dunn and had a pleasant chat. Upon arriving at Newton the Rebel Major was emboldened by the good treatment he had received from Co. E. to ask a favor of General Trowbridge. He asked that his men be allowed to stay the night with some of their friends in the area. General Trowbridge assented very cordially and left no guards in place, only asking their word to report in the morning for formal parole. Such treatment touched the hearts of the defeated and dispirited rebels. In the morning the Rebel officers were surprised to be fitted with horses and restored their side arms and then bid a hearty farewell.*

* (This story was told in the 1870's by the Rebel Major during a visit to Michigan and a chance meeting with Gen. Trowbridge, Adjutant Gen. Robertson, Gen. Wm. B. McCreery, and a banker named Emory Wendell. It has been modified by the Author for accuracy and clarification).

Upon returning to East Tennessee, the 10th MI Cavalry had duty at Lenior Station and Sweetwater until August 1865 under Major John H. Standish (Colonel Trowbridge having won the honorable promotion of Brigadier and Major General by brevet), and Lt. Colonel Smith. Major Harvey E. Light had returned back, having had great success in recruiting, and the ranks were full enough to permit promotion and muster in all the grades. (Reverend

Cherry had petitioned Michigan Governor Crapo hoping to get more relief for the men who were sick and expressed concern for their wives and children back home since there had been a large period of lack of pay. He also mentioned the 11th MI Cavalry).[73] They remained on duty in West TN until November. Attached to Cavalry Brigade, Dist. of East TN, Dept. of the Cumberland. Mustered out at Memphis Nov. 11, 1865 and arriving at Jackson, MI on the 15th. Regiment lost during service 2 Officers and 29 Enlisted men killed and mortally wounded and 240 Enlisted men by disease.[74]

In later years, several G.A.R. reunions would be held among the members of the 10th MI Cavalry. General Luther Stephen Trowbridge died February 2, 1912 and is buried in Elmwood Cemetery, Detroit, MI (Section B, Lot 4). Captain Weatherwax had been returned to the Congregation Church in Grand Rapids and buried in the Fulton Street Cemetery.[75] He had a G.A.R. Post named after him. William H. Dunn (1844-1934) returned to Saugatuck (Ganges) and had two daughters with wife, Mary. He had served in Custer's 5th MI Cavalry with General Trowbridge before the 10th Cavalry was formed and would stay active in the G.A.R. for the remainder of his life where he was remembered for leading Memorial Day parades on a white horse.[76] He is buried in front of the Civil War monument in Taylor Cemetery, Ganges, MI. Also listed are his brothers, whom were also Civil War veterans.[77]

REUNION OF THE TENTH MICHIGAN CAVALRY AT THE HOME OF GENERAL L. S. TROWBRIDGE, AT DETROIT, AT THE TIME OF THE NATIONAL ENCAMPMENT OF THE G. A. R., AUGUST 5TH, 1891.

Chaplain
Henry Cherry

Capt. and Bvt.
Lt. Col.
Edwin J. Brooks

Capt. and Bvt. Maj.
James H. Cummins

Capt. and Bvt. Maj.
William H. Dunn

Capt.
Ben. K. Weatherwax

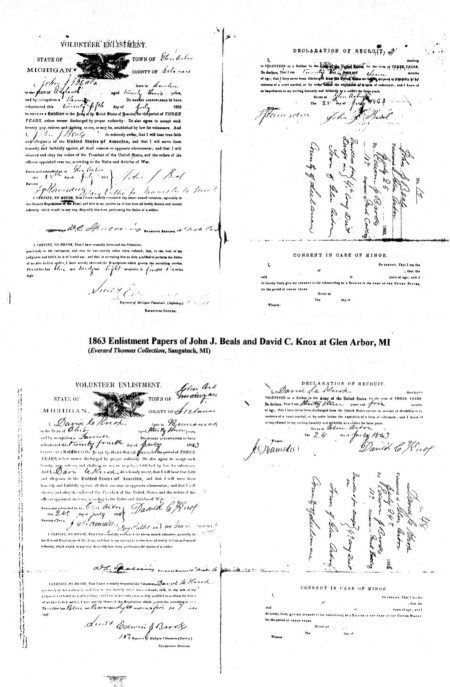

1863 Enlistment Papers of John J. Beals and David C. Knox at Glen Arbor, MI
(Everard Thomas Collection, Saugatuck, MI)

DECLARATION OF RECRUIT.

I, Enslee B Larue, desiring to VOLUNTEER as a Soldier in the Army of the United States, for the term of THREE YEARS,

Do declare, That I am twenty-one years and .... months of age; that I have never been discharged from the United States service on account of disability on by sentence of a court-martial, or by order before the expiration of a term of enlistment; and I know of no impediment to my serving honestly and faithfully as a soldier for three years.

Given at Glen Arbor
The 28 day of July Enslee B Larue

Witness: Ens.B.Ly

No. 50

Enslee B Larue
Volunteered at Glen Arbor
July 23d 1863,
By Edwin J Brooks
12th Regiment of Mich Cavalry
Enrolled for 3
Draft in 3 } 4th Cong Dist
Town of Glen Arbor
County of Leelanaw

CONSENT IN CASE OF MINOR.

I, John Larue of .... do CERTIFY, That I am the .... that the .... years of age; and I said .... is twenty .... years of age; and I do hereby freely give my consent to his volunteering as a Soldier in the Army of the United States, for the period of THREE YEARS.

Given at Glen Arbor
The 28 day of July
Witness: John Larue

Enlistment Papers of Sgt. Enslee B. Larue

Notice that since he was not yet 21, it is signed by his Father, John LaRue, the first permanent white settler on the mainland of Leelanau Co. Also notice recruiter Edwin Brooks of Northport, Surgeon David C. Spaulding, and witness George Ray. (*Everard Thomas Collection*, Saugatuck, MI)

VOLUNTEER ENLISTMENT.

STATE OF Michigan
TOWN OF Glen Arbor
COUNTY OF Leelanaw

I, Enslee Larue, born in Leelanaw Co aged twenty years, and by occupation a Farmer Jump in the State of Michigan Do hereby acknowledge to have volunteered this twenty third day of July 1863 to serve as a Soldier in the Army of the United States, for the period of THREE YEARS, unless sooner discharged by proper authority: Do also agree to accept such bounty pay, rations, and clothing, as are, or may be, established by law for volunteers. And I, Enslee B Larue do solemnly swear, that I will bear true faith and allegiance to the United States of America, and that I will serve them honestly and faithfully against all their enemies or opposers whomsoever; and that I will observe and obey the orders of the President of the United States, and the orders of the officers appointed over me, according to the Rules and Articles of War.

Sworn and subscribed to, at Glen Arbor Enslee B Larue this 28 day of July, 1863.

Before Ens.B.Ly Justice of the Peace

I CERTIFY, ON HONOR, That I have carefully examined the above named volunteer, agreeably to the General Regulations of the Army, and that in my opinion he is free from all bodily defects and mental infirmity, which would, in any way, disqualify him from performing the duties of a soldier.

D.C. Spaulding Examining Surgeon.

I CERTIFY, ON HONOR, That I have minutely inspected the Volunteer, previously to his enlistment, and that he was entirely sober when enlisted; that, to the best of my judgment and belief, he is of lawful age; and that, in accepting him as duly qualified to perform the duties of an able-bodied soldier, I have strictly observed the Regulations which govern the recruiting service. This soldier has brown hair, black eyes, florid complexion, is five feet 10 inches high.

Edwin J Brooks
.... Regiment of Michigan Volunteers, (Infantry.)
Recruiting Officer.

The Forest Haven Soldiers of the 10th MI Cavalry included: [78]

Sgt. Robert D. Adams Enlisted at Antrim in Co.H. 10th MI Cav. Sgt. Aug. 24, 1863. Age 22. Listed as a **Glen Arbor** Draftee. Mustered Sept. 2, 1863. Commissary Sgt. Mustered out at Memphis, TN December 11, 1865.

William J. Bannon Age 23. Enlisted in Co. M. 10th MI Cavalry at Grand Rapids, MI. Mustered Oct. 3, 1864. Joined regiment at Strawberry Plains Nov. 1, 1864. Was listed in Hospital at Knoxville.[79] Discharged at Memphis on Oct. 2, 1865. Later a Resident of **Maple City**, MI. G.A.R. Post 168. (also listed as Brennon). 1837-1910 Buried in Williamsburg City Cemetery, Benzie Co.

John J. Beals Age 23. Enlisted in Co. E. 10th MI Cavalry July 25, 1863 at **Glen Arbor**, MI. Born in London, England. (Listed blue eyes, sandy light hair, 5'6") Mustered Sept. 12, 1863 Mustered out on Nov. 11, 1865 at Memphis, TN.

John M. Benjamin Co. E. 10th MI Cavalry from **Solon** Township. Listed in Solon Township 1894 Veteran's Census. Died at Long Lake (Aug. 2, 1837 - March 29, 1901) Linwood / Neal Cemetery off Church Road.

Cpl. George W. Getchell Age 19. Enlisted in Co. E. 10th MI Cavalry July 23, 1863 at **Glen Arbor**, MI Mustered Sept. 12, 1863 Corporal June 25, 1865. Mustered out on Nov. 11, 1865 at Memphis, TN (Born Nov. 13, 1843 - D. April 22, 1922). Buried in Platte Township Cemetery, East of Otter Creek - Benzie County. (See Moses Getchell 1st Ill. Bat. of Glen Arbor.)

David C. Knox (also listed under David E. / G. & Knight). Age 33 Enlisted in Co. E. 10th MI Cavalry July 24, 1863 at **Glen Arbor**, MI Born in Brunswick, Ohio. (Listed blue eyes, brown hair, 5'7") Mustered Sept. 12, 1863 Mustered out on Nov. 11, 1865 at Memphis, TN The Knox farm was NE of South Bar Lake. David Knox died April 10, 1894. Listed Age 64? Buried at Empire, MI. Maple Grove Cemetery. Founding Member: G.A.R. Post 168. (See Daniel in the 15th MI Inf. and John Knox were listed in the pre-war 1860 Census of Leelanau Township.)

John B. Laillet Age 28. Co. E. 10th MI Cavalry Enlisted at **Glen Arbor** Sept. 26, 1863. Born in New York. (Listed hazel eyes, brown hair, 5'7") Mustered Oct. 14, 1863 Mustered out at Memphis, TN on Nov. 11, 1865.

Sgt. Enslee B. Larue Age 20. Enlisted Sgt. Co. E. 10th MI Cavalry at **Glen Arbor**, MI Sept. 12, 1863. Born in Iowa City. (Listed grey eyes, black hair, 5'10") Enlistment papers signed by his father, John LaRue (Larue). Discharged at Knoxville, TN. May 18, 1865. (In his youth, made trips of 30 miles carrying bushel bags of corn for the winter. He would later marry Kate "Lizzie" Coon and settled in Ohio. He died around 1903. His son, Frank Herman LaRue, became a vaudeville actor.)[80]

Cpl. Chester McIntyre Age 30. Co. E. Enlisted at Grand Rapids, MI Feb. 8, 1864 Mustered March 8, 1864 Corporal June 25, 1865 Mustered out at Memphis, TN Nov. 11, 1865 Resided at **Burdickville**, followed **Thomas McIntyre** who joined the 10 MI Cavalry in 1863. Glen Arbor Township 1890 Fed. Census Civil War Veteran & 1894 Veterans Census of MI. Buried in Kelderhouse/Port Oneida Cemetery. G.A.R. Post 168

Sgt. William W. Morgan Age 22 Commissary Sgt. Co. E. 10th MI Cavalry at **Glen Arbor**, MI enlisted July 23, 1863 Mustered Sept. 12, 1863 <u>Died at Knoxville, TN May 2, 1864</u>. Buried in National Cemetery, Knoxville,TN. (See Jessie Morgan in Leelanau Township & **Edward Morgan** also served in the 10th MI Cavalry.")

Sgt. Jonothan W. Russel Age 30 Co. E. 10th MI Cavalry **Traverse**. Involved with initial enlistment's. Aug. 1863. Corporal Sept. 12, 1863. Wagon Master Dec. 1864. Sgt. Jan. 1865. Mustered out at Memphis, TN Ferrier Nov. 11, 1865. Lived in Long Lake Township. Born in Vermont. Died July 7, 1907. Buried in Oakwood Cemetery. G.A.R. Post 168.

Lucius A. Smith Age 17. Co. E 10th MI Cavalry at Traverse City. Born in New York. (Listed blue eyes, brown hair, 5'6") Enlistment papers signed by his father, Alvin A. Smith. Enlisted Sept. 28, 1863 - out at Memphis, TN Nov. 11, 1865. Buried in East Kasson Evangelical Cemetery, **Maple City**. (Harom B. Smith of Co. D. 10th MI Cavalry also listed in Traverse.)

George W. Stetson Age 27 Enlisted Co. E. 10th MI Cavalry at **Glen Arbor**, MI enlisted July 24, 1863 Mustered Sept. 27, 1863 Mustered out at Memphis, TN Nov. 11, 1865. Listed as Glen Arbor Hunter and Trapper from New York in the pre-war 1860 Census with wife Elizabeth, children Allen and Marria E. (see also Ruben Stetson 164th NY). Founding Member: G.A.R. Post 168. (Listed in Kasson post-war 1870 census, came from PA in 1859 and moved from Glen Arbor to land that is now the area of the Glen Lake Community Schools.)[82]

Additional 10th MI Cavalry Horse Soldiers Associated with Leelanau County -

Albert A. Barnes Co.F. 10 MI Cav. Misc. Leelanau County. (Was listed as a 16 year old Mail Carrier in the pre-war 1860 Census of Leelanau Township. See John Barnes 15th MI Inf.)

Capt./Lt. Edwin J. Brooks of Northport, see 10th Cavalry History. Served in 1st NY Artillery/Chicago Light Infantry before joining the 10th Cav. became Captain of Co. M. (See also Abraham Brooks 10th MI Infantry.)

Anson J. Buckman Co. E. 10th MI Cavalry. Centerville. Age 17. (Listed as Blue Eyes, Light Hair, 5'7") Father, Henry S. Buckman signed consent.

George G. Campbell Age 21. Enlisted in Co. E. 10th MI Cavalry July 25, 1863 at Glen Arbor, MI Mustered Sept. 12, 1863 Deserted out at Grand Rapids, MI Dec. 2, 1863. Listed in pre-war 1860 Glen Arbor Census. His twin older brothers John and Neil are listed with the Glen Arbor Township Veterans.

Sgt. Edgar S. Charter Co. E. 10th MI Cav. Leelanau TS. & 19th MI Cav., Traverse & Northport (Was listed in the pre-war 1860 Census of Leelanau Township as a 22 year old farmer from Ohio, his Dad was from Vermont and Mom from New York. Listed as Hazel Eyes, Black Hair, 6'1") G.A.R. Post 399. Listed in Leelanau Township 1894 Veteran's Census. Died in 1911. Buried in Northport.

James Clark Age 36 Enlisted March 1865. (See Clark's in 15th & 26th MI)

Adam (Abel) Cook Co.I. 10th MI Cav. Age 23. Bingham? Lived in Centerville. (Wagoner).

Rev. Leander Curtiss Co. M. 10th MI Cav., Age 38. Joined regiment at Strawbery Plain, TN Nov. 1864. Discharged at Chattanooga, TN Oct. 2, 1865.Misc. Leelanau County. Died May 4, 1892. Buried at Gilead, MI. (See letter from Dec. 16, 1864 *Grand Traverse Herald*.)

Daniel Flanigan Age 18 Co. E. 10th MI Cavalry. Leelanau County, Enlisted Aug. 21, 1863 - Mustered Sept. 12, 1863. Out Nov. 11, 1865 at Memphis, TN. Later in Atwood, MI. Baxter Post 119. Charlevoix.

Cpl. James J. McLaughlin Co. D. 10th MI Cavalry. His Father had been an early Teacher at Northport (See first Chapter). James went on to become a Judge in Elk Rapids. Died June 26, 1908.

James R. (M.) **Merril** Co. D. 10th MI Cav. Leelanau County. 1838-April 6, 1907. Kalkaska Cemetery.

Lewis P. Ramsdell Co.F. 10th MI Cav. Elmwood Township.

Charles Randall Age 18 Enlisted in Co. E. 10th MI Cavalry from Leelanau Co., MI Sept. 12, 1863 -listed deserted at Knoxville TN Feb. 6, 1865. Though may have been result of George Randall being MIA in the 26th MI (Charles and Gilbert were listed in the pre-war 1860 Census of Leelanau Township.)

Jonathan W. Russell 10th MI Cavalry
(Courtesy U.S. Army Military History Institute
Carlisle Barracks, PA *Clara Hill Collection*)

Sgt. Gilbert Randall Age 23. Sgt. Enlisted in Co. E. 10th MI Cavalry from Leelanau County, MI Sept. 12, 1863 -Mustered out at Memphis, TN Nov. 11, 1865. (See A.W. Randall in 10th MI Inf.)

Sgt. James Spencer Age 20. Enlisted in Co. E. 10th MI Cavalry from Leelanau County, MI Sept. 12, 1863 Sgt. Aug. 11, 1865 Mustered out at Memphis, TN Nov. 11, 1865.

Edwin R. Van Valkenburg Co. E. 10th MI Cav. Age 18. Born in Massachusetts. (Listed Grey Eyes, Dark Hair, 5'11") Served Oct. 1863-Nov. 11, 1865., (See also listing under Sgt. Edward P. Van Valkenberg Co. E./I. 1st MI Eng.) Northport G.A.R. Post 399. Also lived in Traverse City, MI. Buried in Oakwood Cemetery. (Listed in the pre-war 1860 Census of Leelanau Township.) Also: **Major Eli Van Valkenburg** listed as Paymaster of Volunteers.

Joseph Wakazoo 10th MI Cav. Northport. (From 1st MI Sharpshooters & listed in 16th MI Co. H.). Wounded in battle June 6, 1864. (Listed Age 34 in the pre-war 1860 Census of Leelanau Township.)

Additional 10th MI Cavalry Horse Soldiers associated with the Grand Traverse Region:

Sgt. Abram Adsit Co. M. 10th MI Cav. Age 30. Joined regt. at Strawberry Plains, TN Nov. 1864. Discharged at Memphis, TN Oct. 2, 1865. Born Feb. 8, 1834. Died March 29, 1891. Buried in Traverse City, Oakwood Cemetery.

Henry Allison Enlisted in Co. E. 10th MI Cavalry. Age 18. Traverse. Mustered Oct. 14, 1863 - Died at Camp Nelson, KY Dec. 8, 1864.

Gustaff (Augustus) Anderson Co. E. 10th MI Cavalry. Age 25. Traverse. Born in Sweden. (Listed Blue Eyes, Light Hair, 5'11") Sept. 12, 1863 - Nov. 11, 1865.

Albern Atwell Co. M. Age 42. Joined regt. at Strawberry Plains, TN Nov. 1864. Dis. at Memphis, TN Oct. 2, 1865.

Capt. Enos B. Bailey served as Sgt in 3rd MI Cav. & Lt. in Co. I. 10th MI Cav. and became Captain of Co. I. Jan. 1864. after **Capt. Thomas (Amos T.) Ayers** resigned.

Hilman/Hyland S. Beach Co. M. 10th MI Cav. Born in NY 1833. (A May 26, 1899 letter written by F.B. Beach of the 10th MI Cav. to Capt. Dunn years after the War regarding a reunion in Petoskey, MI mentions Daniel Flanigan, Gilbert Randall, and John Runyon.)[83]

David S. Beebee Co. M. 10th MI Cav. Joined unit at Strawberry Plains, Died at Knoxville, TN Dec. 24, 1864 & is buried in National Cemetery. (John Beebee was in the 6th MI Cav.)

William Brakel Co. M. 10th MI Cav. June 26, 1837 – April 29, 1908 Oakwood Cemetery.

John Brown Co. I. Age 19.

Robert Byers Co. B. 10th MI Cavalry & Co. A. 19th MI Inf. Died July 12, 1901 Maple Grove Cemetery, T.C.

James Callaghan Co. E. 10th MI Cav. Joined regt. at Strawberry Plains, TN Discharged at Memphis, TN

David Carisle Co. A. 10th MI Cav. Co. I. 3rd MI Inf. G.A.R. Post 84 Kalkaska. 1840-1908 Yuba Cemetery.

Ira B. Chase Co. M. 10th MI Cav. Age 35. Joined regt. at Strawberry Plains, TN. Oct./Nov. 1864 – 1865. Lived in Neal, Died June 24, 1919 age 90. Oakwood Cem. (See also Albert Norris, 5th MI Cavalry & Edgar Chase in Post 399 listing.)

Sgt. Oscar Chase Co. I. 10th MI Cav. Age 23.

Eugene Cook Co. B. 10th MI Cav. Age 18. Feb. 1865-Oct.1865.

John Crotty Co. C. 10th MI Cav. 1846-Jan. 30, 1906 Oakwood Cemetery.

James R. Dean Co. D. 10th MI Cav. Elk Rapids area.

Sgt. Levi Decker Co. H. 10th MI Cav. Charlevoix, MI Brookside Cemetery.

Charles Denio Enlisted in Co. E. 10th MI Cavalry Age 28. Born in NY. (Listed Grey Eyes, Light Hair, 5'8") Sept. 12, 1863-Nov. 11, 1865.

Charles Deverney Enlisted in Co. E. 10th MI Cavalry Age 21. Penninsula Twp. Grand Traverse. Born in Milwaukee, WS. (Listed Black Eyes, Black Hair, 5') Oct. 14, 1863 - Out at Memphis, TN Nov. 11, 1865.

William R. Durga Co. M. 10th MI Cav. 1827-died at age 80 y 11m 29 d. Williamsburg Cemetery.

Girden H. Fish Co. E. 10th MI Cavalry Age 24. Oct. 14, 1863 - Nov. 11, 1865. 1836 - Nov. 23, 1903. Oakwood Cem.

George E. Fisher Co. F. 10th MI Cavalry.

Michael Gallagher 10th MI Cavalry.

Hebron Hallet 10th MI Cavalry and/or **Hiram Hallock** 10th MI Cavalry. (See Empire Township?)

Amos Hill Co. M. 10th MI Cavalry Age 44. Joined regt. at Strawberry Plains Oct. 3, 1864 out at Memphis Sept. 19, 1865.

Albert Jennings Co. F. 10th MI Cav. Born July 4, 1843. Buried in Fife Lake Cemetery.

George F. Johnson Co. M. 10th MI Cav. Whitewater / Elk Rapids.

William P. Jones Co. D. 10th MI Cav. Age 16. Lived at Big Bass Lake, Baldwin. Died in Nov. 1927.

Joseph Kune (Cune) Co.M. 10th MI Cav. Age 36. Joined regiment at Strawberry Plains, TN Nov. 1864 and was killed in action at Martinsville, VA April 8, 1865 at the close of the war.

Otis Lamunyon Co. F. 10th MI Cav. Died Oct. 30, 1936 Fife Lake Cemetery.

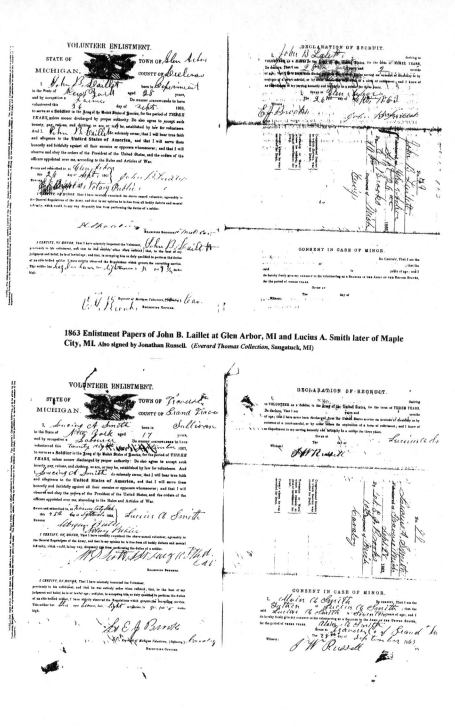

1863 Enlistment Papers of John B. Laillet at Glen Arbor, MI and Lucius A. Smith later of Maple City, MI. Also signed by Jonathan Russell. (*Everard Thomas Collection, Saugatuck, MI*)

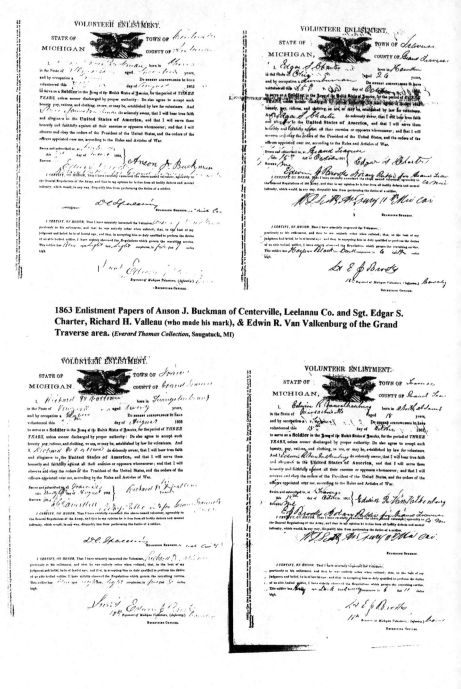

1863 Enlistment Papers of Anson J. Buckman of Centerville, Leelanau Co. and Sgt. Edgar S. Charter, Richard H. Valleau (who made his mark), & Edwin R. Van Valkenburg of the Grand Traverse area. (*Everard Thomas Collection*, Saugatuck, MI)

William S. Merrill Co. E. 10th MI Cavalry. Age 17. Penninsula Twp. Born in NY. (Listed Blue Eyes, Light Hair, 5'5") Mother, Eliza Merril signed Consent. Enlisted August of 1863. (See James Merril Co. D.)

Edward Morgan Co. M. 10th MI Cav. Joined regiment at Strawberry Plains, TN. Died at Manton, MI.

Adolphus Payette 10th MI Cavalry.

Alexander Pratt Co. B. 10th MI Cavalry Age 18. Mustered Sept. 2, 1863 out at Memphis, TN Nov. 11, 1865. Lived in Harlan, MI & member of Pomona G.A.R. Post 396, Cleon Twp. Manistee Co. MI (See photograph).

David Phillips Co. I. 10th MI Cavalry. Died at Knoxville, TN March 15, 1864.

David E. Ralfe / Rolfe Co. I. 10th MI Cav. Buried in Circle Hill Cemetery, Whitewater Township.

(John?) Reuben Reynolds Co. G. 10th MI Cav. Age 43. Feb.1865, at Harper Hospital Sept. 23, 1865, out Oct. 6, 65.

Bartholomew Rhorer/Roher Co. M. 10th MI Cav. Age 24. Manistee

Lafayette C. Rickerd Co. D. 10th MI Cav. & Co. H. 21st MI Cav. 1846 - July 6, 1919. Williamsburg Cemetery.

John M.C. Runyon Co. E. 10th MI Cav.?

Rudolph Scherer Co. E. 10th MI Cavalry Age 25. Traverse City. Joined regiment at Knoxville, TN Jan. 23, 1865. Harper Hospital Aug. 25, 1865. Out at Detroit Sept. 9, 1865.

Nelson C. Sherman Co. M. 10th MI Cavalry at Grand Rapids, Age 27. Died in T.C. Feb. 9, 1896. Oakwood Cem.

Edward Skinner Co. E. 10th MI Cavalry Nov. 17, 1864 - July 12, 1865. Lived in Central Lake.

George Sluyter Co. M. 10th MI Cav. Joined regiment at Strawberry Plains, TN Discharged at Detroit Aug. 3, 1865.

William Sluyter Co. M. 10th MI Cav. Joined regiment at Strawberry Plains, TN Dis. at Memphis, TN Nov. 11, 1865. 1839-1889 Buried in Oakwood Cemetery.

Sgt. Eber A. Springsteen Co. D. 10th MI Cav. 1839-1910. Frankfort area.

Reubin Sutherland Co. K. 10th MI Cav. At Saginaw.

James (or David) Sweeney Co.D. 10th MI Cav. Age 23. Sept. 1863- Aug. 1865.

W. Todd Co.D. 10th MI Cav. Blacksmith.

William Tracy 10th MI Cavalry. Grand Traverse.

J.H. Turner Co. I. 10th MI Cavalry. Died in 1864. Buried in Camp Nelson National Cemetery. Grave # 1473.

Richard H. Valleau (Barney? / Vallon) Co. E. 10th MI Cavalry Age 20. Traverse. Born in NY. (Listed Blue Eyes, Light Hair, 5'8") Father, James Valleau signed Consent. Mustered Sept. 12, 1863 - Died of disease 4 months later at Camp Nelson, KY Jan. 29, 1864. Grave # 1490. (see George Vallean 7th OH).

Zodock Wilcox Co. D. 10th MI Cav. Joined regiment at Strawberry Plains, TN Out at Knoxville, TN May 25, 1865.

George Winnie Co. M. 10th MI Cav. Joined regiment at Strawberry Plains, TN Discharged at Memphis, TN

Richard Wood Co. D. 10th MI Cavalry. Buried in Elk Rapids.

Elliott Wright Co. I. 10th MI Cavalry Age 18. Bingham. Sept. 30, 1863 - Died of disease at Strawberry Plains TN June 11, 1864.

Silas Wright Co. E. 10th MI Cavalry Age 19. Born in Parama, NY Sept. 10, 1845. Died in Petoskey in 1937 at age 91. Greenwood Cemetery. Lombard G.A.R. Post.

(A letter by Charles C. Pemperton of Co. C. is in the MI Archives.)

Alexander Pratt of the 10th MI Cavalry (Back 2nd Row 3rd from left) is shown here with some of the members in the Pomona G.A.R. Post 396 of Cleon Twp. Manistee Co. Also pictured are: 1st Back Row – Robert Fulton Lewis, Jacob Sears of the 9th & 8th MI Inf., T. Cordion 11th MI Cavalry, Jake Rinard 57th PA?, Horatio Snyder 4th NY L.A., 2nd Back Row – Geo. Hall, Geo. Clifton, Alexander Pratt 10th MI Cav., John Stanton MI Eng., 3rd Seated Row – Geo. Henderson, Sgt. William O. Killian 6th MI H.A., A.L. Hunt 13th MI Inf., Daniel Holmes MI Cav., Lt. Alonzo Chubb 105th OH Inf. 4th Front Row – Byron Dean 13th MI Inf. & Oliver C. Gregg. The Post was named after Lt. Charles O. Twist of the 8th MI Cavalry.
(Courtesy Copemish American Legion Post 531 & Bruce D. Overmyer)

Union Soldiers
(Courtesy Military History Institute
Carlisle Barracks, PA)

**The Clarkston Band of the
15th Michigan Infantry**
(Courtesy Ray & Brian Russell)

Forest Haven Soldiers: The Civil War Veterans of Sleeping Bear & Surrounding Leelanau

"The Gallant" 15th MI Infantry

This unit included many men from the Leelanau County area who were drafted in the fall of 1864 into "The Gallant 15th" MI. Colonel John M. Oliver. They joined a unit that had already been through the Battles of Shiloh / Pittsburg Landing, Corinth, Vicksburg, Alabama, Chattanooga, Knoxville, Guntersville, Atlanta Campaign, Resaca, Dallas, Pumpkin Vine Creek, Kenesaw Mountain, and Jonesboro. (In action at Decatur, the 15th's Chas. F. Sanscrainte earned the Congressional Medal of Honor). The men joined these veteran fighters during their operations against Confederate Gen. Hood in North Georgia and North Alabama through Nov. 3. 1864.

The Active service of the 15th during their enlisted time also included: Travel through Marietta, Allatoona, Reconnaissance from Rome on Cave Springs Road, Resaca, Snake Creek Gap, Carr Springs, and in several skirmishes Oct. 12-13. Then Sherman's March from Atlanta to the Sea Nov. 15 - Dec. 10. It was then serving in the Third Brigade, Second Division, Fifteenth Corps. Arrived at Vining's Station, Encountered opposition where they had a slight skirmish at Clinton, GA Nov. 21-23, with three men wounded. Moved Near Bryan's CourtHouse Dec. 8, 1864. Siege of Savannah, GA, Dec. 10-21. Engaged at Saluda Creek, SC, and Fort McAllister,GA, Dec. 13, 1864.

Colonel John M. Oliver was promoted to Brigadier General Jan.12, 1865 and Frederick Y. Hutchinson was commissioned Colonel on the 14th. Campaign of the Carolinas Jan to April, 1865. Embarked upon transports for Beaufort, S.C. Duck Creek, S.C., via Garden's Cross Roads, Orangeburg (engaged), Grangeburg, Salkehatchie Swamps, S.C., Feb. 2-5 with occasional skirmishing in the front. Congaree, Angley's Post Office Feb. 4. Crossed Combahee River. Encamped on Dickinson's Plantation. Feb. 5. Destroying railroad at Bamberg Station Feb. 7. Encamped in South Edisto Feb. 9. Poplar Springs Feb. 11. North Edisto River Feb. 12-13. Sandy Run Post Office Feb. 14. Columbia Feb. 16-17, where they were shelled by the enemy and skirmishing on the banks of the Broad River and Saluda Mills. Ordered to arrest stragglers and incendiaries Feb. 18. Crossed Waterlee River on the 22nd. Through Liberty Hill on the 23rd of Feb. Then on to Camden, Lynch's Creek, Cheraw, Laurel Hill to Fayetteville with more fighting engagements. Support of the 14th & 20th Corps at Falling Creek in line throwing up works. In the Battle of Bentonville, N.C. March 19-21. Detailed guarding train going to Kinston, NC for supplies March 22. Occupation of Goldsboro March 24. (Marched 230 miles in March).

Advance on Raleigh April 10-14 via Pikeville and Lowell Mills. **Napoleon Paulis of Co. B. (Northport) wounded April 12.** Occupation of Raleigh April 14. Bennett's House April 26. Surrender of Johnston and his army. March to Washington D.C. via Richmond, VA. April 29-May 20. Bailey's Cross-roads. Marched from Louisburg,

General John M. Oliver
15ᵗʰ MI Infantry
(State Archives of Michigan)

Correspondence of Colonel John Oliver of the 15ᵗʰ MI Infantry
(Courtesy Western Michigan University Historical Collections)

Lawrenceville NC, Petersburg, VA. Took up line of march to D.C. via Bowling Green, Fredericksburg, and Alexandria, VA. Participated in the Grand Review (Victory Parade) with Sherman's Army May 24, 1865. (Marched 210 miles during May).

The regiment was encamped near Washington until it started for Louisville, KY June 1-6 via the Baltimore and Ohio Railroad, thence moved to Little Rock Ark. via transports to the mouth of the White River June 28, and duty till August 13. Mustered out at Little Rock, Ark. Aug. 13,1865. They delayed departure for a week, no doubt due to the unfortunate deaths of several area men that week. Unit started upon its return to Michigan Aug. 21 where it took transports for Cairo, and then proceeded by rail to Michigan where it arrived in Detroit September 1, 1865 and was last paid. The membership of the 15th was ~ 2371 men with 337 losses. Forty-eight men and two officers were killed in action. Eighteen men and one officer died of wounds. 263 men and four officers died of disease. Those companies with the most men from Leelanau County were: Co. A. Captain John H. Waterman, Co. B. Captain Richard Loranger, & Co. C. Captain R.F. Farrell.[84]

The Forest Haven Soldiers of the 15th MI Infantry Included:[85]

Hiram Bowen /(Brown) Age 25. Co.D. 15th MI Inf. Drafted from **Almira**, Northern Benzie Co. Mustered Oct. 27, 1864. Out at Little Rock, AK Aug. 13, 1865 and died of disease from his service a few months after returning home. His wife was Julia and their 3-month-old infant son, Albert, had died just a month before his departure for the war.[86] Born in Kalaneo, Eaton Co. April 7, 1839. Buried in Green Briar – Almira Union Cemetery.

Jan/Lohn Cizkovsky (Cizkofy/John Criskivooska/Cizkorosky) Drafted in Co. D. 15th MI Inf. from **Glen Arbor**. Age 40. Mustered Oct. 27, 1864 & Mustered out at Little Rock, Ark. June. 13, 1865. Later returned to Chicago like **Vaclav Vileta** and died.

Benjamin Collins Age 37. Co.A. 15th MI Inf. Drafted from **Glen Arbor**. Mustered Oct. 27, 1864. Mustered out at Little Rock, AK Aug. 13, 1865.

John Dorsey Co. A. 15th MI Inf. Age 39. Drafted for 1 Year from **Glen Arbor**, MI Mustered Oct. 27, 1864 & Mustered out at Little Rock, Ark. Aug. 13, 1865 He settled on the Southern shore of Glen Lake on land he had purchased before the war, at $2.00 per acre.[87] Listed on **Empire** Township 1894 Veterans Census of MI. (Dorsey & Parker ate supper at the Soldiers Rest before going to Jackson, MI as mentioned on page 36 of the "Biozard Letters.") He and Elizabeth (Cogshall) had two sons listed in the pre-war 1860 Glen Arbor Census & 5 more were later born.[88] Photograph is featured in "Remembering Empire Through Pictures." He was a native of Dublin, Ireland,[89]born December 25,1825, a Cooper (Barrel maker) who could speak Native Indian language fluently.[90] and was a friend of pioneer John LaRue.[91] He died April 8, 1903. Age 77. Buried at Empire, MI (Maple Grove Cemetery). 1st Commander of G.A.R. Post 168. (See G.A.R. Post 168 photograph on far right of second row.)

<u>**Vaclav**</u> /Wensel (or **Wveusit-Vancella, Vencile**), **Hajek** (or **Highlick-Husick-Higheck-Hagon-Sfagon**) Co. B. 15th MI Inf. Age 40. Drafted for 1 Year from **Glen Arbor**, MI Mustered Oct. 27, 1864 & Mustered out at Little Rock, Ark. Aug. 13, 1865. Listed on Cleveland Twp. 1894 Veterans Census of MI under Vencel Hayek. Died May 17, 1909. Buried in Cleveland Township / Shalda Cemetery by Mary Hajek, in an unmarked grave! Member: G.A.R. Post 168.

Glen Lake G.A.R. Post 168
(Courtesy Empire Area Museum)

William F. Kellogg 15th MI Infantry
(Courtesy Kasson Heritage Group)

John Dorsey 15th MI Infantry
(Courtesy Empire Area Museum)

William Freeman Kellogg Co. B. / K. 15th MI Inf Age 24. Drafted for 1 Year **Maple City** / listed Glen Arbor, MI Mustered Oct. 27, 1864 & Mustered out at Little Rock, Ark. Aug. 13, 1865 Lived in Kasson, MI. Listed in 1894 Veterans Census of MI. Disability for Rheumatism & partial deafness. Photo in "Remembering Yesterday" by Kasson Heritage Group. Served as Justice of the Peace. Farm was at SW corner of Baatz & Fritz Roads. July 5, 1828 – March 3, 1906. Buried in Rose Hill Cemetery, Kasson Township off M-72. Member: G.A.R. Post 18 and 168.

Henry Kirchert (Sometimes listed under Kirkout) Co. A./B. 15th MI Inf. Age 33. Drafted for 1 Year from **Glen Arbor**, MI. Mustered Oct. 27, 1864 & Mustered out at Little Rock, Ark. Aug. 13, 1865. Listed in Centerville Township 1894 Veterans Census of MI. Farm was off SE corner of Shell (Prouse) Lake in North Unity/Port Oneida area. Died Dec. 19, 1916. Buried in Cleveland Township / Shalda Cemetery. Member: G.A.R. Post 168.

Anton (Anthony) Kucera (Kucers) / Antoine Krucera Co. B. 15th MI Inf. Age 41 Drafted for 1 Year from **Glen Arbor**, MI Mustered Oct. 27, 1864 & Mustered out at Little Rock, Ark. Aug. 13, 1865 His farm was located about half way between Big Glen and Lime Lake. Died September 24, 1886. Bohemian Farmer. Age 62. Listed as Buried at North Unity Cemetery, MI now Cleveland Township / Shalda Cemetery. (1824~1886). Member: G.A.R. Post 168.

John Kulanda (Kolando / Kulenda) Co. B. 15th MI Inf. Age 37? Drafted for 1 Year. **Glen Arbor**, MI Mustered Oct. 27, 1864 & Mustered out at Little Rock, Ark. Aug. 13, 1865 (Born in Bohemia April 25, 1830 or 1839 - Died July 1, 1891). Buried at Cleveland Township / Shalda Cemetery or North Unity Cemetery. He and Mary had a young son and daughter in the pre-war 1860 Census of Glen Arbor Township. During an engagement with the enemy a bullet struck him on the brass plate of his belt. The force of the ball was so great that it caused him to reel and fall but he was caught by a comrade and laid gently on the ground. The effect of this shot he never recovered from and it is believed was the ultimate cause of his death. His old comrades in the G.A.R. visited him in his last sickness and as a Post were in attendance at his funeral.[92] Member G.A.R. Post 168.

George Lee Co. E. 15th MI Inf. Age 19. Substitute for Fred Warner, Drafted from **Glen Arbor**, MI Mustered Oct. 27, 1864 No further record.

Joseph Massupoert/Masopust (Masepust/Massuport) Co. B. 15th MI Inf. Age 38. Drafted for 1 Year from **Glen Arbor**, MI Mustered Oct. 27, 1864 & Died Aug. 15, 1865. Buried in National Cemetery, Little Rock, Ark. Section I Grave # 639. Killed by runaway team.

Mathias/Matej (Nathias) **Nemeskal** Nemischer/Nemescher or Nymschull Co. C. 15th MI Inf. Age 42. Drafted for 1 Year from **Glen Arbor**, MI Mustered Oct. 27, 1864 & Died of disease at Little Rock, Ark. July 18, 1865. Buried at Little Rock, Ark. Widow: Nemeskal drew Pension in **Maple City**, MI. (John Nemeskal Age 25 is listed on the post-war 1870 Sleeping Bear Census.)

James Nolon Co. C. 15th MI Inf. Age 38 of Centerville. Mustered Oct. 27, 1864. Discharged at Louisville, KY June 26, 1865. **Solon** Township 1894 Veteran's Census. Buried in Holy Rosary Cemetery, Isadore / Mt. Cavalry. (Maurice Nolan was also listed in draft.)

Daniel Parker Co. C. 15th MI Inf Age 30. Drafted for 1 Year from **Glen Arbor**, MI Mustered Oct. 27, 1864 & Mustered out at Little Rock, Ark. Aug. 13, 1865 (Captain R.F. Farell of Detroit, 1st Lt. John Considine, 2nd Lt. John Stewart) Glen Arbor Township 1890 Fed. Census Civil War Veteran. Daniel Parker died Dec. 20,1889. Buried in the old Glen Arbor, MI Township Cemetery, near M22-Forest Haven Road within the Sleeping Bear Dunes National Lakeshore. Daniel was a Founding Member: G.A.R. Post 168. (Mary Parker is also listed in some of the local Glen Arbor History, Burr Parker in Empire, A. Parker is buried in Frankfort, MI who served as the first Commander of Carver Post 123 & Sewell Parker served in 26th MI).

William Pierce Co. C. 15th MI Inf. Age 44. Drafted for 1 Year from **Glen Arbor**, MI Mustered Nov. 11, 1864 & Mustered out at Little Rock, Ark. Aug. 13, 1865

Zimariah (Zimri/Zeimer/Zennia) **Pratt** Co. C. 15th MI Inf. Age 39. Drafted from **Almira**, Northern Benzie Co. Mustered Oct. 27, 1864. Died of disease July 11, 1865. Buried in National Cemetery, Memphis, TN. Grave # 4134. Listed Gray eyes, Dark hair, 5'6 ½" Farmer from Milton, Vermont.[9] Damaged headstone in Almira Cemetery. Also listed with his widow, Tryphena. (See Adonison Pratt 106th NY G.A.R. Post 168.)

George N. Sites Co. C. 15th MI Inf. Age 20. Drafted for 1 Year from **Manitou**, MI Mustered Oct. 27, 1864 & Died of disease at New Berne, N.C. March 16, 1865 Buried in old cemetery, New Berne, NC.

Sgt. John W. Van Nostrand (Van Ostrand) Sgt. Co. C. 15th MI Inf. Age 37. Drafted for 1 Year **Glen Arbor**, MI Mustered Oct. 27, 1864 & Corporal May 1, 1865. Sgt. June 30, 1865. Mustered out at Little Rock, Ark. Aug. 13, 1865. Lived in Burdickville. Listed in **Empire** Township 1894 Veterans Census of MI. He later had a farm a few miles east of Glen Lake Schools. Born 1827 in NY? Buried in Kasson Cemetery (**Maple City**). Member: G.A.R. Post 168. (Wilson Van Ostrand of Glen Arbor was also listed in the draft.)

James Veleter or **Valaday/ Veleton** Co. C. 15th MI Inf. Age 43. Drafted for 1 Year from **Glen Arbor**, MI Mustered Oct. 27, 1864 & Mustered out at Little Rock, Ark. Aug. 13, 1865

Alfred E. Willard (Millard) Co. C. 15th MI Inf. Age 20. Drafted from **Almira**, Northern Benzie Co. Mustered Oct. 27, 1864. Died of disease at Little Rock, AK Aug. 8 or 9, 1865. Buried in National Cemetery, at Little Rock, AK Section I Grave No. 627. Marker also placed in Almira Cemetery in Benzie County.

Additional Soldiers of the 15th Michigan Infantry Associated with Leelanau County

John Barnes Co. A. 15th MI Inf. Age 20 Centerville. Substitute for Simeon Pickard. (see Albert Barnes in 10th MI Cavalry and Barnes under Leelanau County listings.)

Matihias (Bridehout/Breithoup) Breithaupt (Wattice Bridehout) Co. A. 15th/18th MI. Elmwood. Township. Born Nov. 4, 1826 - Died Dec. 14, 1898? Oakwood Cemetery.

John Bremer (Bramer) Drafted from Centerville into Co. D. 15th MI Inf. Age 28. Mustered Oct. 5, 1864. Out at Little Rock, AK June 13, 1865. Served earlier in Co. M. 43rd MO Militia (or 42nd). Leland TS 1894 Veteran's Census. East Leland Cemetery. G.A.R. Post 399.

Kerr (Cornelius) Bud Co.A. 15th MI Inf.(Leelanau Twp.1894 Veteran's Census), Age 22. G.A.R. Post 399. (Listed at age 17 in the pre-war 1860 Census of Leelanau Township.) Northport Cemetery. See Henry Budd 26th MI.

**Insert of: John P. Howell
15th MI Infantry, from**
"A History of Leelanau
Township" (Courtesy
Leelanau Historical Museum)

Elk Rapids,
Mich.

Mr. & Mrs. John Bremer
MO & MI Civil War Veteran
(Courtesy Louise Bremer & Leelanau
Historical Museum)

Narcissus Cardinal Co.B. 15th MI Inf. Centerville. Age 28. Substitute for John Porter.

George L. Clark Co.H. 15th MI Inf. Age 33. From Leelanau. (See Charles in 26th MI)

James A. Clark Co. A. 15th MI Inf. (from Honor).

Robert/Phillip Easternight (Easterwright) Co. A. 15th MI Inf. Age 33. (Leelanau TS.1894 Veteran's Census), Northport G.A.R. Post 399. (Listed at age 28 from Baden, Germany in the pre-war 1860 Census of Leelanau Township.) Northport Cemetery.

Phillip Goldrick Co. A. 15th MI Inf. Age 33. Drafted for 1 Year from Leelanau, MI Mustered Oct. 27, 1864 & Mustered out at Little Rock, Ark. Aug. 13, 1865 (Listed at age 29 under Philip Garlicke from Ireland in the pre-war 1860 Census of Leelanau Township.)

John P. Howell Co. B. 15th MI Inf. Age 35. (Leelanau Twp.1894 Veteran's Census), Mustered Oct. 27, 1864 & Mustered out at Little Rock, Ark. Aug. 13, 1865 Died May 30, 1903. Northport G.A.R. Post 399. (Listed from England in the pre-war 1860 Census of Leelanau Township.) Northport Cemetery.

Charles Irish Co. F. 5th MI Elmwood Township. Died May 8, 1914 Age 76 Oakwood Cemetery.

Daniel S. Knox Co. B. 15th MI Inf. Age 32. Drafted from Leelanau, MI Mustered Oct. 27, 1864 & Mustered out at Little Rock, Ark. Aug. 13, 1865. (Listed from Ohio in the pre-war 1860 Census of Leelanau Township with John Knox, Sailer.) Northport Cemetery. (See David Knox 10th MI Cav.)

David/Daniel Lawabee/Larabee Co. C. 15th MI Inf. Age 34. Northport.

John Leikman Enlisted in Co.C. 15th MI Inf. Age 26. Northport. Wounded in action at Shiloh, TN.

John I. (J.or F.) **Miller** Co. B. 15th MI Inf. Age 43. Drafted from Centerville. Leland. (Postmaster). (Listed from Canada in the pre-war 1860 Census of Leelanau Township with 3 daughters.) Born in Quebec, Canada Sept. 3, 1822. Died Sept. 10, 1889. St. Mary's Cemetery, Lake Leelanau.

Robert Moore Enlisted in Co.C. 15th MI Age 30. Northport. <u>Buried in Corinth National Cemetery</u>. (Listed in the pre-war 1860 Census of Leelanau Township, wife Mary was 19 & Daniel Moore's family was listed in Glen Arbor Township.)

Charles Norris Co. C. 15th MI Inf. Elmwood Township 1894 Veteran's Census also Solon Twp. Died Feb. 2, 1904 Age ~ 71. Buried in Oakwood Cemetery. T.C. McPherson G.A.R. Post 18. (Listed in the pre-war 1860 Census of Centerville Township, was son of Seth W.) See Albert Norris 5th & &7th MI Cavalry.

John O'Riley Co. A. 15th MI Inf. Leland.

Walter C. Palmer Enlisted in Co.C. 15th MI Inf. Age 22. Northport. <u>Killed in action at Shiloh</u> April 6, 1862. Buried in Shiloh Nat.Cemetery. (Veteran Melville Palmer of the 26th MI is listed in Suttons Bay and was age 17 in the pre-war 1860 Centerville Census.)

Napoleon Paulus Co. B. 15th MI Inf. Age 27 of Centerville-Leland TS 1894 Veteran's Census, was wounded April 12, 1865. Northport G.A.R. Post 399. Listed Napoleon Paul Age 22 from Canada in the pre-war 1860 Census of Centerville Township with wife Phelomen age 18 from Wisconsin. Lost two daughters in a terrible drowning accident at Carp Lake (Leelanau) in June of 1884. Story in Leelanau Enterprise. Listed buried in Paulus Cemetery on north edge of Leland.

Henry Peck Co. C. 15th MI Inf. (Northport) Enlisted Nov. 26, 1862. Age 31. (Peck family photo in "Remembering Yesterday" by Kasson Heritage Group. (See Edrick Peck 11th MI Cavalry.)

Andrew& John Scott[94] Co. F. 15th MI Inf. Joined regiment in Beafort, SC. (Leelanau Twp.1894 Veteran's Census), Northport G.A.R. Post 399. (John was 26 and Andrew was 28 in the pre-war 1860 Census of Leelanau Township from Canada with Mary Scott 18 and Mary Avery age 4 . John later served as Sheriff.) John was born Jan. 20, 1831 & died Aug. 11, 1911. Both brothers are buried in Northport Cemetery. See Daniel Scott 12 Ill. Cleveland Township.

Matthias Snyder Co. C. 15th MI Age 31. Elmwood Township 1894 Veteran's Census. Traverse City. Born in Germany Aug. 3, 1833 - June 28, 1900 in California. Oakwood Cemetery. Traverse City.

David S. Sutton Co.D. 15th MI Inf. Bingham. <u>Died of disease at Shiloh,</u>[95] TN June 1, 1863.

Theobald Joseph Umlor (Umbler) Jr. Co.C. 15th MI Inf. Age 27. Centerville & Elmwood Township. Lived in Traverse City. 1836-1927 Oakwood Cemetery, old Catholic section. McPherson G.A.R. Post 18

Edward Welch Co.C. 15th MI Inf. Age 32.

John White Co.C. 15th MI Inf. Age 24.

And many additional men of the Grand Traverse area in the 15th MI Infantry including:

John H./N. Bradshaw Co.K. 15th MI Inf. Died 1903. 1844-1903 Mt. Hope Cemetery, Green Lake.
Courtland Brownell Co.D. 15th MI Inf. Age 30. Benzonia. Died Aug. 25, 1914 Age 86. Oakwood Cemetery.
Milo N. Corning Co. C. Lived in Mayfield Twp. in late 1800's.
Abial Crandall 15th MI Inf. Charlevoix.
George Dair Co. B. 15th MI Inf. Oct. 2, 1842 – March 17, 1890. Joyfield Cemetery, Benzie Co.
Edward C. Davis Co. B. 15th MI Inf. T.C.
Lewis Gebeau (Geboo) Co.B. 15th MI Inf. Age 30. Charlevoix. Drowned Oct. 27, 1887.
George Greenwood Co.G. 15th MI Inf. Age 36. Manistee. Died June 25, 1900. Buried at Soldiers Home, MI.
Eli Horton Co.B. 15th MI Inf. Age 33. Charlevoix. <u>Killed in action at Chattanooga, TN.</u> Dec. 2, 1864.
Justus D. Johnson Co.K. 15th MI Inf. Thompsonville Cemetery.
Charles Kroupa 15th MI Inf.
Andrew LaForge Co. B. /I 15th MI Inf. 1838-1904 Maple Grove Cemetery-Elk Rapids.
Martin Liginvan 15th MI Inf. Lived in Kingsley. Evergreen Cemetery Lot 115, No marker!
Francis Martin Co.B. 15th MI Inf. Age 38. Crystal Lake.
Peter Matheson Co.K. 15th MI Inf. Died May 13, 1932. Gilmore Cemetery, Benzie Co.
Mark F. McMichael Co.K. 15th MI Inf. 1843- April 17, 1890 or 1891. Oakwood Cemetery, Traverse City.
James A. Morgan Co.G. 15th MI Inf. Age 40.
Soloman E. Morgan Co.B. 15th MI Inf. Age 22. Crystal Lake. (See William M. 10th MI Cavalry & Jessie in Leelanau Twp.)
Sgt. Henry Ostrom Co.H. 15th MI Inf. Charlevoix.
August Otto Co.A. 15th MI Inf. Age 35.
Elijah L. Ransom Co.H. 15th MI Inf. 1848-1896/1921? Oakwood Cemetery, Traverse City.
William A. Sanders Co. C. 15th MI Inf. Peninsula Twp.
Crosby Whitney Co. A. 15th MI Inf. Born 1843, in Walton Cemetery?
(Others likely with Solon of Kent County but may possibly be connected: Edwin J. Rodgers, George Rome, Elmer Rose, and Manley Rounds of the 15th MI Infantry.)

After Col. John Oliver was promoted to Brigadier General,
Frederick Y. Hutchinson was commissioned Colonel of the
15th MI Infantry (National Archives and Records Administration)

Lt. Charles H. Holden of Northport
26th MI Infantry
(Michigan Archives)

Men of the 26th MI Infantry including
Sewell S. Parker (Bottom Right)
(State Archives of Michigan)

Forest Haven Soldiers: The Civil War Veterans of Sleeping Bear & Surrounding Leelanau

26th MI Infantry The Lakeshore Tigers

Service under 25 Yr. old Colonel Judson S. Farrar and later Colonel Lemuel Saviers who had served with other men from Leelanau County in the 1st Michigan Sharpshooters before he became Captain of Co. F. of the 26th MI. **Captain L. Edwin Knapp** of Co. A. was from Grand Traverse, **Lt. Charles H. Holden** of Northport, and **Lt. Jacob E. Seibert** of Manistee. Lt. Holden left with 60 gallant men who left their families, plows, and workshops to fight the battles of their country. In 1862 the *Grand Traverse Herald* reported, "When we take into consideration the fact that our population is composed mostly of farmers who are struggling against all hardships and privations incident to clearing up new farms in the wilderness, it must be conceded that our infant county has sent forth her full quota to the war."[96] (Unfortunately, many more would follow.)

26th MI Active Service: from Jackson MI to Alexandria VA they were said to have past through Toledo, Cleveland, OH then Erie, PA, to Almira, NY, to Williamsport, Harrisburg, PA, Baltimore, MD, and Washington where a letter by Charles Gunn of Co. H. described the Capital as one of the most beautiful buildings he ever saw and Washington, as a City, as one of the dirtiest. They passed by the old Bull Run Battlegrounds going to Union Mills to meet General Stuarts Rebel Cavalry where they saw old shells, bayonets, and knapsacks.[97] On to Suffolk where a letter by Oscar Eaton was sent to the *Grand Traverse Herald* describing much of the action, (see insert), then to Windsor, Dix's Peninsula Campaign, Bottom's Bridge, New York City to assist in sustaining the laws during the famed New York Draft Riots. The *New York Times* wrote of the 26th MI Infantry:

" The Twenty-sixth Michigan arrived here last night from Potomac, and will be assigned to duty in this city, until the great riot is quelled. The regiment bore evidences of the hard services it has undergone in the field; but it is composed of as fine a body of brave, intelligent American young men as ever shouldered a musket in the cause of civil liberty and civil order. We welcome it to the city, and we trust our citizens, by their thoughtful attentions, will show their appreciation of such a regiment. At the present moment the Peninsular State is represented in the three great armies of Grant, Rosecrans, and Meade, as well as in those of Banks, Gillmore and Dix, and the Michigan soldiers have won renown for their bravery and discipline throughout the war and on almost every battle-field."

The regiment was later ordered from Fort Richmond, on Stanton Island, to cross the Rappahannock, and after its engagements at Mine Run the regiment returned to Stevensburg in Dec. of 1863 for winter quarters. In joining the Army of the Potomac, it was assigned to the 1st Brigade, (Miles), of the 1st Division, 2nd Army Corps, and was recognized as the skirmish regiment of the division.

The Grand Traverse Herald

MORGAN BATES, Editor and Proprietor

TRAVERSE CITY
FRIDAY MORNING, JUNE 26, 1863.

Letter from Capt. Eaton.

DISBANDED FARM, Ns____son Co. Va.,
May 20, 1863.

MR. BATES—Feeling an inclination to inflict a letter upon some person or persons, I have about made up my mind to bore the readers of the Herald for a short time this excessively warm afternoon (with your permission of course,) in regard to the where-abouts and whatabouts of the 29th Mich., Co. A, of which regiment contains most of the Traverse boys, who volunteered in our County, some over 9 months ago. On the morning of the 20th of April we were aroused at daybreak by the hideous screeching of a railroad locomotive in front of our camp, and the announcement of the Conductor that he held in his hand an order for Lieut. B. S. Parker, (who now commands this company during the temporary absence of Capt. Knapp, by sickness,) to report, with his command, at Alexandria instantly. We, soldiers, as we are supposed to be, were not long in waking up to the subject, and in a very short time we had prepared a cup of coffee, and swallowed the same, packed our knapsacks, transferred the Company movables (tents excepted) to the cars and were whirling along toward Alexandria, which place we reached a few minutes before 6 o'clock in the morning, stopping some 15 minutes to pick up a squad that were detached at Edsell's on guard duty. At ten o'clock, A. M., the regiment had embarked on board a transport and were steaming down the Potomac. In leaving Alexandria we were obliged to bid adieu to our good old Sibley tents, which for the last 8 months had sheltered us from many a heavy storm both of rain and snow, and in which we had enjoyed so many soldierly comforts, and betake ourselves to shelter tents. This, of course, we understood to mean active service in the field, in lieu of guarding cities and handling cord-wood. Our regiment reached Suffolk, Va., via Fortress Monroe, Norfolk, &c., on Tuesday at 11 o'clock, P. M., and were soon basking in the construction of ride-pits, with rebel bullets flying over and around their heads. Mr. Hubbard and myself with some 25 or 30 others belonging to the regiment, remained behind on duty connected with the Quarter Master's Department, and followed the regiment with Quarter Master Holden, on Friday afternoon, the 24th; Lieut. Holden was formerly first Lieut. in Co. A, but some six weeks since received the appointment of regimental Quarter Master, which ranks as 1st Lieut. We were very sorry to part with him from the Company, but hope that the regiment may not be the loser by the change. We left the city 3.30 P. M., having fine fair weather, a commodious boat, pleasant and agreeable Captain, plenty of cabin room and to spare, (our party and another about the same kin, being, the only passengers,) of course we had rather of an unusual pleasant trip. We crossed Mt. Vernon, Aqua Creek, &c., before dark, and came to anchor at Marsha Point just at dark; resuming the voyage again at daylight next morning, reaching Fortress Monroe about 5 o'clock P. M., on Saturday. The next morning we took boat for Norfolk, distant some 16 miles, from thence cars to Suffolk, some 24 miles, where we arrived about half past two o'clock P. M., very much pleased with our tedious journey of a few days,...

THE REBEL INVASION.

Lee's Whole Army Moving Northward.

NEW YORK, June 17.

The Herald's special, 16th inst. night, says the rebel movement now in progress towards the North is being made by Lee's whole army. The advance is by Ewell, with Jackson's old corps of two divisions, 13,000 men. The third had not come up. Lee, with Hill's and Longstreet's corps, are also moving north and will act in conjunction with Ewell, but at present is keeping between Ewell and Hooker. If Stonewall is in possession of Ewell who will undoubtedly move on Pennsylvania when piloted by his third division. Lee's force engaged in this movement is fully 98,000. There can be no doubt but we have at once into the interior of Pennsylvania, endeavoring to do so before Couch can organize a defence.

The Herald's Washington dispatch says:—From rebel sources the following is learned: I do not know what value may be attached to it, it comports, however, with what sympathizers here have mysteriously whispered from time to time for a week past. Lee's army, number 96,000 men, has been divided into three parts. Number one started six days ago from Gordonsville for Fortress-ville, Va., number two left Culpeper Court House and proceeded by by way of Gratton to Wheeling and Pittsburg, with instructions, after occupying the latter, to unite with number one, in proceed through Ohio into Kentucky; number three is to proceed by way of Winchester and Harper's Ferry into Maryland and Pennsylvania towards Harrisburg or Baltimore, with a design to make a diversion to occupy the attention of the Federal Army of the East. This last division of the rebel army comprised every largely of cavalry and mounted artillery.

Richmond is, for the present, abandoned with the exception that conscription and a new levee will be brought there in sufficient numbers to garrison the defence. It is expected that a force of from 20,000 to 30,000 rebel sympathizers will be in readiness in Maryland to co-operate with the Third Division. It was also stated that very generally believed here, that Bragg had found Lee, and that the rebel army moving in that direction amounts to 150,000 men.

To corroborate this, Union officers here from the Southwest state that all the points in that part of the country have been fortified with the highest degree of art and to such an extent that there was nothing more left in the front, another instead of sending reinforcements to their garrisons in the Southwest from the mere liberally sending reinforcements from the western army. Lee, with a view to offensive operations.

NEW YORK, June 17.

Headquarters Army of the Potomac; a dispatch, 15th, to the Herald, states that this morning we started again, and to-night the whole country south of the Occoquan is left to the enemy.

It is reported that rebel cavalry are at Chambersburg, and that the country are at Brook's Station, five miles from Aquia. The rebels will undoubtedly follow closely, though an engagement with the pursuing forces is not anticipated.

It would probably be improper to state where our exact line of defence will be established, although the enemy will doubtless know before the publication of this letter. But Hooker's balancing will file cattle early to the defence of Washington, and will occupy a position best adapted to defeat the designs of Lee. To-day all is quiet.

Whether Lee will attack us, or attempt another expedition in Maryland remains to be determined. It has been we shall be ready for him, and the fate of rebel army of North's Virginia may be decided in the next few days.

THE VERY LATEST NEWS.

The Alleghany arrived here from Chicago on Wednesday afternoon, and we are indebted to Capt. Boynton for a copy of the Chicago Tribune, of Tuesday, the 23d. That paper says:

"We do not prefer our readers any safe pilotage through the mazes of our dispatches from Virginia. The mystery has not yet lifted from Lee's movement, and his whereabouts are still matters of conjecture. We incline to the belief that the invasion of Maryland has its increasing formidable look and if so it is Baltimore that is the point of attack, with a view to cut off Washington from the Loyal States. A short time will definitely decide what will then will be the blindest guess work. Lee is certainly in heavy force and means mischief in a movement is too imperious to have undertaken on so large a scale, without a plan."

The Missouri State Convention is unlikely to reach any definite action on the Emancipation question. It is something, however, for Liberty to be able to make a draw battle with Slavery on the domain of the latter.—Error wounded writhes in pain sore enough, and will be likely to die among her Missouri worshippers at no distant day.

...

A PROCLAMATION.

WHEREAS, The armed insurrectionary combinations now existing in several of the States are threatening to make inroads into the States of Indiana, Western Virginia, Pennsylvania, and Ohio, requiring immediately an additional force for the service of the United States: Now, therefore, I, Abraham Lincoln, President of the United States, and Commander-in-Chief of the Army and Navy thereof, and of the Militia of the several States, when called into actual service, do hereby call into service of the United States 100,000 militia from the States following, namely: from the State of Indiana, 10,000; from the State of Pennsylvania, 50,000; from the State of Ohio, 30,000; from the State of Western Virginia, 10,000; to be mustered into the service of the United States forthwith, and to serve for the period of six months from the date of such muster into said service, unless sooner discharged, to be mustered in as infantry, artillery and cavalry in proportions which shall be made known through the War Department, which Department will also designate the several places of rendezvous. These militia are to be organized according to the rules and regulations of the volunteer service and such orders as may hereafter be issued. The States themselves will be respectively credited, under the enrolling act, for the military services rendered under this proclamation.

In testimony whereof I have hereunto set my hand and caused the seal of the United States to be affixed.

Done at the city of Washington, this 15th day of June, 1863, of the independence of the United States the 87th.

ABRAHAM LINCOLN.

By the President:
WILLIAM H. SEWARD, Secretary of State.

From Port Royal.

NEW YORK, June 17.

The steamer Arago arrived from Port Royal. Gen. Hunter and staff came passengers.

An English engineer who invented a floating press which will print 25,000 sheets of a newspaper, on both sides, is on board...

...we are content to leave the keeping of our fame to those who shall give to the world the impartial history of the war. – War Correspondent for the 26th MI Infantry.[98]

In January of 1864 a group of six recruits left Northport for Traverse City. They included Joshua Middleton, Chauncy Woosley, John Kehl, Charles Waltz, Jacob Haines, and Thomas McCormick. Joshua S. Middleton wrote of their journey in his diary:

"We arrived in Traverse City Friday night, tired, cold and hungry. Snow had been three feet with much of the road not broken through most of the way. From Traverse we had hired a team of horses, but through our haste proved only worthy of carrying our baggage. The teamster turned back within five miles of Benzonia, and it was snowing, cold and disagreeable. We managed to find a place to stay over night with some new settlers whose women folks took a great fancy to some cheese we had.

We ate dinner in a woods on the way the next day. We kept going until nightfall when we realized we had taken the wrong road (but eventually found the right guide marker). We slept over night with the Smith's in their small log house, with no bed. We had very little extra clothing with which to cover us, and were so cold we could not sleep at all. We did have plenty to eat though...John Kehl told the woman that I had fourteen children, that there was only one inch height difference in their sizes, from the oldest to the youngest – standing them in a row was looking like a line of steps.

We reached Manistee at 4:00 p.m. the next day. Eventually traveled to Pentwater, Muskegeon, took train cars from Perrysburg for Grand Rapids, having had no sleep or anything to eat since leaving Pentwater. We arrived before dinner, the 23rd of January 1864.

In February we came through on the Detroit and Milwaukee Railroad to Detroit, Toledo, Pittsburg, Little York, arriving at Harrisburg, PA about sundown. In Baltimore we had our breakfast, and arrived in Washington about 3:00 p.m. Friday where we went to Alexandria, VA about nine miles from Washington. Here we received our equipment. We are near Dixie. We stayed here two days, then it was off to the front. First to Brandy Station, then on to our camp. We built us a little cabin and began to be soldiers, doing picket duty through the winter on the Rappahanock.

We have been assigned to the 26th Michigan Volunteers, Company A. Here we also found Henry Holcomb of Northport."[99]

In the spring of 1864, under the command of Major Lemuel Saviers, the 26th MI Infantry crossed the Rapidan with General Grant's Army May 4, 1864 to the James River to begin the Battle of the Wilderness. This battle began a sustained offensive known as the Overland Campaign. Fighting was fierce but inconclusive as both sides attempted to maneuver in the dense woods. General Grant wrote in his *Personal Memoirs*, "More desperate fighting has not been witnessed on this continent than that of the 5th and 6th of May."[100]

The 26th MI was engaged in some of the severest and deadliest engagements of the campaign at the Battles of the Wilderness, Corbin's Bridge, and Spotsylvania where the 26th made its assault just as the Union lines moved forward to charge. Those battles took the lives of more men from Leelanau County than any other in the War. To reach Spotsylvania, the 26th had been in a sharp encounter across the Po River and made an all night's march in a storm. They reached the ground of the first line of the Division just as they massed for the assault, never halting to rest and moved up in gallant style. The 26th was one of the first regiments to plant its colors in the Rebel's works during vicious hand-to-hand struggles. It was near where the 26th fought that witnesses told of a tree 22 inches in diameter (& 61 inches in circumference) that was cut down by the intense fire of mini balls and fell within the Confederate lines. In support in this action was also the 1st MI Sharpshooters who also suffered great losses in this battle.

The regiment fought for more than one hour over the Rebel works, almost musket to musket, losing a large number killed and wounded. When the enemy made signals of surrender, firing ceased but as the enemy advanced a fresh line of supports came up and most of those that had started to surrender turned and jumped into the works again. The regiment then fought this new line until it was relieved to the left, joining the Brigade into the night. During the fourteen hours of battle, Major Saviors, commanding the regiment, was struck four times by the enemy's bullets while gallantly doing his duty, and seven out of the nine color-guards were killed or wounded. The regiment was specially complimented by Generals Barlow and Miles for its noble conduct and persistent and vigorous fighting during the day. Colonel Lemuel Saviers was eventually discharged for wounds from Spotsylvania.

Action continued at Salient (Bloody Angle) which "offered the most horrible sights of the war. In places, the trenches held corpses piled four and five deep, and sometimes at the bottom of such a pile a living wounded man would be found. The firing had been so intense that many bodies had been hit over and over again and were mutilated beyond any chance of identification."[101] This two-week battle consisted of a series of ferociously sustained combats along the Spotsylvania front. Unit moved to cross the North Anna River over Jericho Bridge where it was heavily attacked. Joshua S. Middleton wrote of his experience in this action from his diary:

"May 3, 1864. I was on picket line when we were ordered to break camp, at around 11 p.m., marching all night, crossing Eli Ford about 8 o'clock in the morning. We reached Chancelorville about noon, having stolen a march on Lee, and gotten possession of our field ahead of him, in the Wilderness. We were put right away out on the line, where we were kept until 6 o'clock in the morning. In the swamp you could hear the (mini) balls whiz past – spat – chug. Two struck near me, one beside me in a tree, another over my head. But thank God none touched me. We took three prisoners and that night we were moved to the left of the front line. The next morning we went to work building breast works. The Rebs began shelling our lines...We then made a drive to flush them out of the woods in front of us. On the 6th of May (Friday) we drove them back 2 miles. I was wounded in the wrist just as we were getting through with this fight. They sent me to Division Hospital, along with Henry Holcomb, who was mortally wounded. I left there that night, crossing over Eli Ford, having been ordered back to Chancelorville to Fredericksburg. I was knocked over a thirty-foot embankment, from which I hurt real bad.
May 10, 1864. Arrived at Fredericksburg. I am almost crazy with pain, and have had no provisions since leaving the field Hospital. It has been awful hot and dirty, and we have been forced to drink muddy water. Even this we were happy to get." [102]

On June 30, 1864, Joshua Middleton wrote more about these events to his sister from the Jarvis U.S. Hospital:

"Little Tom McCraney was shot dead in the Wilderness, Charley Clarke and John Eglas (Egeler) were both wounded at the same time... Our friend Chancy Woolsey is gone. He was shot, on the 31st of May and Charley Waltz, a young fellow who went with us was wounded at the same time, shot through both thighs." [103]

View from Beverly House looking toward Spotsylvania Court House
(Library of Congress)

Operations along the Totopotomoy Creek opened with cavalry combats at the Pamunkey River crossing at Dabney's Ferry. On to Cold Harbor, the regiment made a desperate charge on the Confederate works at Gains Mills across an open field, meeting with severe losses. It was continually under fire for 10 days and finally crossed Wilcox's Landing at the James River to arrive at Petersburg to join the assault.

They fought gallantly at Deep Bottom where they were part of the skirmish line that led the assault, then on to White Oak Swamp. The regiment was specially complimented by General Hancock in his general orders for their action between New Market and Charles City where they drove back the enemy twice their own size in number. In August of 1864, after duty at Weldon Rail Road, they briefly joined other soldiers from Leelanau County in the 10th MI Cavalry at Strawberry Plains, and then they occupied positions in front of Petersburg where they were daily engaged for five months. In April of 1865 they saw action at Hatcher's Run, Farmville, and other battles during the Appomattox Campaign where General Grant sent the flag of truce through their lines to General Lee when the terms of surrender were made. After the surrender of Lee and his Army they went to Washington D.C., marched in The Grand Review May 23, & Mustered out June 4, 1865.[104]

(For an additional detailed descriptive of some of the battles the 26th were in, see "A Stillness at Appomattox" by Bruce Catton (1953) and the 1997 book "The Battles For Spotsylvania Court House and the Road to Yellow Tavern May 7-12, 1864" by Gordon C. Rhea, Louisiana State University Press, Baton Rouge.)

Civil War Re-enactors
Civil War Muster, Jackson MI
(Leonard G. Overmyer III)

Civil War Veterans of the Sleeping Bear Dunes National Lakeshore
(Courtesy Leelanau Historical Museum)

Lakeshore Tigers of the 26th MI Inf. Glen Lake Area or Membership with Glen Lake G.A.R. Post 168. [105]

Sgt. Levi Bailey Enlisted in Co. K. 26th MI Inf. at Pittsfield. From **Glen Arbor.** Age 26. Mustered Dec. 12, 1862. Wounded in action at Spotsylvania, VA May 12, 1864. Became Sgt. May 1865. Discharged June 3, 1865. Later acquired a government homestead three miles northeast of Empire, MI. His wife, Virginia, was an early school teacher. [106]

Cpl. John (F.T.) Dechow (Dago) Sr. Enlisted in Co. B. / K. 26th MI Inf. & 14th Reg.

Veteran Res. Co. D. Age 21. Grand Rapids. Mustered March 21, 1864. Family history says he drew his name out of a hat for the right to volunteer. [107] Listed as being 5'7 ½" with light hair and blue eyes. [108] Wounded in action after the Battles of the Wilderness May 12th at Spotsylvania. The mini-ball went into his right arm at the elbow and came out halfway down his arm. His only treatment for his wound was "cold water dressings" for twelve days until he was admitted at the 29th Ward at Harwood Hospital, Washington D.C. where Y. Logan Sample of the Christian Commission assisted him with writing a letter home. [109] He would later be moved to Hospitals in Maryland and Pennsylvania. Transferred to Veteran Reserve Corp. Jan. 10, 1865. (Where is said to have served as a guard for President Lincoln and others.) Discharged at Washington D.C. **Port Oneida / North Unity area** resident, near School Lake. Listed in Cleveland Township 1894 Veteran's Census. (He also had a Glen Arbor Postal Address and was listed in the pre-war 1860 Census of Glen Arbor Township at age 18). Member G.A.R. Post 168. John's daughter, Mrs. Manney in the "Remembering Yesterday" Kasson Heritage Group, tells of stories about the G.A.R. Post 168 celebrations:

"The family would travel into the fair grounds at Maple City where they would meet all the members of their father's company who fought in the Civil War. The men would organize for a parade to the Fair Grounds, where the soldiers gathered and the service began consisting of a prayer by a minister, then the G.A.R. Ritual. This included naming the Company & Regiment, time & place of enlistment, and the name of the veteran who had passed away during the year, and flowers were placed on a covered mound. Sometimes there were several names and when there were none mentioned, the leader would say, 'In memory of our fallen comrades who fell in the battle of the Wilderness or Spotsylvania or elsewhere.' After the ceremonies, the soldiers would gather to visit and recall experiences. John Dechow likely telling of how a 'colored' southern woman made hot cakes from corn meal for some of the men. They were so very hungry and had been living on hardtack (a very hard bread) and sometimes a piece of salt pork if they were lucky."

A photograph of John & Ellanora (Ellen/Eleanora Shalda) Dechow is also featured. [110] The chipped bone in his right elbow from his war injuries rendered his right arm and hand nearly useless within a few years. He also became blind in his right eye and applied for a disability pension in 1871. [111] Buried in Cleveland Township / Shalda Cemetery. Dago/Dechow Family Marker. (April 22, 1842-Sept. 7, 1907).

Henry C. Fuller Enlisted in Co. H. 26th MI Inf. at Mason/Delhi as a Drummer. Age 21.

Aug. 11, 1862. **Glen Arbor** Draftee. Mustered in September 25, 1862. Discharged at Washington D.C. June 9, 1865. (Orlando S. Fuller was a Corporal in Co. H.)

Sgt. Charles Manns (Manes/Maus) Sgt. Enlisted in Co. A. 26th MI Inf. at Traverse City, Age

18. Mustered Sept. 11, 1862. Wounded in action at Totopotomoy Creek June 3, 1864. Gunshot wound in right buttock. Sgt. May 1, 1865. Out at Alexandria, VA June 4, 1865. Relations also in Milwaukee, WS. Listed in **Centerville** Township 1894 Veteran's Census. Listed also as Mane. G.A.R. Post 168.

John (Dago) Dechow 26th MI Infantry
(Courtesy William H. Steib, Don, Fred & Paul Dechow)

John (Dago) Dechow 26th MI Infantry
(Courtesy Kasson Heritage Group)

The Baileys & Manns around 1908
with Glen Lake Narrows in background.
(Courtesy U.S. Park Service, Sleeping Bear Dunes
 National Lakeshore)

Civil War Letter Sent By John Dechow (Dago)
Letter sent to his brother Fred, in Glen Arbor, MI that mentions
news of Levi Bailey, Charles Manns, President Lincoln and others.
(Courtesy Donald L., Fred & Rose Dechow)

(2)

U. S. Christian Commission.
Broadr Chie, 500 B sheet.
WASHINGTON, D. C.

Frederick Dago
Teleses
Glenn Harbor
Michigan

7th St Wharf Washington D.C.
May 10th 1865

Dear Brother:-
Yours 20th ult came duly to hand
and I take this opportunity of dropping
you a few lines, to let you know
that it found me still in the
land of the living, and in the
enjoyment of tolerable good health
and am glad to hear you are all
getting along so well.
Well Fred, the war is near to
an end at least the fighting is over;
and they are making preparations for
sending the troops home. The whole of
the armies of the United States are ordered
to assemble here at or near Washington
and on the fifteenth day of this month
they will have a grand review prep
paratory to going home. I think the
Volunteers will all be mustered out of

Service, and none but the regular
Army will be kept
I received a letter from Levi Bailey a
short time ago, in which he says he
went through the fight all safe but that
a good many of the boys in 26th Michigan
were killed and wounded. Chas. Manns
was taken prisoner but soon after was
re-captured by our men again.
You heard all right when you heard that
President Lincoln was shot. it happened
at Fords Theatre; he and his wife were
sitting in their private box in the theater
and about half past ten oclock P.M.
a man by the name of Booth steped
out and shot him in the back of the head
the bullet lodgeing in his brain. he lived
untill seven oclock the next morning
his remains have been sent to Springfield
Illinois for interment.
Booth escaped and got out of the City that
night, but he was pursued and found

(3)

Concealed in a barn about 70 miles
below this place on the night of
the 26th of last month. He would
not give himself up, and Sergent
Corbert of the 16th N.Y. Cavalry shot
him through the head. he died about
three hours after
Well Fred, think I shall have to get
home again as soon as possible and
give my attention to some of the girls
its a shame you fellows allow other
young men to come there and take
our girls away, if I was there I would
not allow it. give my regards to
Miss Burdick and other enquireing friends
As ever your true Brother
John D—

The men in the 26th MI from the Grand Traverse region called themselves the "Lake Shore Tigers." Reverend George Smith gave them all Bibles upon their departure.

Some of the men of the 26th MI said to have been associated with the Leelanau Co. area who gave the last full measure of devotion: [112]

James (Jason Goodell) Adameson Co.D. 26th MI Inf. At Arcadia. Listed in 1862 Grand Traverse Herald Drafted from Centerville Twp. Died at Washington D.C. June 30, 1864 of wounds received in action at Spotsylvania VA May 12, 1864.

Mortimer K. Boyes Co.A. 26th MI Inf. from Northport Age 18. Died of disease at Ft. Richmond NY Sept. 4, 1863. Buried in a Military Cemetery, Brooklyn NY. (Listed in the pre-war 1860 Census of Leelanau Township as the only son of Henry C. Boys.)

Henry Budd Enlisted in Co. A. 26th MI Inf. at Northport. Wounded in action May 25, 1864 & Died on Davis Island, NY Harbor June 4, 1865 at De Camp General Hospital. Buried in National Cemetery in Brooklyn, NY Grave # 4413, (Born Sept. 23, 1818. Listed Age 42. Carpenter in the pre-war 1860 Census of Leelanau Township with 9 children!) See Kerr Budd 15th MI Inf.

Charles E. Clark Co. A. 26th MI Inf. Age 19. Leland. Wounded in action at Spotsylvania, VA May 12, 1864. Killed in action (with George B. Allen of Traverse City) at Farmerville, VA April 7, 1865. Just two days before General Lee surrendered. (Isaac 8th MI Cav., James 10th MI Cav., George 15th MI)

John Egeler Jr. (Egler) Enlisted in Co. A. 26th MI Inf. Age 43. At Centerville. Mustered Sept. 11, 1862. Died of wounds May 31, 1864 received in action at Spotsylvania, VA May 12, 1864. (Listed from Westernburg, PA? Also NY & WS, in the pre-war 1860 Census of Leelanau Township with 4 children. Younger brother **Phillip** said to have joined later in the War. See Centerville Listings).

Jacob Hans (Haines) Co. A. 26th MI Inf. Centerville or Centreville? Listed in 1862 Grand Traverse Herald from Centerville Twp. Died at Washington D.C. July 20, 1864 of wounds received in action at Spotsylvania VA May 12, 1864. (See Fred Haines 1st MI Inf.)

Cpl. Henry L. Holcomb Enlisted in Co. A. 26th MI Inf. Age 21. At Northport. Killed in action at the Battles of the Wilderness May 7, 1864.

Henrich Klintworth Co. K. 26th MI Inf. Age 39. Leland. Mustered in Dec. 12, 1862. Died of disease in Philadelphia, PA Sept. 1, 1864. National Cemetery Grave # 251.

Henry Lemmerwell (Lemmerman/Limmerman) Co. I. 26th MI Inf. Age 32. Killed in action at Spotsylvania May 12, 1864. (Listed from Hanover in the pre-war 1860 Census of Centerville Township, Day-Laborer for Otto Ghires.)

Thomas McCraney / Mc Creary (or McCormick?) Co. A. 26th MI Inf. Age 26. Centerville. Killed in action at Spotsylvania, VA May 12, 1864. (Listed from Canada in the pre-war 1860 Census of Centerville Township. Was a SchoolTeacher who stayed with the Frederick Cook family.)

George H. Randall/ Ramsdell Co. A. 26th MI Inf. Age 20. Suttonsbay. (Centerville) - Missing in Action. (See A.W. Randall in Glen Arbor, Charles and Gilbert Randall, Lewis Ramsdell in the 10th MI Cavalry.)

Section of the Wilderness
May 1864
(Library of Congress)

Federal casualties of the
Battles of the Wilderness and
Spotsylvania at a temporary
Hospital in Fredericksburg, VA
May 20, 1864
(Library of Congress)

William M. Remar Co. A. 26th MI Inf. Age 26. Centerville. Mustered Sept. 11, 1862 and died at Jackson, MI Nov. 16, 1862 just 2 months later. (Listed from New York in the pre-war 1860 Census of Centerville Township.)

Stephen Simmons (Simminson) Centerville Draftee. Enlisted in Co. C. 26th at Muskegon. Died of Disease July 20, 1863 at New York City & Buried in Brooklyn National Cemetery Grave # 697.

Sgt. William H. Voice (Boice) Co. A. 26th MI Inf. Age 20. Enlisted from Northport. Mustered Sept. 11, 1862, died of disease at Camp Jackson, MI Sept. 22, 1862 less than 2 weeks later of Typhoid Fever. (Listed in the pre-war 1860 Census of Leelanau Township.) An incredible story of how he had Herman Dunkelow get a doll for his baby sister before he died is told in "A History of Leelanau Township." Dunkelow was over 90 years old when he told this story to William Voice's baby sister who had come by for a visit, unaware it was Dunkelow who had helped retrieve the sentimental gift.

Voice had promised his worried 3 year old sister he would get her a doll. According to the story by Dunkelow, "The poor fellow kept raving about a doll...He begged for someone to get him a doll for his baby sister.

The doctors and nurses paid little attention to the young man's delirious talk, but Dunkalow was so touched he went out and spent his last cent on a beautiful china doll... Dunkalow said the young man grew calm and peaceful when he saw the doll and Dunkalow propped it up at the foot of the bed where he could see it. He died before morning."[113]

His body was escorted by several soldiers for a massive funeral in Northport.

Joseph Warwick Enlisted Co. A. 26th MI Inf. Age 40. Centerville or Centreville? Listed in 1862 Grand Traverse Herald from Centerville Twp. Died on Dec. 6, 1863 from wounds received in action at Mine Run, VA. Nov. 29, 1863. (Joe Warbock? In 1860 Centerville Census.)

Cpt. Chauncey Woolsey Co. A. 26th MI Age 45. Enlisted in Grand Rapids, MI. Jan. 23, 1864. Killed in action after the Battle of the Wilderness[114] at Totopotomoy during a skirmish at Sheldon Farm. "John Kehl was with him that day. The company was lying prone, firing on the enemy line, when the order came to retire. As Kehl got up he saw that Woolsey was dead from a bullet to the head."[115] May 31, 1864. Buried in National Cemetery at Yorkstown, VA Grave # 69. Post 399 is named after him. Chauncey was listed with 5 children in the pre-war 1860 Census of Leelanau Township. [116] It was not clear if he had been elected Captain by his men or was given the title posthumous by the G.A.R. His Grandfather, Adolphus Woolsey, served in the War of 1812, died in 1875 at the age of 80 in Leelanau Twp.[117] See Wallace Woolsey in the 1st MI Sharpshooter & Byron Woolsey 26th MI Inf. who was presented with the Bible given to his Father by Rev. George Smith. This same Bibile would later be given to Byron's son Clinton F. Woolsey who was killed in WWI with the same Bible being again presented back to Byron. The Woolsey Memorial Airport was named in Clinton's honor. (Also soldier Dare Woolsey's tin photograph is in the MI Archives in Lansing.)

<u>Possible additional Lakeshore Tigers who died are listed further in the Leelanau list.</u>

John Kehl
26th MI Infantry
(Courtesy Leelanau Historical Museum)

Joshua S. Middleton
26th MI Infantry
(Courtesy Leelanau Historical Museum)

Chauncey Woolsey
26th MI Infantry. Killed in action.
(Courtesy Leelanau Historical Museum)

George B. Allen
26th MI Infantry. Killed in action.
(Michigan Archives)

John Kehl (Kept) Enlisted in Co. A. 26th MI Inf. Grand Rapids. Served Jan. 23, 1864 - June/July 3, 1865. Leelanau Township 1894 Veteran's Census, **Northport** area. He was born in Alsace, France in 1825 and emigrated from Prussia/Germany areas to New York with his parents in 1828. Served as a Justice of the Peace and Township Treasurer.[118] Listed in Northport Cemetery. G.A.R. Post 168 and Post 399. (Was listed in the pre-war 1860 Census of Leelanau Township at age 35 from France with 4 children.) Ship-maker.

William H. Pratt Drum Major. Co. A. 26th MI Inf. Age 41. Musician/Drummer. Elm Hall. Listed under Putt, Leelanau Twp. Draftee. Believed to be the same Mjr. Pratt later listed as returned from New York in 1876 to settle at **Glen Haven** on a farm south of Pierce Stocking Drive, Sleeping Bear Dunes National Lakeshore. Bill Pratt was a known Fiddler.[119]

Additional Lakeshore Tigers of the 26th MI Inf. Northport / Leland Areas & Surrounding Leelanau: [120]

George W. Bigelow Co. A. 26th MI Age 28. Northport. Aug. 1862 - Deserted in New York City Aug. 1, 1863, though may have been victim of foul play. (Listed in pre-war 1860 Census of Leelanau Township with wife and small child.) Samantha Bigelow died in 1897, buried in Almira Cemetery.

John A. Brainard Co.A. 26th MI Inf. T.C. Leelanau Misc.

Asa V. Churchill Co. A. 26th MI Inf. Age 30 of T.C./Leelanau Sept. 1862, Transf. to V.R.C. 1865.

Manrod (Minrod) Buckler/ Bergler / Bughler Co. A. 26th MI Inf. & 14th Vet.Res. Centerville/Good Harbor. Age 25. Enlisted Aug. 13, 1862-June 26, 1865. Wounded in Action. Lost left hand index finger. Lived on South Manitou Island. Buried in Good Harbor Swedish Cemetery. (A Jacob Burger is listed in the pre-war 1860 Census of Leelanau Township.)

Sgt. Frederick Cook Sr. Co. A. 26th MI Inf. Centerville. Age 39. (See opening stories at beginning of book). Discharged for Disability Nov. 24, 1864. G.A.R. Post 399. Listed in Leland Township 1894 Veteran's Census. Born in France in 1828? Buried in Beechwood Cemetery, Leland, MI. Dec. 5, 1902. (Listed in pre-war 1860 Census of Centerville Township as a Shoe-maker. Son Fred lived in Maple City.)

Herman Dunkelow Co. A. 26th MI Inf. Age 27. Leland Twp. 1894 Veteran's Census/ Centerville. Lost right arm above elbow in action at Deep Bottom, VA Aug. 16,1864. (Listed in the pre-war 1860 Census of Centerville Township, Day-Laborer with Henry Lemmerwell for Otto Ghires.) Lived past the age of 90 and had been the soldier who bought a doll for William Voice's baby sister. Oct. 12, 1832 – Oct. 24, 1925. Oakwood Cemetery (Dunkelau).

Nelson Gallup Co. A. 26th MI Inf. Centerville.

L. & Cyriel (Syriel) **Grant** Co. A. 26th MI Age 32. Centerville. Suttonsbay. Sept. 11, 1862 - June 4, 1865. (Syriel was listed in the pre-war 1860 Census with 3 daughters.) Nov. 19, 1828 – May 9, 1880. St. Mary's Cemetery, Lake Leelanau. G.A.R. Post 168 Marker.

Lewis Gremmulbaker Co. A. 26th MI Inf. Age 36. Centerville/Centreville?. Died in Hospital of wounds received in action at Spotsylvania, VA May 12, 1864. Buried in National Cemetery in Philadelphia, PA Grave # 131.

John George Haft (Hoft/Hoeft) Co. K. 26th MI Age 28. Leland. Dec. 12, 1862. Transf. to Co. D. 21st. V.R.C. Leland (Beechwood) Cemetery. (Martin Hoft of Glen Arbor was also listed in the draft.)

James (Haggerty) Hagen 26th MI Inf. Drafted from Leelanau Twp.

Lt. Charles H. Holden Co.A. 26th MI Inf. Northport. Age 30. Quartermaster. Discharged for Disability April 5, 1864. RIP? (Listed as an Attorney in the pre-war 1860 Census of Leelanau Township.)

David Hollinger Co. A. / K. 26th MI Age 44. Leland. Dec. 12, 1862. Wounded in action at Spotsylvania in neck and left hand finger. Leland Twp. 1894 Veteran's Census. Died April 19, 1896 at Leland. (Beechwood Cemetery) Northport GAR Post 399.

James C. Johnson Co. A. 26th MI Inf. Age 35.

85

Fermund (Korp) Kord 26th MI Inf. Wounded in action near Petersburg, VA June 16, 1864. Misc. Leelanau Co.

William H. Lawson Co. A. 26th MI Inf. Age 23 Centerville. Enlisted at Northport. Mustered Sept. 11, 1862. Taken Prisoner at Po. River, VA May 10, 1864. No further record.

James R. Lee Co. A. 26th MI Inf. Age 20. Centerville. (Listed in pre-war 1860 Census, son of Thomas Lee from England.) While in the Army, he lost an ill child in Sept. 1864.[121] Later moved to Manistee, MI. (See Charles & Thomas in 1st NY L.A.)

Sgt. Charles E. Lehman Co. A. 26th MI Inf. Age 30. (Northport). Wounded in action at Cold Harbor and later at Farmville. April 7, 1865 with Charles Clark and George Allen just before the end of the War. No further record. RIP? (Listed as a Mason from Saxony in the pre-war 1860 Census of Leelanau Twp.)

Thomas McCormick Co. A. 26th MI Inf. Northport.[122] (See James McCormick 19th WS)

Joshua S. (R.) Middleton Co. A. 26th MI Inf. Age 39. Leelanau TS 1894 Veteran's Census. Wounded at the Battle of the Wilderness,[123] See stories told in 26th MI Infantry. GAR Post 399. (Listed as a Farmer from Pennsylvania in the pre-war 1860 Census of Leelanau Township with 6+ children.) Northport Cemetery.

George H. Mills Co. A. 26th MI Inf. Age 20. Centerville/Northport. (Joined with Jessie Mills Age 16 from Pentwater.)

George W. Miller Co. A. (or I.) 26th MI Inf.Centerville/Northport. Discharged for Disability at Alexandria, VA. (In part may have been his age, he was listed age 9 in the pre-war 1860 Census of Leelanau Township?)

William W. Nash Co. A. 26th MI Inf. / Co. J. 20th Regt. Age 37. Northport. (Listed in the pre-war 1860 Census of Leelanau Township with 4 children.) Died May 22, 1882. Listed under Monroe Center / or Maple Grove Cemetery, Blair Township. (See John Nash in 42nd Ill.)

Melville Palmer Co. A. 26th MI Inf. Age 19. Centerville/Suttonsbay Twp. 1894 Veteran's Census. Served 1862-1865. Born May 24, 1843 in Ohio. Died March 15, 1913.[124] Buried in Keswick/Maple Grove Cemetery - Bingham Township near Veteran's Rock Monument. (Listed in the pre-war 1860 Census. Father was from New York.) Tin Type photograph in uniform is held at the Leelanau Historical Museum.

Sewell S. Parker Co. A. 26th MI Inf. (Photo in MI Archives).

Hiram Quackenbush 26th MI Inf. Centerville. Age 18. Dec. 12, 1862, Cpl. Jan. 1, 1865. Discharged June 4, 1865.

Martin Wachel (Mathias Wagle) Co. I. 26th MI Inf. Age 34. Centerville? Enlisted March 8, 1864. Discharged by S.O. No.140 June 3, 1865.

Charles Waltz Enlisted Co. A. 26th MI Inf. Northport.[125]

Richard (Deetrick/Deidrick) White Co. A. 26th MI Inf. Age 32. Leland. Listed deserted in NY City Aug. 6, 1863? Listed in Leland Township 1894 Veteran's Census. East Leland Cemetery.

Byron Woolsey Co. A. 26th MI Inf.? Listed as a Leelanau draftee. Said to have entered with a group of men from Northport in January of 1864.[126] Teamster (Wagoner) but was not likely enrolled due to his young age.

Some of the Additional 26th MI Inf. from the Grand Traverse Region: [127]

George B. Allen. Co. A. Age 18. Sept. 11, 1862. Killed in action (with Charles Clark of Leland) at Farmville, VA April 7, 1865 . Just two days before General Lee surrendered. Shot through the head and killed instantly. [128] Marker in Yuba Cemetery, Acme Township. (See Charles Allen 1st MI Sharpshooters.)

Charles Avery Jr. Co. K. 26th MI Inf. Age 18/30? Grand Traverse Co. Died of disease at Alexandria,VA. March 13,1863.

Joseph Baldwin Age 42. Manistee.

Thomas R. Bates Co. A. 26th MI Inf. Age 29. Traverse City. Sept. 1862 - June 1865. 1838-1883 Oakwood Cemetery, T.C.

John Duncan Co. A. 26th MI Inf. Age 43. T.C. later lived in Bad Axe, MI.

Oscar Eaton Co. A. 26th MI Inf. Age 42. Wounded at Totopotomoy Creek June 3, 1864. Letter written to Grand Traverse Herald in 1863 tells of action in Suffolk, Virginia. (See Henry Eaton 7th OH)

Ashley A.E. Elder Co. E. 26th MI Inf. Born July 4, 1844. Died Nov. 20, 1928. Buried in Oakwood Cemetery, Traverse City.

Giles Gibson Co. A. 26th MI Inf.

John Gillison Co. A. 26th MI Inf. Killed in action at Spotsylvania.

Augustus Gould Age 21. Manistee. (See Edward Gould 8th VT)

Preseroid D. Greenman Co. A. 26th MI Inf. Cpl. Age 33. Sept. 11, 1862. Discharged for disability at Alexandria, VA March 10, 1863. Reported in the "Grand Traverse Herald" that he died at Fairfax, VA July 15, 1863 or March 27.

Richard Haas Co. H. 26th MI Inf. Age 37. Joined in Ingam. Taken prisoner at Deep Bottom and died of starvation at Salisbury, NC Feb. 25, 1865. (See George Haas 5th MI Inf. and John Haas 16th MI Inf.)

John Hopkins Co. A. 26th MI Inf. Age 21. Wounded at Spotsylvania & had RH Leg amputated. No further record.

Cpt. L. Edwin Knapp Co. A. 26th MI Inf.

Cpt. Charles R. Lackey Co. A. 26th MI Inf. Cpl. Age 25. Joined in 1862 later becoming a Lieutenant & the Captain of Co. K. 26th MI Inf. Mustered out at Alexandria, VA June 4, 1865. Died April 9, 1889 Age 43. Oakwood Cemetery.

Gilbert Lackor (LaCore) Co. A. 26th MI Inf. Age 21. T.C. Died of disease at Alexandria, VA March 5, 1863. (See Charles 8th NY H.A and other LaCore listings: Henry Marvin in 7th MI Inf.)

Elias Langdon Co. A. 26th MI Inf. Age 27. Sept. 11, 1862 - June 9, 1865 out at Philidelphia, PA.

George H. Lawrence Co. A. 26th MI Inf. Age 38. T.C. Drummer

Robert McAly Co. E. 26th MI Inf. Fife Lake area. (Jame McAly Co. I. 1st MI Eng. & Mech.)

John McLaughlin Co. D. Enlisted from down state. Age 18. Wounded in action at Petersburg. (See various McLaughlin's listed.)

George Moody Co. A. 26th MI Inf. Age 33. T.C. Died of disease at Yorktown, VA July 15, 1863 Grave # 1106 YkTn Nat. Cemetery. Captain Knapp, in a letter in the *Grand Traverse Herald* announcing his death stated, "George was a faithful soldier – always discharging his duty well." Charles Moody 1840-1910 also served. Grand Traverse Soldier **Myron A. Moody** (brother of Joseph) died of measles at the age of 18 in a Grand Rapids Hospital.[129]

Henry O'dell Co.A. 26th MI Inf. Age 21. Whitewater Twp. Sept. 11, 1862. Killed in action before Petersburg June 18, 1864.

Horace Phillips Co. A. 26th MI Inf. Age 26. Sept. 11, 1862. - Wounded at Totopotomoy Creek June 3, 1864. Discharged at Philadelphia, PA June 13, 1865. 1839-Oct. 22, 1915 in Yuba Cemetery.

Riley L. Stearns Co. A. 26th MI Inf. Age 21. T.C. Service Sept. 11, 1862 - June 4, 1865.

Milton Stites (Stiter) Co. A. 26th MI Inf. Age 20. Musician. Fifer. Sept. 1862 – March 1865.

Anisa D. Stinson Co. E. / F. 26th MI Inf. Died at Davenport, Newago Co.

Ziphaniah Swan Co. H. 26th MI Inf. lived in Traverse City after 1905.

John A. Thayer Co. A. 26th MI Inf. Age 19. T.C. Service Sept. 11, 1862 - June 4, 1865.

Lt. Andrew J. Underhill Co. A. 26th MI Inf. Age 27. Disability Oct. 15, 1863. Lived in Chicago. Died Nov. 1, 1908. Age 76. Buried at Pentwater, MI.[130]

Francis Wait Co. A. 26th MI Inf. Age 19. T.C. Service Sept. 11, 1862 - June 4, 1865. Had been a paroled P.O.W.

Note: Many men from the Pentwater area served with our soldiers and were also considered fellow Lakeshore Tigers.

Civil War Re-enactors
Charlton Park, Hastings MI
(Leonard G. Overmyer III)

**Monument of the 1st Michigan Sharpshooters
at the Capital in Lansing, MI.**
(Leonard G. Overmyer III)

1st MI Sharpshooters

A large number of Native American Indians from Northport quickly joined the MI Sharpshooters (some so eager for the chance, they were not all registered) and were very able in their task. A monument to the 1st MI Sharpshooters resides on the lawn of the Michigan Capital Building in Lansing. Several books have been written on these men including: "Between the Fires: American Indians in the Civil War" 1995 Laurence M. Hauptman, The Free Press 866 Third Ave. New York, NY 10022. Also, "These Men Have Seen Hard Service: The First Michigan Sharpshooters in the Civil War" 1998 Raymond J. Herek, Wayne State University Press, MI.

Company K of the First Michigan Sharpshooters, under Colonel Charles Victor DeLand, was considered the most famous Indian unit in the Union army fighting east of the Mississippi. The unit was led by Captain Edwin V. Andress, Lt. William J. Driggs, and Lt. Garrett A. Gravaraet, who had been teaching at the Ottawa (Odawa) community at Little Traverse Bay. He could speak several modern languages, besides Chippewa, and was known as a fine portrait artist, landscape painter, and thorough Musician. Lt. Gravaraet was the son of Bear River band chief Mankewenan (Sgt. Henry G. Gravaraet of Mackinac Island) who was killed in the Battle of Spotsylvania, and Chippewayan Sophie Bailey of Little Traverse. Lt. Gravaraet would also die during the war of wounds received in action at the Battle of Petersburg and was later buried on Mackinac Island. Colonel De Land cited these men for their courage and gallantry.[131]

Even before its ranks were filled, the First Michigan Sharpshooters were called into action to fight General John Hunt Morgan's incursions into the North. After guarding rebel prisoners at Camp Douglas, the Indian Sharpshooters were eventually attached to Burnside's Corps. Joining the Army of the Potomac in the Campaign from the Rapidan to the James River. Like the 26th MI Infantry, they took heavy casualties in the Battles of the Wilderness and Spotsylvania, where in this desperate encounter, they poured volley after volley at the on-coming foe. The Federal line, advancing with a cheer, met the charging Rebel enemy in a dense thicket of pines during vicious hand to hand struggle. On a rise of ground, where their rifles commanded the country, rallied the 1st MI Sharpshooters under Colonel Deland and the 27th MI Infantry under Major Moody. Behind them stood the 14th NY Battery supported by the 2nd MI Infantry. Col. Humphrey of the 2nd MI Infantry yelled, "Boys, this must be stopped!" The charging Confederates fired their guns with terrific furor, but the little band stood firm. Every now and then the bold rebels laid their hands on the battery only to be shot down by the Sharpshooters. Everything on the left of the Sharpshooters had been swept away, and the attack on their front and flank, with both infantry and artillery pouring in shot and shell, was terrific. As they gallantly held their ground, on the left of the Sharpshooters stood a small company of Indians commanded by Lt. Graveraet who suffered dreadfully, but never faltered or moved, sounding a "War-whoop" with every volley. Their unerring aim quickly taught the Rebels they were standing on dangerous ground. Col. DeLand was twice wounded in the attack. Other area soldiers in the 26th MI Infantry also suffered great losses here.

After Salient, they experienced more action at North Anna River, Ox Ford, Pamunkey, Totopotomoy, Cold Harbor, and they particularly distinguished themselves in the Battle before Petersburg, Virginia where they lost Lt. Gravaraet.

Lt. Garret Graveraet
Co. K. 1ˢᵗ MI SS
(Courtesy Detroit Public Library
John Buckbee Files, Burton Historical Collection)

Flag of the First Michigan Sharpshooters

With Battle Stripes.

Indians of Michigan
(Courtesy Grand Traverse
Pioneer & Historical Society)

The death of Lt. Gravaraet was written about in the July 1864 *Grand Traverse Herald*:

"In the fight before Petersburg, June 18, Liet. Garrat A. Graveraet, of Little Traverse, gave his life for his country. He was Second Lieutenant of Company K, 1st Michigan Sharpshooters, Burnside's Corps. He was a young man of extraordinary attainments, and was highly esteemed as an officer and gentleman. His bravery and accomplishments endeared him to the company, and at their request he was promoted to a Lieutenancy. In the fight before Petersburg on the above date, he was with his father in the trenches, and had the misfortune to see (his) father shot dead by his side. He bore the body of his parent from the trenches to a safe spot, where weeping bitterly, he dug a grave with an old tin pan, in the sand, and buried him. This done, the devoted son dried his tears and returned to the battle. His rifle told with terrible precision among the rebel officers, until he fell, badly wounded in the left arm. Lieut. G. was brought to Washington, where his arm was amputated at the shoulder, which resulted in his death..." (July 10th)

On July 30, 1864, the Union forces detonated four tons of black powder in a tunnel that had been dug directly under the Confederate works at Petersburg, known as the Mine Explosion. Four Divisions of Union troops rushed into the enemy works and over 4000 soldiers were lost as Confederate forces surrounded the crater and poured devastating rounds into the hole, while the Union forces tried to fight their way out of the crater.

In the midst of the confusion, Sgt. Antoine Scott, an Ottawa Indian in Co. K., with a companion, refused to take cover and deliberately drew the enemy fire so their fellow soldiers might escape. Major Asahel W. Nichols wrote in a report, "They stood boldly up and deliberately and calmly fired their pieces until the enemy was almost upon them, when instead of laying down their arms and surrendering, ran the gauntlet of shot and shell and escaped..."[132]

During 1864, Indian presence was frequently noted in combat as well as in the daily events of camp life. Besides their distinctive physical appearance, the Indians in this unit were set apart from other soldiers in the Army of the Potomac by their "battle flag, a large live Eagle" which was perched "on a pole some six feet long on a little platform." The Indians took heavy casualties in nearly every engagement.[133]

Action continued on at Weldon Rail Road, Poplar Springs, Vaughan & Squirrel Level Roads, Hatcher's Run, Fort Stedman where Co. K. took part in the final charge capturing more prisoners than they had men engaged, Appomattox Campaign, continued action at Petersburg while Admiral Porter was hammering away with his gunboats up the James River. The 1st MI Sharpshooters, leading the skirmishers and pressing hard upon the rear of the Rebel forces, were the first to enter the long fought for city.[134]

They were later among the first troops to enter Richmond, then on to Washington D.C., in the Grand Review May 23, 1865. Mustered out July 28, 1865.[135] Of the hundred plus men in Co. K. who left home to fight for their country, more than half were killed in battle and practically all the rest were wounded.[136]

Besides the area Indians, a number of local men served with the First Michigan Sharpshooters. Two 18-year-old friends from Northport, Wallace Woolsey and Doug Hazel, left their homes near the end of July aboard Woolsey's boat leaving word that they were sailing for "salt water,"as they did not want their parents to follow. In a few weeks the folks at home learned that the boys enlisted in Company I.[137] (1st Annual Reunion was held at Jackson, MI Sept. 14, 1886. Proceeding copy held in the State Library of Michigan.)

Indian Leaders of the Grand Traverse Region
(Courtesy Grand Traverse Pioneer & Historical Society)

Wounded Indian Soldiers at Fredericksburg, VA, May 1864 (Marye's Heights).
Believed to be members of Co. K. 1st MI Sharpshooters.
(Library of Congress)

Sleeping Bear / Glen Lake area: [138]

Wade B. Daniels Co. A. 1st MI Sharpshooters? or Light Artillery.? (see Histories), G.A.R. Post 168. Listed in Glen Arbor Township 1894 Veteran's Census. Listed also under W.H. Daniels. (see also Samuel Daniels 147th Ind., Glen Arbor).

Peshawbestown and remaining Leelanau County: [139]

Sgt. Charles Allen Sgt. Co.K. 1st MI Sharpshooters. Age 19. Northport. Died of wounds received in action at the Battles of the Wilderness VA June 6, 1864.

James Arwonogefic (Arnowogzice) Co. K. 1st MI Sharpshooters G.A.R. Post 399.,

George Ashe-Ke-Bugaskberg (Ashe-ke-bug/Askberg) Co.K. 1st MI SS (Northport). Age 28. Onominee Indian Cemetery. & Amos.

C.B. Fowler Co. D. 1st MI SS. Died Oct. 19, 1864. Buried in Hampton National Cemetery, VA.

Douglas Hazel Co. I. 1st MI Sharpshooters (Northport). Age 18.

John Keen 1st MI Sharpshooters (Northport). Returned home on sick leave.[140]

Kewaquiskum 1st MI Sharpshooters (Northport).[141] Believed died of Illness. (Kashgo-gria? In 1860 Centerville Census.)

Rob McLaughlin 1st MI Sharpshooters. Northport.[142]

Thomas McLaughlin 1st MI Sharpshooters. Northport. (See various McLaughlin's in MI E&M, 10th., 15th & 26th Inf.)

Lewis Miller Co.K. 1st MI Sharpshooters. Northport. Listed in November 1864 Grand Traverse Herald.

Thomas Miller Co.K. 1st MI SS. Age 19. From Omena/(Northport), Omena Cem./Pres. Church Yard.

William Mixinasaw Co.K. 1st MI Sharpshooters (Northport). Age 20. Listed as died a prisoner in Camp Sumpter, GA. / at Andersonville Nat. Cemetery Oct. 26, 1864 Grave # 11511. & also as discharged at Philadelphia, PA. (Mixsumaz listed with wife, Mary, and son, Peter, in 1860 Centerville Census.)

Louis Muskoquan (Joseph Muskoguon) 1st MI Sharpshooters (Northport). Prisoner at Andersonville and survived the "Sultana" ship explosion.[143] Died in late 1890's in Hayes Twp. Charlevoix, MI.[144]

William Nevarre Co.K. 1st MI SS? Age 18.

William P. Newton Co. K. 1st MI Sharpshooters (Indian), Northport G.A.R. Post 399 (See Frank 5th MI)

Jocko Penaeswonoquot (Aaron Peqongay). Co. K. 1st MI Sharpshooters (Indian) Age 21. Leelanau Township 1894 Veteran's Census, also listed as **Aaron (Jacko Sargarnargeeton)** **Peniquonqayt/Penaisnowoquot** Co. K. 1st MN Sharpshooters. or as **Aron Sargarnargeeton / Aaron Sahgahnahquato/Sarconquatto** Co. K. 1st MI Sharpshooters Leland. **Aason Tas-qas-was-geto** Northport G.A.R. Post 399. (A Census listing also lists a **Jacko Pe-nais-now-o-quot**.) 1837?-1916. Omena Cemetery. Grave reads Aaron Sargonquatto known as Aaron Pequongas.

Sgt. Edward F. Rodgers Co. D. 1st MI SS. Leelanau Township. Northport G.A.R. Post 399. Died Nov. 1, 1906. Northport Cemetery.

Sa-qua-non Co. K. 1st MI Sharpshooters Northport (1860 Centerville Census lists Sahgosega/Shawakgutt.) Once reported dead.[145]

Shake Co. K. 1st MI Sharpshooters Northport[146] Believed died of Illness. (1860 Centerville Census lists Sahgak Age 12.)

Louis Shouman (Shomin) Co.K. 1st MI Sharpshooters. Peshawbestown Immaculate Conception Cemetery.

John H. Thomas Co. I. 1st MI Sharpshooters Age 18. Wounded in Battle of Wilderness (Listed in pre-war 1860 Leelanau Twp. Census.) Northport G.A.R. Post 399. Oakwood Cemetery.

Joseph Wakazoo Co. K. 1st MI Sharpshooters. Northport. Later joined 10th MI Cavalry. (Listed in pre-war 1860 Leelanau Twp. Census.)

Payson Wolfe Co. K. 1st MI Sharpshooters. Northport. Taken Prisoner at Petersburg (to Savannah) interned at Andersonville & Millen, GA. (Listed in pre-war 1860 Leelanau TS. Census with 3 young children.) G.A.R. Post 399. Born in 1831. Died Dec. 7, 1900.[147] Buried by Petoskey, MI near Cross Village Cemetery that also holds **Sgt. Frank Tabasasch** of Co.K., **Zena D. Ransom** of Co. C., and **Joseph Ach-Au-Nach**.[148]

N.H. (Wallace) Woolsey Co.I. 1st MI Sharpshooters (Northport). Age 18. Cpl. (Listed in pre-war 1860 Leelanau TS. Census.) Mustered out at Delaney House, D.C. July 28, 1865. Said to have died of T.B. as a result of his service in the Civil War.[149] Northport Cemetery. (See Chauncey Woolsey 26th MI Infantry.)

Some of the Additional 1st MI Sharpshooters from the Traverse Region: [150]

Peter A-won-O-Quot Co. K. 1st MI SS. Age 25. Little Traverse area.

Louis Bennett Co. K. 1st MI SS. Age 31. Little Traverse area.

Capt. Allen E. Burnham 1st MI SS. Lived in Kalkaska. Was also a Mexican War Veteran.[151]

Augustus Bushaw Co. K. 1st MI SS. Age 20. Little Traverse area. Buried in Lakeview Cemetery, Harbor Springs. Mar. 23,1887.

Jonah Dabasequam Co. K. 1st MI SS. Age 20. Little Traverse area.

Joseph Gibson / Louis G. Gibson Co. K. 1st MI SS. Age 23. Bear Lake.

Samuel Kaquatch Co. K. 1st MI SS. Age 18. Little Traverse area.

Cpl. Leon O-Tash-Qua-Bon-O Co. K. 1st MI SS. Age 23. Little Traverse area. (See photograph.) Died April 3, 1902. Age 61.

Jacob Prestawin Co. K. 1st MI SS. Age 24. Traverse City.

John F. Rainbow Co. H. 1st MI SS. Lived in Kalkaska.

John Shomin Buried in Lakeview Cemetery, Harbor Springs. Died July 3, 1895 &

John B. Shomin Co. K. 1st MI SS. Age 20. Grand Traverse area. Buried in Lakeview Cemetery, Harbor Springs Sept. 10, 1913 .

William H. Stubbs Co.E. 1st MI Sharpshooters. Died May 5, 1907. Blaine Cemetery, Benzie Co.

Antoine Tab-Yant Co. K. 1st MI SS. Age 35. Little Traverse area. Buried in Lakeview Cemetery, Harbor Springs May 22, 1894.
Others in the 1st MI Sharpshooters with possible ties to Leelanau may have included: Cpl. Enos Bolton, Thomas Smith, & Freeman Sutton as well as many more Native American Indians.

Leon O-Tash-Qua-Bon-O
Co. K. 1st MI SS
**(Courtesy Detroit Public Library
Deland Files, Burton Historical Collection)**

Federal Prisoners at Andersonville (National Archives)

The Sultan (Courtesy Kansas State Historical Society, Topeka)

Federal Soldiers by gun in captured fort at Atlanta, GA.
(George N. Barnard – Library of Congress)

Civil War Re-enactors portray Bat. E.
Camp Grayling, MI. See William Nickloy
(Leonard G. Overmyer III)

Forest Haven Soldiers: The Civil War Veterans of Sleeping Bear & Surrounding Leelanau

Michigan Units [12]

MI Light Artillery

Cpl. James U. Auton (Anton) Battery L. 1st MI L.A., & Co. K. 9th MI Cav. (Both regiments from the same area and served together). Age 18. Mustered April 16, 1863. Unit service: Lebanon KY, Knoxville TN, Jonesboro, Cumberland Gap, detached to Strawberry Plains. Reported as of Co. M. 9th MI Cavalry Corporal June 15, 1865. Duty at Concord, NC. Mustered out at Lexington, NC July 21, 1865. (Empire Township 1890 Fed. Census Civil War Veteran & 1894 Veterans Census of MI.) Oct. 1, 1846 – April 10, 1919. Buried in Rose Hill (Ziegler) Cemetery. G.A.R. Post 168.

Cpl. William Nickloy also under William (James) Nickaloy. Cpl. Battery E. 1st Michigan Light Artillery. Age 22. From Adrian. Began May 6, 1863. Nashville & La Vergne TN. Mustered out July 30, 1865. Lived in Fountain, MI & Buried in Platte Township Cemetery. East of Otter Creek - Benzie County. G.A.R. Marker.

Lt. John (James) M. Tilton Sgt. Battery A. 1st Regiment MI Light Artillery "Cyrus O. Loomis' Battery, Coldwater Artillary" Glen Arbor Draftee. Enlisted Oct. 1, 1861. One of the state's most famous military units. After Rich Mountain, the battery exchanged its old brass guns for ten pound Parrotts sent by General McClellan as a reward for driving the enemy from a position he had regarded impregnable. Some times the battery was divided; one Captain would take a gun on board a Steamer for work along the rivers; another would mount his cannon on a flat car, protect it with a screen of iron, and go dodging up and down the railroads about Nashville. Unit at: Cheat Mt., Louisville KY, Nashville TN, Bridgeport AL, Battle of Perryville (where, led by General Sheridan, they were engaged by 24 Rebel cannons in a crossfire, "but the Michiganders were too much for them all." – Silas Parker – MI Archives).

The battle of Perryville was opened and closed by the Loomis Battery. In the thickest of that fight the Colonel was holding the enemy in check to permit the withdrawal of other regiments; orders came to spike his guns and retreat, but such was Colonel Loomis' fondness for his Parrotts that he decided to stay with them. So he fought on in spite of orders, and after repelling five charges and losing eighteen men and thirty-three horses, he brought out every one of his guns.

In an artillery duel at Murfreesboro, Colonel Loomis, "the envy of all artillerists" as a *New York Herald* correspondent called him, in rapid succession dismounted five of the enemy's guns and drove a second battery off the field. In the battles at Stone River and Chickamauga where Lt. Van Pelt commanded the famous battery to his death with sword in hand, "Scoundrels," he cried, "don't dare lay hands on those guns." As he spoke he fell dead.[153] Tilton was then Commissioned Junior 2nd Lieut. Sept. 21, 1863. At Mission Ridge they recaptured three of the Loomis cannon lost at Chickamauga and the other two were eventually recovered at Atlanta. Tilton was again

Loomis' Battery   (Courtesy Library of Congress and Burton Historical Collection, Detroit Public Library)

Cannon from Loomis' Battery at Coldwater.
(Betty L. Overmyer)

Mustered April 1, 1864. Commissioned Junior 1st Lieut. Sept. 6, 1864. Battles of Chattanooga. Mustered Dec. 9, 1864. Resigned March 6, 1865.

One historical account of this Michigan Battery was in Parkersburg, VA where the MI men had a stirring unexpected welcome from several pro-union locals. Correspondent "Spencer" of the Free Press described the scene:

> Three young ladies, one dressed in red, one in white, and one in blue, each holding a flag, were standing in front of a very large U.S. flag, which was held by several other ladies in the background. "The group formed a scene at once so beautiful and from the fact of its being on the banks of a seceded State, roused the artillery boys so completely – the officers especially – the our 'Lyon' Capt. Loomis, roared above the wild cheering the command: 'Cannoneers of the Ringgold gun, to your posts!' The command set them to work so vigorously on their 'pet' that her 'noisy barking' roused the people for miles around." This impromptu salute may well have been typical of Captain Loomis.[154]

Loomis' Battery A of the 1st Regiment MI Light Artillery was considered the most famous of the unit, renowned for effectiveness of its service, its dramatic history and the equally dramatic history of its commander.[155] One of the ten-pounder Parrott guns of this battery is on display in a park in Coldwater at the junction of US-27 and US-12.[156] Others were at the Capital in Lansing until they were scrapped for World War II. John Tilton's grave is listed as being found along the road going into the Leelanau Boy's Camp,[157] or now called Leelanau Schools (Glen Arbor / Port Onieda area) just off the road in an old graveyard. It also holds other settlers including Mrs. Fields and her twin babies who had escaped with her husband from Mormon King Strang; and Sailors possibly from the wreck of the schooner "Phelps."[158] Born in 1835. He owned land west of Wells Lake.[159] Listed in Kasson Township 1894 Veterans Census of MI.

Surrounding Leelanau:

Elden S. Bryant Bat. E. 1st MI L.A.

Cpl. William Core/Cove. Bat. H. 1st MI L.A. & 17th Army Corps. Bingham Township 1894 Veteran's Census. Born in Liverpool England in 1842.[160] – Aug. 12, 1920. Oakwood Cemetery. Member of Traverse City McPherson G.A.R. Post 18.

Thomas Haynes Bat. H. 1st MI L.A. G.A.R. Post 399.

James Mason Bat. G. 1st MI L.A. & U.S. Navy. Leland Township. G.A.R. Post 399. St. Mary's Cemetery, Lake Leelanau.

(also Grand Traverse: Ora E. Clark and James N. Mason in Bat. G. MI L.A., Ferdinand Dord?, and John Sutherland Age 27 in unassigned L.A. Jan. 1864. Also possibly Charles G. Day.)

Grave of Lt. John M. Tilton by entrance to Leelanau Schools, Glen Arbor, MI.
(Nathaniel G. Overmyer)

BATTERY A FIRST MICHIGAN LIGHT ARTILLERY
ORGANIZED IN COLDWATER AND KNOWN AS
LOOMIS' BATTERY

THIS IS ONE OF THE SIX TEN POUNDER PARROTT GUNS SENT TO
LOOMIS BATTERY BY GENERAL McCLELLAN AT RICH MOUNTAIN, WEST
VIRGINIA, TO REPLACE THE OLD SIX POUNDER BRASS GUN ORIGINALLY
SUPPLIED THE BATTERY, AND WAS IN SERVICE IN WEST VIRGINIA FROM
JULY 1ST UNTIL DECEMBER 16TH, 1861 WHEN THE BATTERY WAS
ORDERED TO REPORT TO GENERAL BUELL AT LOUISVILLE, KY.
IN ADDITION TO ITS SERVICE IN WEST VIRGINIA, IT WAS IN ACTION
AT BOWLING GREEN, KY., FEB. 14, 1862, HUNTSVILLE, ALA., APRIL,
1862, BRIDGEPORT, ALA., APRIL 29, 1862, GUNTHERS LANDING, ALA.
MAY 15, 1862, ATHENS, ALA. MAY 29, 1862, WHITESBURGH, ALA., JUNE,
1862, PERRYVILLE, KY. OCT. 8, 1862, STONE'S RIVER, TENNESSEE,
DEC. 31, 1862, JAN. 1, 2 AND 3, 1863, HOOVER'S GAP, JUNE 25, 1863
CHICKAMAUGA, GA. SEPT. 19 AND 20, 1863, MISSIONARY RIDGE, NOV. 25,
1863, CHATTANOOGA, TENN., NOVEMBER, 1863 TO JULY, 1865
THIS GUN, WITH FOUR OTHERS OF THE BATTERY, WAS CAPTURED BY
WALTHALL'S AND GOVAN'S BRIGADE OF WALKER'S CORPS OF THE CONFED-
ERATE ARMY IN THE BATTLE OF CHICKAMAUGA ON THE 19TH OF SEPTEMBER
1863, IN WHICH BATTLE LIEUT. VAN PELT AND THIRTEEN MEN WERE KILLED
OR WOUNDED, THIRTEEN MEN MISSING, AND FORTY HORSES KILLED.
THE GUNS WERE RECAPTURED BY WILLICH'S BRIGADE OF THE UNION
ARMY, BEFORE THE DAY'S FIGHTING CEASED.

John M. Tilton

Lt. John M. Tilton
1ˢᵗ MI Light Artillery
("Loomis Association Album"
M.C. Switlik Collection)

Abner Fritz 1ˢᵗ MI Cavalry
(Courtesy Kasson Heritage Group)

Sgt. Charles Clifton
U.S. Navy
1ˢᵗ MI Engineers & Mechanics
(Courtesy Elaine Burgin-Orvis
Stoddard Collection)

MI Engineers & Mechanics

Sgt. Chas (Charles W.) Clifton U.S. Navy Co. D. 1st MI Eng./Mechanics. Mustered Dec. 6, 1861 with Isaac Clifton. Re-enlisted Jan. 2, 1864 at Chattanooga, TN Feb. 1, 1864 Artificer & Corporal Feb. 3. Sgt. Nov. 1, 1864, Mustered out at Nashville, TN Sept. 22,1865. Served with George & Peter Stoddard. Buried in Maple Grove (Empire Union) Cemetery.

David McLaughlin Enlisted in Co. K. 1st MI Eng. & Mechanics & 1st MI Inf. Age 35 (listed as 25). Aug. 9, 1864. Joined regiment at Graysville, GA Sept. 1864. Atlanta March to the Sea, Carolina Campaign, Battle of Bentonville, Goldsboro, Richmond, Grand Review May 24, Discharged June 6, 1865 at Washington D.C. In 1894 Veteran's Census. Buried in Kasson Cemetery. (Aug. 4, 1829-Nov. 13, 1908). G.A.R. Post 168. (See McLaughlin's in 1st MI SS, 10th Cav., 15th MI, 16th MI, & 26th MI Inf.)

David Wright Enlisted in Co. K. 1st MI Eng. & Mechanics. Age 41. Mustered Dec. 31, 1861. Unit Service: KY, Nashville TN, Shiloh, Corinth, Huntsville AL, Louisville KY, Perryville, Battle of Stone River, Repulse of Gen. Forest's Attack, Murfreesboro, Chattanooga, Discharged at Nashville TN, June 4, 1863. (also later listing under Co.B. 1st Ind. Cavalry). Listed in Oakwood Cemetery. G.A.R. Post 168.

David L. Hillard Co.H. 1st MI Eng.& Mechanics. Wayland, MI. Born in Canada, died Jan. 11, 1925. Lived in Empire, MI.

Surrounding Leelanau:
Ebenezer Fillmore Co. L. 1st MI Eng. & Mech. 1815-1895, Linwood / Neal Cemetery, Long Lake area.
Sgt. Edward P. Van Valkenberg Co. E./I. 1st MI Eng. also see Edwin 10th MI Cav., Northport G.A.R. Post 399. Also Cpl. Morris B. Jennings Co. I. MI Eng. & Mech. Traverse City area.

1st MI Cavalry

Abner S. Fritz Enlisted in Co. G. 1st MI Cavalry Bugler. Age 21. Mustered Sept. 7, 1861. (1st Cavalry would be part of General Custer's Woverines.) Unit Service: Washington D.C., Loudoun Heights VA, Shenandoah Valley under General Banks & Sheridan, Berryville, Leesburg, Snicker's Gap, Battle of Winchester. Disabled at Winchester, VA (in left hand), in Bank's retreat down the valley May, 1862[161] & Discharged June 6, 1862. Lived in Maple City/ Burdickville P.O. Was elected Kasson Township Supervisor for 18 terms.[162] Lost three of his children (to illness?) in July of 1880. Photograph featured in "Remembering Yesterday - Kasson Heritage Group" Kasson Township 1894 Veteran's Census. Died April 12, 1913. Aged 72 Yrs. 11 Months. Buried in Rose Hill (Ziegler) Cemetery.[163] G.A.R. Post 168.

Robert J. Middaugh (Middeaugh/Meddough) 1843-1899 Listed with 1st MI Lancers. Age 18. Mustered Nov. 6, 1861. Listing Deserted? Though unlikely. Buried in Maple Grove (Empire Union) Cemetery. Listed in Empire Township 1894 Veterans Census of MI. G.A.R. Post 168.

Surrounding Leelanau:
Cornelius Fogarty 1st MI Cav. & see also 17th MI Inf. Suttonsbay.
Squire Loomis Co. A. MI Lancers Suttonsbay.
(Also **Edward Stormer** Co. L.1st MI Cav. lived in Petoskey. A detailed transcript of Daniel Lee Spencer Co. D. 1st MI Cavalry is held at the MI State Library in Lansing compiled by Margaret Mastick of Milford, MI 1961.)

1st MI Infantry

When the First Michigan Infantry arrived in Washington DC, President Lincoln was credited with exclaiming "Thank God for Michigan!"[164]

Gooding Adams Enlisted in Co. I. 1st MI Inf. Age 18. Mustered July 31, 1861. Joined unit after Battle of Bull Run but was discharged at Weldon RR VA Aug. 31, 1861. Re-enlisted in Co. A. 8th U.S. Veteran Volunteers March 29, 1865. Camp Stoneman. Discharged at expiration of service, Washington D.C. March 28, 1866. G.A.R. Post 168. Buried in Crystal Lake Cemetery, Benzie Co.

John Jackson Fredrick Age 31. Enlisted in Co. I. 1st MI Inf. / 1st MI Sharp Shooters. Mustered Aug. 13, 1863 Listed deserted out? (Empire Twp. 1890 Fed. Census Civil War Veteran)

Fred'k Haines Age 44. Co. I. 1st MI Inf. Drafted June 11, 1864 from **Manitou**. Mustered June 23, 1864. This Veteran Unit had already been through the Battles of: Bull Run, Antietam, Fredericksburg, Chancellorsville, Gettysburg, the Wilderness, & Spottsylvania. Joined regiment near Petersburg, VA Oct. 1, 1864 during Siege. Mine Explosion, Weldon Railroad, Hatcher's Run, Dabney's Mills, Appomattox Campaign, Battle of Five Forks, Surrender of Lee and his Army, Participated in the Grand Review May 1865, Ordered to Louisville, KY. Mustered out near Jeffersonville, Ind. July 9, 1865. Died Nov. 4, 1893. Age 73. Buried in Maple Grove (Empire Union) Cemetery near Empire, MI. G.A.R. Post 168. (See Jacob Haines 26th MI Inf. & Thomas Haynes MI Lt A.)

Paul Half Jr. Age 37. Co. I. 1st MI Inf. Drafted June 11, 1864 from **North Manitou Island**. Mustered June 23, 1864. As mentioned, this Veteran unit had already been through the battles of: Bull Run, Antietam, Fredericksburg, Chancellorsville, Gettysburg, the Wilderness, & Spotsylvania. Joined regiment near Petersburg, VA Oct. 1, 1864 during Siege. Died of disease at City Point, VA on Dec. 20, 1864.

1st Michigan Colored Infantry (102nd)

John Holland / Hallad Co. A. 1st (&102nd) MI Colored Inf. With 1st NY Cav. Known as 'Lincoln's Troops.' Glen Arbor Draftee. Age 20. Enlisted at Detroit. Service under **Patrick McLaughlin** (see 16th MI). Nov. 6, 1863. **1st Colored Infantry**. Joined 9th Army Corps. at Annapolis, MD., Hilton Head & St. Helena, SC. Designated **change to 102nd U.S. Colored Troops** May 23, 1864. Attack on Baldwin FL, Raid on FL Central RR, Beaufort SC, Skirmish at Cuckwood Creek (where Capt. Patrick McLaughlin was Killed in action at Salkehatchie, SC Feb. 8, 1865) Carolina Campains. Mustered out at Charleston, SC Sept. 30, 1865. Also:
Russell Woodford Co. I. 1st MI Colored (102nd Colored) Inf. Fife Lake/Union Twp.

2nd MI Cavalry (Often joined in action by the 2nd Iowa Cavalry)
John C. Cook 2nd MI Cav. Traverse City. Died at age 91 in 1926. Woodville Cemetery, Big Rapids.
Nason/Neason Finch Co. E. Bugler, 2nd MI Cav. Died in 1913 at age 94. Long Lake area. Linwood/Neal Cemetery. Lot. 6E, Unmarked Veteran.
Charles Gardner Co. D. 2nd MI Cav. Suttonsbay. (Died in 1877 Age 68. Buried in Bingham Cemetery, Flag but no Veteran's Staff Marker). Also veteran **Manleus F. Gardner** in Bingham Cemetery.
William Hawkins Co.D. 2nd MI Cav from Point Betsy Leelanau County. (See Thomas Hawkins 2nd MI SS.)

1st **Michigan Infantry** (Michigan Archives)

Historical Re-enactor Gerome Peebles,
himself a U.S. Veteran, speaks at the
Civil War Muster in Jackson, MI.
(Leonard G. Overmyer III)

2nd MI Infantry

Benjamin A. (or O.) Demming See 4th MI Infantry. (Deming) P.O.W. Age 18. 2nd & 4th MI Inf. Enlisted in Co. K. 4th MI Inf. June 30, 1861. Discharged for Disability at Miners Hill Jan. 6, 1862. Re-enlisted in Co. G. 2nd MI Inf. March 31, 1864 at Centerville, MI. Taken Prisoner near Petersburg, VA July 30, 1864. No further record. (see R.E. Deming 1st WS in G.A.R. Post 168).

2nd MI Sharp Shooters

Thomas J. Hawkins Co.B. 2nd MI Sharpshooters. Centerville Draftee. Died July 1864 of wounds received in action at the Battles of the Wilderness May 6, 1864. Buried in Arlington VA National Cemetery. (See William Hawkins 2nd MI Cavalry.)

3rd MI Cavalry

Joseph Prickett Co. L. 3rd MI Cav. Leelanau TS 1894 Veteran's Census. (Indian) Northport G.A.R. Post 399. Onominee Indian Cemetery.

3rd MI Infantry

William E. (or L.) Bickle Enlisted in Co. G. 3rd MI Inf. Age 24. Mustered Sept. 7, 1864. Reorganized Unit Service: Decatur AL, Murfreesboro TN against Gen. Hood, Huntsville AL, Nashville TN, New Orleans LA, Regiment went on to Texas. Admitted to Harper Hospital Aug. 24, 1865. Discharged at Detroit Aug. 29, 1865. Maple City resident. Kasson Township. Buried in Oakwood Cemetery. G.A.R. Post 168 Adjutant. Was the last member of the Post to file a G.A.R. report (May 25, 1913, a Month after Abner Fritz died), with Nathaniel Harrington. Died in 1923.

Louis Ruthardt Enlisted in Co. C. 3rd MI Inf. Age 19. Originally from Grand Rapids, MI. Entered March 1, 1862. Unit: Battle of Fair Oaks or Seven Pines, Savage Station & Peach Orchard, Charles City Cross Roads & Glendale, Malvern Hill, Harrison's Landing. Discharged for Disability at Detroit Sept. 2, 1862. Listed in Solon Township 1894 Veteran's Census. Born June 30, 1842. Died Sept. 9, 1926. Solon Township Cemetery.

Surrounding Leelanau:

Charles Leroy Co.G. 3rd MI Inf. Centerville. Wounded in action at Malvern Hill July 1, 1862.
Morris Franklin Quackenbush Co.F. 3rd MI Inf. Reported in Grand Traverse Herald that he died of Typhoid Fever at the Military Hospital in Murfreesboro, TN Jan. 10, 1865 Age 20y, 10m, 12d. (See Hiram in 26th MI)

This June 1861 *New York Illustrated News* woodcut depicted the Third Michigan Infantry parading down Detroit's Jefferson Avenue on its way to Washington, DC.

4th MI Cavalry

William H. Amidon Sr. Enlisted in Co. B. 4th MI Cavalry. Age 24. Dark Hair 5'9" Mustered Aug. 19, 1864. Siege of Atlanta, Jonesboro, Against Gen. Hood in GA & AL, Nashville TN, Chickasaw & Montgomery AL, Capture of Macon & Confederate President Jefferson Davis. Mustered out at Nashville, TN July 1, 1865. Became deaf in right ear due to service. Cleveland Township 1894 Veteran's Census. Buried in Kasson Cemetery with a newer marker. (Mar. 2, 1840-Jan. 31, 1913). G.A.R. Post 168.

Sgt. William D. Burdick Sgt. Co.G. 4th MI Cav. & Co.B. 15th Reg.Vet. Res. Corps.

Enlisted as Commissary Sgt. At Quincy. Age 29. Mustered Aug. 29, 1862. Stanford, Cumberland River, Stone River, Pea Vine Ridge, Chickamauga, Transferred to Invalid Corps. Sept. 30, 1863. Discharged at Springfield, Ill. (where John Boizard was serving) July 7, 1865 from Co. B. 15th Reg. Vet. Res. Corps. See pre-war stories at beginning of book. He was listed age 27 from New York with wife Annie in the pre-war 1860 Census of Glen Arbor Township. (Also listed as William H.) Listed as a Glen Arbor Draftee. (See Theadore Burdick in 6th MI Cavalry.)

Henry Cooper Enlisted in Co. M. 4th MI Cavalry. Age 21. Mustered Aug. 29, 1862. Service: Stanford, Cumberland River, Taken Prisoner at Stone River Bridge between Lebanon & Nashville Nov. 12, 1862. Paroled. Unit went on to Battle of Stone River, Pea Vine Ridge, Chickamauga, Chattanooga, Pumpkin Vine Creek, Dallas, Atlanta, Jonesboro, Capture of Confederate President Jefferson Davis (with the 1st WS). Mustered out at Nashville TN July 1, 1865. Listed in Kasson Township. Died April 27, 1872. Buried in Round Top (Friends) Cemetery.

Surrounding Leelanau:
John A. Miller Co.C. 4th MI Cav., Misc. Leelanau County.
Joshua R. Moe Co.A. 4th MI Cav., Traverse City area as well as several others.

4th MI Infantry

4th MI Infantry Service: Manassas / Battle of Bull Run, Washington D.C., Virginia Peninsula, Battle of Hanover Ct. House, Seven Days Battles (Richmond, VA), Battle of Mechanicsville, 2nd Battle of Bull Run, Battle of Antietam, Battle of Fredericksburg, Battle of Chancellorsville, Battle of Gettysburg, Mine Run, Battle of the Wilderness, Spotsylvania & Court House, Salient, North Anna River, Jericho Mills, Pamunkey, Totopotomoy, Cold Harbor, Petersburg, Veterans & Recruits transferred to **1st MI Infantry** June 30, 1864. (See Frederick Haines record). Reorganized Oct. 1864. Decatur, Maysville, Rebel Gen. Hood's attack on Murfreesboro, Huntsville AL, Knoxville, Strawberry Plains, Bull's Gap, Jonesboro, Nashville TN, New Orleans LA, San Antonio Texas and other points until May 1866.[165] (See Book: The 4th Vol. Michigan Infantry at Gettysburg: The Battle for the Wheatfield. by Martin Bertera and Ken Oberholtzer, Morning Side House, Inc. 1997 Dayton, OH.). The MI Archives in Lansing also holds many photo's of this unit.

George Cook Enlisted in Co. C. 4th MI Inf. Age 21. Mustered June 20, 1863, out July 30, 1864. G.A.R. Post 168. (See John Cook in 2nd MI Cav., Adam Cook in 10th MI Cav. & Frederick Cook in 26th MI Inf.)

John F. Crain Enlisted in Co. C. 4th MI Inf.& 1st (with **Samuel Crain**). Mustered June 20, 1861. Wounded in action at Gettysburg on July 2, 1863. Re-enlisted for Jan. 1, 1864. On detached service with Co. C. 1st MI Inf. July 2, 1864. Listed deserted? at New Orleans, LA June 25, 1865 (though this date was after the war). G.A.R. Post 168.

Benjamin A. (or O.) Demming (Deming) P.O.W. Age 18. 2nd & 4th MI Inf. Enlisted in Co. K. 4th MI Inf. June 30, 1861. Discharged for Disability at Miners Hill Jan. 6, 1862. Re-enlisted in Co. G. 2nd MI Inf. March 31, 1864 at Centerville, MI. Taken Prisoner near Petersburg, VA July 30, 1864. No further record. (see R.E. Deming 1st WS in G.A.R. Post 168).

Charles E. Lawyers (Law) Enlisted in Co. C. 4th MI Inf. Age 23. At Sturgis, originally from La Grange, IN. Listed Glen Arbor Draftee. Mustered June 20, 1861. Discharged for disability July 30, 1862.

John Post Co. F. 4th MI Inf. Age 36. Feb. 28, 1863 at Liberty. On detached service with Co. C. **1st MI Inf.** July 2, 1864 Petersburg, VA. Transferred to Co. K. Feb. 15, 1866. Discharged at San Antonio, TX Feb. 28, 1866. (Listed as Empire Township 1890 Fed. Census Civil War Veteran) Died April 8, 1877. Green Briar Cemetery - Almira Union.

Surrounding Leelanau:
Lorenzo Rose Co.A. 4th MI Inf. Leelanau Township Draftee.

General George A. Custer
Michigan Cavalry Brigade
(Michigan Archives)

5th MI Cavalry

Soon after the arrival of this regiment to Washington in the early part of the war, the 5th MI Cavalry under Colonel Joseph T. Copeland was assigned to the Michigan Cavalry Brigade. This was composed of the First, Fifth, Sixth and Seventh Michigan Cavalry. These regiments served together during the war. After Col. Copeland became a Brigadier General, Russell A. Alger took over.

In June of 1863, General George Armstrong Custer was assigned to command the cavalry division. Shortly after, the brigade met Confederate General J.E.B. Stuart's cavalry on June 30, near Hanover, PA, and drove them back in a spirited charge.

At the Battle of Gettysburg, the 5th Cavalry, with the Michigan Brigade, had one of the severest cavalry engagements of the war with General Stuart's forces on July 3. Their determined gallantry won a decisive victory in repelling Stuart's attack, driving him back so he could no longer threaten the rear of the Union lines. Action continued on at Williamsport, Boonsboro, and Falling Waters.

This regiment also included Major Luther S. Trowbridge who would later command the 10th MI Cavalry and William H. Dunn of Saugatuck who would also serve in the 10th MI Cavalry over many men from Leelanau County. In August of 1862, Dunn had joined at the age of 18 in Co. I under Captain William B. Williams of Allegan and 1st Lt. George N. Dutcher of Saugatuck. Major Trowbridge had his horse shot out from under him at Gettysburg and was rescued by William Dunn.[166] They were both promoted into the 10th MI Cavalry under Thaddeus Foote of the 6th MI Cavalry, - see earlier histories. It was John A. Huff of the 5th MI Cavalry who shot and killed Confederate General J.E.B. Stuart later in the War.[167] John Huff was mortally wounded at Hawes' Shop and is buried in Armada, MI.

Sleeping Bear / Glen Lake & upper Benzie Co.

Charles F. (or T.) **Severance** Enlisted in Co. E. 5th MI Cavalry. Age 19. March 30, 1865 (5th Cavalry was part of General Custer's Wolverines.)[168] Appomattox Campaign, Five Forks, Surrender of Lee and his Army. Expedition to Danville. Discharged - May 5, 1865. Lake Ann G.A.R. Post 423 and Glen Lake Post 168.

Surrounding Leelanau:

Wilbur H. Canfield from Lyons Co. D. 5th MI Cav. Suttonsbay. (Buried in Bingham Cemetery). No Veterans Marker.

George Leslie Co. M. 5th MI Cav. Died in Shenandoah Valley Sept. 22, 1864.

Albert S. Norris Co.G. 5th MI Cavalry & 7th Bingham Twp. Wounded in action at Gettysburg July 3, 1863 & Listed as having Died of disease Dec. 7 Buried in Richmond,VA. & also listed in Neal. (Where Ira Chase of the 10th MI Cavalry lived. See Charles Norris in 15th MI Inf.) Listed in Linwood/Neal Cemetery Sept. 5, 1840 – Feb. 6, 1902.

Harrison G. Stewart Co.E. 5th MI Cav. Died in War June 8, 1864. Age 19. Ogdensburg Cemetery. (See William Stewart 1st NY L.A.)

5th MI Infantry

In September of 1861 the 5th MI Infantry left Fort Wayne for Virginia under the command of Col. Henry D. Ferry. With bands playing and flags flying gaily, the regiment marched to the steamer; but the silk banner borne so proudly at the head of the regiment was soon to have its gold fringe torn and its shining folds shot away, piece be piece. Soldier after soldier snatched the standard from the hands of the falling color-bearer and bore it into the thick of the fight. Ten men lost their lives in defending that flag.

The 5th MI stood fourth among infantry regiments in the entire Union army with respect to the number of men who were killed in action or who died of wounds received while fighting.[169]

Glen Lake:

Samuel A. Axtell (Extell) Age 44 Co. C. 5th MI Inf. Drafted from Glen Arbor & Benzie Co. Mustered June 30, 1864. Siege of Petersburg, Weldon RR, James River, Strawberry Plains, Poplar Springs Church, Hatcher's Run, Discharged March 20, 1865. (Listed in 1870 Empire post-war Census with 4 children. Also Franklin Axtell served in 17 NY L.A. Buried in Gilmore Cemetery, Benzie, Co.)

George Haas Co. K. 5th MI Inf. Enlisted at **Manitou**. Age 38. From Bavaria.[170] Mustered June 11, 1864 Substitute for Mr. Burton. He left his wife and six children for three years with no word heard of him. Battles of the Wilderness, Spotsylvania, Salient (Bloody Angle), North Anna River, Totopotomoy, Cold Harbor, Siege of Petersburg, James River, Strawberry Plains, Poplar Springs Church, Hatcher's Run. Discharged at Alexandria, VA June 28, 1865. He returned to his family on Manitou. Listed in South Manitou Township 1894 Veterans Census of MI. Birth year should actually read 1825. Died 1909? (1860 pre-war Census had George listed at 42?) Listed as buried on the Haas/Hass Farm on **South Manitou Island**. (See John Haas 16th MI Inf.)

Charles B. Taylor Enlisted in Co. I. 5th MI Inf. Age 33. Mustered Sept. 14, 1862 Washington D.C., Battle of Fredericksburg, Battle of Chancellorsville, Wounded in action at Gettysburg July 1, 1863. Transferred to Co. B. June 10, 1864. Battles of the Wilderness, Spotsylvania, Salient (Bloody Angle), North Anna River, Totopotomoy, Cold Harbor, Siege of Petersburg, James River, Strawberry Plains, Poplar Springs Church, Hatcher's Run where listed deserted at Petersburg, VA Oct. 27, 1864. Though this was same day Nathan Gutherie was captured & may have been the same fate. Later listed with **3rd MI** Inf. Member G.A.R. Post 168. (See Edmund P. Taylor 10th Ill. Cavalry under Leelanau Township.)

Surrounding Leelanau:

Henry Davis Co. H. 5th MI Inf. Centerville. (Substitute for Walter W. Barton.)

Mattew H. Glen Denning / (M.) Glendening Age 33. Enlisted 5th MI Inf. Co. H. June 11, 1864 Drafted from Centerville (Centreville?) Mustered July 6, 1864. Wounded in action October 17, 1864. (Decatur).and at the battle of Burgesses Farm Oct. 27th and was taken prisoner on the morning of the 28th. He was carried to Richmond and kept over three months when he was parolled and returned home on a thirty days furlough.[171] Mustered out at Jeffersonville, IN July 5, 1865. Born 1830 – Died Jan. 6, 1908 Age 78y, 8m, 11d. Traverse City Oakwood Cemetery.

Nathan Gutherie Age 36 Co. H. 5th MI Inf. Enlisted at Centerville. July 3, 1864. Taken prisoner Oct. 27, 1864. Returned to Regiment at Burksville, VA April 27, 1865. Listed in Leland TS 1894 Veteran's Census. Leland (Beechwood) Cemetery. (see Samuel Gutherie under 16th MI Inf.).

Frank Newton (Nowanten /Nowlty/ Newonton) Co.G. 5th MI Inf. Centerville. (See Martin Novotny 7th Cav.?)

The Grand Traverse Herald.

MORGAN BATES, Editor and Proprietor.

TRAVERSE CITY:

FRIDAY MORNING, JULY 10, 1863.

For the Grand Traverse Herald.
Interesting Correspondence.

ELK RAPIDS, June 30, 1863.

FRIEND BATES,—A younger sister of mine has recently gone to labor as a Missionary Teacher among the Contrabands at Corinth, Miss. Some of her letters to me are of more than ordinary interest, and from the topics of which they treat, would not fail, I think, to interest and profit your readers. I send you some extracts, which, if you think best, I should very much like to have you publish.

Yours, truly,

LENORE WARREN.

CONTRABAND CAMP, CORINTH, Miss.
June 5, 1863.

DEAR BROTHER LEROY,—My first invoice of letters from the North, came yesterday—and yours among them. I hope you received my letter from Cincinnati.—We left that great dirty city on the 5 o'clock train Wednesday morning, and reached Cairo the next morning. The journey was pleasanter than we anticipated.

THE WAR IN THE EAST.

Brilliant Cavalry Victory—Great Battle Supposed to be in Progress—Interesting Details of the Situation—Successful Federal Skirmishing.

From the Harrisburg Telegraph.

HARRISBURG, July 1, 9.30 p. m.—A battle took place yesterday afternoon, at Hanover Junction, between Gen. Pleasanton and the rebel cavalry, which lasted nearly the whole afternoon.

THE SIEGE OF VICKSBURG.

Special Dispatch to the Chicago Tribune.

CAIRO, July 1st, 1863.

Cavalry General Benjamin H. Grierson
owned cottages in Omena, Michigan.
(Ostendorf Collection)

General George A. Custer led the
1st, 5th, 6th, and 7th Michigan Cavalry
(Library of Congress)

George A. Custer and General Alfred Pleasonton
(Library of Congress)

Famous Cavalry Generals Associated with Leelanau County

General George Armstrong Custer was a visitor in Leelanau County at Omena, MI where his in-laws owned property.

General Benjamin Grierson (6th Ill. Cavalry) who led a famous screening movement through Mississippi during Grant's Vicksburg Campaigns, also owned land in Omena. Like General Custer, Grierson would serve out West after the War commanding the 10th U.S.Cavalry (Buffalo Soldiers). These Black Soldiers were famous for their courage and devotion.

5th or 6th U.S. Cavalry (& 6th Colored Infantry)

Arnold Freeman Listed Negro. Black Soldier. Co. C. 5th or 6th U.S. Cavalry. Listed in 6th Colored Inf. Co. C. in National Archives, unit served with Cavalry. (KY, VA, AK, Carolinas). Listed in Kasson Township 1894 Veteran's Census of Michigan. Buried in East Kasson Evangelical Cemetery. (West of Large White Pine). Grave reads: Co. C. 6th U.S. Cavalry but may actually mean 5th U.S. Cavalry or 6th Colored Infantry. Died Jan. 28, 1899. G.A.R. Post 168.

6th MI Cavalry

Frank Weiler Co.I. 6th MI Cav. Enlisted 1864. Age 18. (Transf. to 1st Cav. Nov. 1865). East Leland Cemetery.

Some from the **Grand Traverse Region** included:
John H. Adams 6th MI Cavalry Buried in Gilmore Township, Benzie Co.; **John F. Beebe** 6th MI Cavalry of Elk Rapids.; Also - **Joseph Buck** Co. A. 6th MI Cavalry; **Theodore Burdick** Co. I. 6th MI Cavalry Died at Andersonville Prison Aug. 8, 1864. Grave # 6990.[172] (See W. Burdick 4th MI Cav.); **David O'Connel** Co.I 6th MI Cav. Age 26. From Stronach. Wounded & taken prisoner at Seneca, MD June 11, 1863. Discharged Nov. 2, 1863. Also - **Luman A. Cutler** 6th MI Cavalry Gilmore. Died in 1863.; **Jonathan Fuller** 6th & 5th MI Cavalry Oakwood Cemetery G.A.R. lot.; **Robert S. Garner** 6th MI Cavalry. Died 1916. Oakwood Cemetery, T.C. (See 2nd MI Cavalry listings.); **George W. Osborne** 6th MI Cavalry Oakwood Cemetery. Also - **Freling H. Potter** 6th MI Cavalry; **Charles Riley** Co. I. 6th MI Cavalry. Manistee. Died in Andersonville Prison July 20, 1864. Grave # 3732.[173] & **Eber Stanley** Co. K. 6th MI Cavalry. Later lived in Petoskey, MI.

6th MI Infantry

Cpl. Francis (Franklin B.) Todd Co. K. 6th MI Inf. Glen Arbor Draftee. Enlisted Aug. 6, 1861 Age 24. Mustered Aug. 20, 1861. Against New Orleans on Transport "Constitution," Ship Island, Baton Rouge, Warrenton, Vicksburg, action with Steamer "Cotton," Ponchatoula, Amite River & Jackson RR, Port Hudson, converted to a Regiment of Heavy Artillery by General Banks & retained Infantry number. Action at Tunica Bayou, became Corporal Oct. 26, 1863. Duties in LA, Vicksburg, AK, Fort Morgan AL. Discharged at Kalamazoo, MI Aug. 23, 1864. Expiration of term of service. Listed as being buried in an unidentified marker at the old Glen Arbor Township Cemetery in the woods near M22-Forest Haven Road within the Sleeping Bear Dunes National Lakeshore. (The Todd family owned an Inn at Glen Arbor).

George W. Slater Co. E. 6th MI Inf. Enlisted Jan. 8, 1864 at Jackson. Age 46. Duties in Vicksburg, AK, Fort Morgan AL. Campaigns of the South. Mustered out at New Orleans, LA. Aug. 20, 1865. George W. Slater was a Charter Petitioner for the Murray Post 168 G.A.R. (Co. E. also included Thomas J. Overmyer who died in Andersonville Prison Aug. 6, 1864. Grave # 4874.)[174]

1863.

MAJOR GEORGE K. NEWCOMBE,
Traverse City, Mich.

Major George K. Newcombe. Born at Westfield, Chautauqua County, N.Y., August 16th, 1833. He enlisted at Owosso, Shiawassee County, Michigan on October 12th, 1861 as Captain of Co. F. 9th MI Infantry. He was later promoted to Major 7th MI Cavalry on December 10th 1862. At Gettysburg, in Custer's famous mounted charge, he was wounded by a rifle shot in the leg. He was honorably discharged and mustered out at Owosso, MI Oct. 12, 1863. Lived in the Traverse City area. (Insert from Personal and Historical Sketches and Facial History of and by members of the Seventh Regiment Michigan Volunteer Cavalry 1862-1865, Compiled by Q.M. Sgt. William O. Lee, Seventh Michigan Cavalry Association, Detroit, MI 1901-1902.)

7th MI Cavalry

Thomas Daly Enlisted in Co.B. 7th MI Cav. Age 28. Glen Arbor Draftee. Feb. 4, 1864 at Detroit. Joined regiment at Stevensburg, VA March 18, 1864. Service: Morton's Ford, Kilpatrick's Raid on Richmond, Wilderness, Todd's Tavern, Beaver Dam Station, Yellow Tavern, Meadow Bridge, Hanover Court House, Hanovertown, Haw's Shop, Old Church, Cold Harbor, Trevillian Station, Front Royal, Kearneysville, Shepherdstown, 3rd Winchester, Luray, Port Republic, Taken prisoner at Middletown, VA on Oct. 19, 1864. He was eventually discharged June 23, 1865.

Isaac Huff Co. G. 7th MI Cavalry Enlisted at the age of 16 in Grand Rapids on Feb. 13, 1865. Mustered March 13, 1865 Appomattox Campaign, Battle of Five Forks, Surrender of Lee and his Army, Danville Expedition, Washington D.C. Grand Review May 23, 1865. Moved to Leavenworth KS, Powder River Expeditions and operations against the Indians in District of the Plains and Dakota & Transferred to Co. A 1st Cavalry Dec. 7, 1865. Duty in District of Utah where they had to use part of their final pay just to get home.[175] Mustered out at Salt Lake City, Utah March 10, 1866. Member of the Traverse City McPherson G.A.R. Post 18. Buried in the woods off the County Line at Bland Cemetery, Empire Township. Oviatt Rd. (1849-1910). (Matthew Bland named the Cemetery after his son Thomas Bland who was killed at the age of 20 in an explosion at Manistee in 1868.[176] His grave is unmarked. Also called Osborne or Jacktown.)

Casten (Carl) Miller Enlisted in Co.A. 7th MI Cav. Age 27. Glen Arbor Draftee. Mustered at Detroit Jan. 18, 1864. Unit Service: Buckland's Mills, Stevensburg, Morton's Ford, Kilpatrick's Raid on Richmond, Wilderness, Todd's Tavern, Beaver Dam Station, Yellow Tavern, Meadow Bridge, Hanover Court House, Hanovertown, Haw's Shop, Old Church, Cold Harbor, Trevillian Station, Front Royal, Kearneysville, Shepherdstown, 3rd Winchester, Luray, Port Republic, Tom's Brook, Cedar Creek, Loudoun Co., Gordonsville, Liberty Mills, Sheridan's Raids. Discharged on Surgeon's certificate of disability at Jackson, MI March 3, 1865.

Surrounding Leelanau:

Jacob Jane Burger (Burgess – See Henry 23rd OH & Herman 86th NY) Co.F. 7th MI Cavalry Centerville. Misc. Leelanau County. Enlisted March 18, 1864. Served in Kansas, out June 24, 1865. (Listed age 24 from Westernburg, PA like the Egler/Egeler family in the pre-war 1860 Census of Leelanau Township with a young son.)

Thomas (John) Harmer Co.F. 7th MI Cav. Age 40. Enlisted March 2, 1864. Transferred to 1st MI Cavalry Co.B. Nov. 17, 1865 after the War. Out at Salt Lake City, Utah March 10, 1886. Misc. Leelanau County. (Listed from England with James Harmer as a Carpenter in the 1860 Census of Leelanau Twp.)

Albert S. Norris Co.G. 5th MI Cavalry & 7th Cavalry. Bingham Township. Wounded in action at Gettysburg July 3, 1863 & listed as <u>Died of disease Dec. 7 Buried in Richmond,VA</u>. & also listed in Neal. (Where Ira Chase of the 10th MI Cavalry lived. Also see Charles in 15th MI) Listed in Linwood/Neal Cem. Sept. 5, 1840 – Feb. 6, 1902.

Martin Novotny (Nowoting/Nowatmey) Co.F. 7th MI Cav. Centerville. Wounded in action at Five Forks April 1, 1865. Listed as Martin Novetone age 12 from Bohemia in the pre-war 1860 Census of Leelanau Township. (See Frank N. in 5th MI Cavalry?)

A POWERFUL REËNFORCEMENT TO THE RIVER FLEET

THE MONSTER IRONCLAD "CHOCTAW"

This huge vessel was one of the first attempts to develop the Eads type of gunboat. She, with the "Tus... 100-pounder in her forward casemate. She had a second casemate forward of the wheel where she cumbia," the "Indianola," the "Lafayette," and the "Chillicothe," was added to the Mississippi squadron... mounted two 24-pounder howitzers, and a third casemate abaft the wheel containing two 30-pounder after Admiral Porter took command, and all received their baptism in the operations of the Vicksburg cam... Parrott rifled guns. Under Lieutenant-Commander F. M. Ramsay, she was active in the flotilla co-paign, the "Indianola" being captured and destroyed by the Confederates. They were flat-bottomed ves... operating with General W. T. Sherman against Haynes' Bluff and Drumgould's Bluff, Mississippi, to dis-sels with side-wheels three-quarters of the way aft, each wheel acting independently of the other so as to give... tract attention from Grant's famous movement to the south of Vicksburg. She accompanied the expedition facility in turning in narrow channels, which rendered the broadside guns more effective. They were designed... that captured Yazoo City on May 21, 1863, and destroyed $2,000,000 worth of Confederate vessels, yards, as light-drafts, requiring from five to seven feet of water. The "Choctaw" and her sister-vessel, the... mills, and other property. On June 7, 1863, she, with the little "Lexington," drove off the Confederate at-"Lafayette," required nine feet. The "Choctaw" mounted three 9-inch smooth-bores and a rifled... tack on Milliken's Bend, Louisiana. In 1864, she accompanied Admiral Porter on the Red River expedition.

Insert from the Photographic History of the Civil War
(James Barnes, Patriot Publishing Co. Springfield, Mass. 1911 Pg. 206)

7th MI Infantry

John B. Chapman possible match under Co. I. 7th MI Inf. Age 35 Originally from Barry Co., Service: Aug. 22, 1861 Discharged for disability at Camp Benton, MD. Nov. 22, 1864. Almira Union / Green Briar Cemetery. (See Thomas Chapman, U.S. Navy.)

Lt. Henry Marvin LaCore Listed as age 24 (25). 2nd Lieutenant Co. C. 7th MI Inf.

Enlisted Sgt. at Jonesville Aug. 19, 1861 Mustered Aug. 24, 1861. Left state for Washington D.C. attached to Army of the Potomac. Duty at Harper's Ferry, Virginia Peninsula Campaign, Siege of Yorktown, Wounded in action at the Battle of Fair Oaks, VA May 31, 1862. Duty at Harrison's Landing, Malvern Hill, Bull Run, Battle of Antietam, Discharged to accept promotion Nov. 10, 1862. Commissioned 2nd Lt. Nov. 13, 1862. Wounded in the arm in action at the Battle of Fredericksburg Dec. 13, 1862. Despite healing from wounds and an incredible career, an absense without leave incident happened shortly after 21 year old Gilbert Lackor (LaCore), (who had enlisted at Traverse City in Co. A. 26th MI Inf.), died of disease at Alexandria, VA on March 5, 1863. (Henry may have taken the body back home?) A dismissal from the service followed April 27, 1863. That Fall we find him serving his country again in:

United States Navy Listed as Marvin (Marion) Henry La Core (Lacoy/Lacour) Enlisted Sept. 2, 1864 at Chicago age listed 29? (28). Transferred from Mississippi Squadron to U.S. Steamer "Portsmouth" "Choctaw" (see insert) Discharged Sept. 9, 1865. Born May 18. Grave reads: Died Sept. 26, 1916. Listed in 1894 Veterans Census of MI. (also as Marion Lacoy/Lacour). Buried in Maple Grove (Empire Union) Cemetery north of Empire, MI. Founding member of G.A.R. Post 168.

His mother had died young from a fall from a horse and the family was broken up. At the age of 16 he ran away and embarked on a whaling vessel at New Bedford, Mass. After which he returned to Michigan to farm until the outbreak of the war. He was active in Fourth of July celebrations in Empire and lectured annually at the Empire High School on whales and whale fishing. He also served as Justice of the Peace. His son, John of Elk Rapids, was a Dentist.[177] Another son, Otto, was a Doctor in Muskeagon.[178] He had established a farm which bordered on the corner of roads M-22 and M-72. (See also Randall LaCore under Empire listings and Lt. Chas. Lackor 8th N.Y. H.A. in Glen Arbor listings. LaCore's daughter was a school teacher at the Kriger/Voice Road school, who's picture is displayed in the Empire Museum with students in 1890. * LaCore's pond is off M-22 just about a mile Northeast of Empire.)[179] *Author's note: One of my favorite spots as a youth.

Leelanau & Grand Traverse Region:

Frank Hodgman 7th **MI Inf.** was a surveyor in the Grand Traverse area. He and his brother wrote letters almost every day of the Civil War. One of the many letters of interest was from January 4, 1863 at camp opposite Fredericksburg where he mentions many of the area Michigan units. "We are encamped about two miles from the Mine... here also the 1st, 5th, and 16th MI. The 2nd, 3rd, 8th, and 20th MI are in our brigade. I hear the 26th MI are in this region. The 24th (MI) are not far from here." He goes on to write, "Two regiments in our brigade (the 79th NY and 8th MI) had a happy New Years day..." They brought down the Quarter Master's shanty "so he rolled out a barrel and they had a merry time, officers and all." He also wrote about when he had left Knoxville and went by rail to Washington where he found the 26th MI Infantry and wrote that he had a good visit. He later stayed with his nephew in the 1st MI at Falmouth, VA. The Hodgman collection is held in reserve at Western Michigan University in Kalamazoo, MI. (Note: The State Archives in Lansing, MI also hold an excellent diary by Surgeon Cyrus Bacon, M.D. of the 7th MI).

8th MI Cavalry

Thomas (Tilden) Avery Co.D. 8th MI Cav. Centerville Township Draftee.
John Cambell? (Possibly? See Glen Arbor Area.)
Isaac Clark Sr. & Jr.? Co.E. 8th MI Cav., Misc. Leelanau County.

8th MI Infantry

John W. Eckman /Ackman Co.I. 8th MI Inf. Bingham Township 1894 Veteran's Census. Misc. Leelanau County.
Mattew H. Dougherty (Mather) Co.E. 8th MI Inf. 1845 – 1908 Downs Cemetery. Wexford, MI.
John Dube Co.F. 8th MI? Inf. or other State. Died Aug. 3, 1905. Age 71. St. Mary's Cemetery, Lake Leelanau. No veteran's marker.
(Unit contained 14 year old Drummer Boy Charlie H. Gardner who was killed from wounds received in action.)

9th MI Cavalry

See **James U. Auton** in 1st MI Light Artillery.

9th MI Infantry

See **S.S. Benjamin** in 18th MI Infantry.

10th MI Cavalry

See earlier chapter.

10th MI Infantry

Abraham A. Brooks Co. I. 10th MI Inf. (Empire Township 1890 Fed. Census Civil War Veteran). or under Abran./Abram. Brooks Co.D. Age 28. Was a farmer from Ohio.[180] Mustered Feb. 6, 1862. Unit History: Pittsburg Landing, Corinth, Nashville, Murfreesboro, Mission Ridge, Chickamauga Station, Rocky Faced Ridge, Pumpkin Vine Creek, Dallas, Kenesaw Mt., Jonesboro, Atlanta to the Sea, Bentonville, in Grand Review. Discharged Feb. 6, 1865. Born Dec. 16, 1832 - April 27, 1908. Buried in Green Briar Cemetery - Almira Union. (Also other marker for L.A. Brooks possible matches in 2nd MI Cav., 13th MI Inf., 17th MI Inf., or 47th OH Inf.)

11th MI Cavalry

11th MI Cavalry Service: Left Kalamazoo, MI Dec. 17, 1863 under Colonel Simeon B. Brown (formerly of the 6th MI Cavalry). Traveled through a blinding snowstorm for Lexington, KY, where they arrived on Dec. 22, and went into camp.

On Jan. 1, 1864 the Regiment had only green wood to burn, and with the thermometer at eight below zero. Encampment until April, 1864 when it was sent to Louisa, KY where it would begin a time of continuous active service. Skirmishes through May 25, 1864 and engaged and defeated Morgan at Mt. Sterling, KY June 13. Scouting and skirmishes in Eastern Kentucky until August 23, where it took part in defeating Wheeler's attempt to cross the Cumberland River near Pt. Burnside Aug. 30.

The Regiment returned to Mt. Sterling Sept. 17 and participated in the First Saltville Raid where, as rear guard of the Division at Sand Mt., punished the enemy so badly that they abandoned pursuit. At Lexington Oct. 19 and then more scouting and skirmishes from Mt. Sterling until Nov. 17, when it moved to Crab Orchard to take part in the Second Saltville Raid. In camp the night of the 21st was a high wind and the air full of flying and drifting snow. The men took to what cover they could find.

Other forces arrived with General Burgridge and Colonel Brown was assigned command of the First Brigade, composed of the 11th MI, 11th KY, 12th KY, and 12th OH. The snow and mud made the next day's marching tiresome and camp that night was at London, KY and later it began to rain while heading for Bean Station.

Leaving Cumberland Gap, Nov. 28, and after Rogersville and capturing Col. Dick Morgan at Kingsport, went by way of Bristol, TN and Abingdon, VA to Wytheville, VA, where a Captain held a revolver at the head of a southern telegraph operator to capture information about the enemy. The 11th MI Cavalry returned to Marion, VA, where General Gillem led an engagement against Confederate Commander Vaughn of thirty-six hours that resulted in defeat of the enemy to allow the command to enter Saltville Dec. 22, and aid in the destruction of the Salt Works.

The early morning of the 24th they arrived at Clinch River where they saw a large number of "colored" families crossing the ford. During the crossing a Rebel band on a hill continued to fire upon the 11th MI Cavalry. Seeing the Rebel officer standing in plain view one of the men of the 11th, who was a fine shot, fired a single shot and the Rebel officer did not appear again. The mountainous march continued with many of the horses in poor shape and the little rations they had were from the country. It was said that the only difference between what the men ate and the beasts was the men stuck their ear of corn in a campfire and parched it.

They traveled back to Lexington, KY, Jan. 3, 1865 and on the 19th moved to Mt. Sterling to scout until Feb. 23, where it traveled to Knoxville via Louisville and Nashville by rail and boat until arriving March 15.

Assigned as part of the Second Brigade, First Cavalry Division, Army of the Ohio, it joined other Grand Traverse men in the 10th MI Cavalry with Stoneman's Expedition taking part in numerous engagements into North Carolina, Virginia, South Carolina, and Georgia.

On May 11, 1865 near Washington, GA, they assisted in the round up of Confederate President Davis' escort. On June 4 they returned to Lenoir Station, TN and on the 24th were ordered to Ft. Pulaski where they were consolidated with the 8th MI Cavalry July 20. Later mustered out Sept. 22 and returned to Jackson, MI on the Sept. 28, 1865. Entire enrollment had been 1375 men with 23 killed or died of wounds, two died in Confederate prison, and 22 died of disease.[181]

The Forest Haven Soldiers of the 11th MI Cavalry included:

Alonzo Kenney Enlisted in Co. H. 11th MI Cav. Age 23. Mustered Dec. 10, 1863. Lexington & KY Expeditions, Cumberland River, Saltsville, Laurel Mt., Cedar Bluffs, Sandy Mt., Against Williams, Mt. Sterling, VA Campaigns, Taken Prisoner at Clinch River, VA Dec. 26, 1864. Discharged at Camp Chase, OH June 21, 1865. Buried in Kasson Cemetery. (Died Mar. 16, 1905. Aged 65 Yrs.). G.A.R. Post 168.

Alfred Levere (Lavere) Enlisted in Co. F. 11th MI Cav. Age 24. Mustered Nov. 3, 1863 at Mendon. Service in KY, Rockhouse Creek, Pound Gap, Pursuit of Morgan (with 10th Cav.), Cumberland River, Saltsville, Laurel Mt., Cedar Bluffs, Sandy Mt., Against Williams, Mt. Sterling, VA Campaigns, Stoneman's Raid with 10th MI Cav. (see history), Carolinas, Salisbury, Catawba River near Morgantown relieving 10th MI Cav., Pulaski, TN, Transfered to 8th MI Cav. Co. K. July 20, 1865. Mustered out at Nashville, TN Sept. 22, 1865. Also lived in Williamsburg. Buried in Solon Township Cemetery.

Oliver Neddo Enlisted in Co. F. 11th MI Cav. Age 27. Nov. 3, 1863, Crab Orchard, Cumberland Gap, Morristown, Stoneman's Raid, VA Campaigns, Saltsville, Lexington KY, Ferrier Feb. 1864, Carolinas Campain, Scouting from Pulaski TN, Blacksmith. Transferred to **8th MI Cav**. Co. K. July 20, 1865. Mustered out at Nashville, TN Sept. 22, 1865. Joined with Frank Neddo who lived in Leetsville, MI and attended 1911 reunion in Kalamazoo, MI. Centerville Township 1894 Veteran's Census. Died April 20, 1916. 80 Yrs, 11 Mos, 20 Days. Buried in Solon Township Cemetery. G.A.R. Post 168.

Edrick W. Peck Enlisted in Co. F. 11th MI Cavalry. Age 16. Mustered Oct. 23, 1863. Battle of Chattanooga & Race to the Summit on Missionary Ridge, Cumberland Gap, Morristown, Stoneman's Raid, VA Campaigns, Saltsville, Lexington KY, Died at Catletsburg Kentucky of wounds in action. Jan. 6 (or 7th), 1865. At the age of 18 Yrs. 9 Months. (This period was after the Saltville raid where the Federals lost ~ 150 men and the Confederates 600.) Buried in Green Briar Cemetery - Almira Union. (See Henry Peck 15th MI)

(**Cpl. Royal G. Teachout** of Co. G. 11th MI Cavalry was listed as the last surviving Civil War Veteran of Charlevoix Co. Member of the Lombard Post # 170. He had also served in the 1st OH Light Artillery Co. B. Buriel at Walloon Lake, Clarion Cemetery).

Soldiers filling canteens at Fredericksburg, Virginia
(Library of Congress No. 0291)

Summit of Lookout Mountain
(Library of Congress)

11th MI Infantry

Robert S. Day Enlisted in Co. E. 11th MI Inf. at Centerville. Age 21. Mustered Aug. 5, 1862. Joined regiment at Murfreesboro, TN Jan. 1863. Battle of Chickamauga, Rocky Faced Ridge, Resaca, Pumpkin Vine Creek, Dallas, Kenesaw, Chattanooga where the 11th MI Infantry joined in one of the most spectacular charges of the war. They were ordered to advance and take the rifle pits at the foot of Missionary Ridge. "The troops moved forward, drove the enemy out of the trenches, and, without further orders, started climbing the slope in hot pursuit. From the ridge a torrent of canister and bullets hit the Federals; halfway up the rugged height the Eleventh's commanding officer and two color bearers were killed."[182] The 11th considered themselves the first unit to win the race of the summit. Robert later transferred to re-organized Co. E. April 15, 1865. Knoxville, Nashville, TN. Discharged at Chattanooga, TN June 10, 1865. Pension for Thigh & Neck 1881. Empire area resident (Oviatt). Buried at Rose Hill (Ziegler) Cemetery. G.A.R. Post 168. (Served with James Day and Color Sgt. John M. Day of the 11th MI who carried the flag at Chickamauga and was killed in action at the Battle of Missionary Ridge. Possible relatives. Co. E. played a vital role at Chickamauga and lost their Captain C.W. Newberry Sept. 20, 1863.)[183]

Charles Franisco Enlisted in Co. A. 11th MI Inf. at Centerville. Age 24. Mustered Aug. 24, 1861. Guard Duties KY, Louisville & Nashville RR. Discharged for disability July 1, 1862. G.A.R. Post 168.

Surrounding Leelanau:
Lovell H. Gage 11th MI Elmwood Township 1894 Veteran's Census. (Oakwood Cemetery).
William H. Nelson 11th MI Inf. Assistant Surgeon. 1830-1884. Oakwood Cemetery. (See Theador Nelson 45th U.S. Vet. Inf.)
William Spafford 11th MI Killed at Stone River, TN in 1862. (see Morris D. Spafford 2nd OH – Kasson Twp.)

12th MI Infantry

Charles L. Barrett Enlisted Co.F. 12th MI Inf. Age 18. Glen Arbor Draftee. Mustered in Feb. 29, 1864 at Kalamazoo. Service: Ak - Little Rock, Clarendon, Gregory's Landing, DeVall's Bluff. Mustered out at Camden, AK Feb. 15, 1866.

13th MI Infantry

Marvin D. Beeman 13th MI Enlisted in Co.A. 13th MI Inf. Age 30. Mustered Feb. 29, 1864. Engineer duty Chattanooga & Lookout Mt. Constructing Hospitals, Pursuit of Gen. Forest into AL, Joined Sherman to Kingston, March to the Sea, Dalton, Savannah, Campaign of the Carolinas, Wash. D.C. Grand Review. Out at Louisville KY July 25, 1865. Also listed under Marion Bearman. Resident Kasson Township. Buried in Rose Hill (Ziegler) Cemetery.

Miles A. Densmore Enlisted in Co. D. 13th MI Inf. Age 18. Mustered Feb. 27, 1864. Engineer duty Chattanooga & Lookout Mt. Constructing Hospitals, Pursuit of Gen. Forest into AL, Joined Sherman to Kingston, March to the Sea, Dalton, Savannah, Campaign of the Carolinas, Sick in McDougal Hospital, NY in 1865. (Unit was in Grand Review). Lived with his sister in Mancelona during the last year of his life.[184] Died Dec. 21, 1893 & Buried in Maple City, Kasson Cemetery. (Listed as 1844 - 1893). G.A.R. Post 168.

Surrounding Leelanau:

C. Burton Co.H. 13th MI Inf. Lake Ann G.A.R. Post 423. Northern Benzie Co.
John Mc Connell Co.F. 13th MI Inf. Centerville Township.
George De Long Co.H. 13th MI Inf. Drafted from Centerville Township. East Leland Cemetery.

14th MI Infantry

Edmund W. Trumbull Listed as: Trumball = Saginaw County. Enlisted in Company E, 14th MI Infantry Dec. 14, 1861, at Owosso, for 3 years, age 44. 5'11" Dark Brown Hair and Grey Eyes. Widowed with 5 children that remained at Owosso with his parents and a sister. Mustered Jan. 7, 1862. Colonel Robert P. Sinclair & later Col. Henry Mizner, Lieut. Col.s Robert W. Davis, George W. Grummond; Majs., M.W. Quackenbush, Thomas C. Fitz Gibbon, and Caspar Ernst. Stationed at Camp Mizner, Ypsilanti, MI Feb. 13 in Captain Alpheus M. Beebe's Company E, the active service of the 14th during his enlisted time included: Left State for St. Louis, MO. April 17, thence moved to Pittsburg Landing, Tenn. joining General Grant's army. Attached to 2nd Brigade, 1st Division, Army of Mississippi. Advance on and siege of Corinth, Miss., April 29-May 30, 1862. Actions at Farmington, Miss., May 3 & 9 engaged with the enemy. Reconnaissance toward Corinth May 8 and again engaged the enemy. Pursuit to Boonville May 31-June 12. Reconnaissance toward Baldwyn June 3. Camp Big Springs. Gen. Buell's operations along Memphis & Charleston Railroad in Northern Alabama and Middle Tennessee June 13-July 18, 1862 against Confederate General Bragg. Edmund had contacted Typhoid Fever in Corinth, MS from which he never fully recovered and after July of 1862 he spent much of his time at the Hospital in Evansville, IN. His unit went on to Florence & Tuscumbia, AL till Sept. 1. Lavergne, TN, March to Nashville, Tenn. Sept 1-6 and Siege duty there. Then assigned to the First Brigade, Second Division of the Fourteenth Corp. Edmund was Discharged at Evansville, Ind. Sept. 14, 1862. Edmund was born in Allegany County NY to Rufus & Hulda Trumbull in 1818. He had a Burdickville Postal address, was a Cooper (Barrel/Wheel maker)[145] and Died Feb. 22, 1885. Buried in the Glen Arbor, MI Township Cemetery, in the woods off M22 - Forest Haven Road. Sleeping Bear Dunes National Lakeshore.

Surrounding Leelanau:

Ernest Crane(Crain) Co. F. 14th MI Inf. Elmwood Township 1894 Veteran's Census. (Born Nov. 8, 1846 in Ohio, Died March 8, 1924. Buried in Oakwood Cemetery).
Myron Harcourt (Harcomb) 14th MI (Kalkaska)., Misc. Leelanau County.
Daniel (David) Mc Carty Co.D. 14th MI Inf., Centerville Draftee. June 1, 1810 – April 14, 1876. Buried in St. Mary's – Lake Leelanau Cemetery.
Lewis Stevenson 14th MI Inf. Grand Traverse area.

(Several letters written by Co.E. Sgt. Nathan Monroe during this period mentioned the battle of Pittsburg Landing, the prisoners taken, and the news on the war on other fronts. A July letter describes the camp near Franklin, TN, the beautiful countryside, and the food to be found in the area. Other letters written by Nathan Monroe and Sgt. William B. Monroe of Co.E. 14th MI were also once held in the Bentley Historical Library Collections at The University of Michigan.)

15th MI Infantry
See earlier chapter.

16th MI Infantry

Owen M. Higgins Co. D. 1st Co. Sharpshooters & Attached to 16th MI Inf. Glen Arbor Draftee. Age 21. Macomb Co. to Detroit. Joined regiment at Hall's Hill, VA. Feb. 14, 1862. Service: Yorktown, Hanover Ct. Hs., Mechanicsville, Gain's Mills, White Oak Swamp, Turkey Bend, Malvern Hill, Harrison's Landing, Ely's Ford, 2nd Bull Run, Antietam. Discharged at Antietam, MD. Oct. 25, 1862. Rejoined at Pontiac, MI. 2nd Reg. Vet. Res. Corps. Co. B. Age 23. Dec. 5, 1864. Discharged at Jackson, MI Nov. 14, 1865.

Samuel L. Holsted (Halstead/Hilsted) Enlisted in Co. C. 16th MI Inf. Age 25. Mustered Aug. 24, 1861. (Stockton's Independent Regiment), Butterfield's Brigade, Washington D.C., Manassas, Virginia Peninsula, Yorktown, Seven Days before Richmond, Mechanicsville, Gain's Mill, Savage Station, Malvern Hill, Harrison's Landing, Battle of Bull Run, Wounded in Action 1862. (Unit eventually at Gettysburg). Discharged at Petersburg, VA Sept. 7, 1864. Centerville Township 1894 Veteran's Census. Pensioned for Gunshot wounds to left hand and leg. Buried in Solon Township Cemetery on June 8, 1915. G.A.R. Post 168 and also later with McPherson G.A.R. Post 18 of Traverse City. Margaret Halsted listed in Woman's Relief Corps. Died in 1915. Solon Twp.

Surrounding Leelanau:

Samuel (Sanford) Gutherie 16th MI Inf. Centerville. (Wounded in action at the Battle of the Wilderness & died at Fredricksburg). Listed as a 32 year old Carpenter from New York in the pre-war 1860 Census of Leelanau Township (See Nathan Gutherie 5th MI Inf.)

John Haas Co. D. 16th MI Inf. Age 18. Enlisted Aug. 24, 1861 at White Pigeon. Wounded and taken prisoner at Gains Mills VA, June 27, 1862. Died in the hands of the enemy. (See George Haas 5th MI)

Capt. Patrick McLaughlin Co.E. 16th MI Inf. Age 24. Leelanau/Centerville Draftee. Joined in Detroit. 1st Lt. Aug. 1861. Service: Washington D.C., Manassas, VA Peninsula, Big Bethel, Yorktown, Battle of Hanover Ct. Hs., Seven Days Battles - Mechanicsville, Gain's Mill, Savage Station, Malvern Hill, Harrison's Landing, Battle of Bull Run, Antietam, Sharpsburg, Capt. of Co. C. Nov. 3, 1862. Battle of Fredericksburg, Mud March, Falmouth, Resigned April 16, 1863. Re-entered as **1st Lt. And Quartermaster Commissioned** Nov. 6, 1863. of **1st Colored Infantry.**[186] Joined 9th Army Corps. at Annapolis, MD., Hilton Head & St. Helena, SC. Designated **change to 102nd U.S. Colored Troops** May 23, 1864. Attack on Baldwin FL, Raid on FL Central RR, Beaufort SC, Skirmish at Cuckwood Creek where Killed in action at Salkehatchie, SC Feb. 8, 1865.

17th MI Inf.

Cornelius Fogarty 17th MI Inf. & 1st MI Cav. Suttonsbay.

George Hawkins Co. H. 17th MI Inf. Suttonsbay. (Wounded in action at Knoxville, TN Dec. 1863, arm amputated. See Thomas in 2nd MI SS & William in 2nd Cav.)

John F. Miller Co. B. 17th MI Inf. Sept. 3, 1822 – Sept. 10, 1883. St. Mary's (Lake Leelanau) Cemetery.

18th MI / 9th Infantry

Sidney C. (Smith) Benjamin / Benjamin C. Smith (or ViseVersa) Enlisted in Co. C. 18th MI Inf. Age 37. 9th/18th MI Inf. Mustered April 10, 1865 Joined Regiment at Huntsville, AL May 3, 1865. Duty & Transferred to Co.D. 9th Inf. June 25, 1865. Mustered out at Nashville, TN Sept. 15,1865. (Glen Arbor Township 1890 Fed. Census Civil War Veteran & 1894 Veterans Census of MI.) Vol. 18 pg. 88. Listed St. Michael's Cemetery, Suttons Bay Twp. Cemetery. Grave reads S.S. Benjamin. (See John Benjamin, 10th MI Cavalry or any of the Smith families in Glen Arbor.)
Cpl. Benjamin Campbell 18th MI Infantry is buried in Oakwood Cemetery?

123

19th MI Infantry

Justin B. (Doane) Donne Enlisted in Co. K. 19th MI Inf. Age 20. Mustered Sept. 5, 1862. Danville & Louisville KY, Nashville TN, Franklin, Spring Hill where many were captured & later exchanged, Murfreesboro, Lookout Valley, Rocky Faced Ridge, Wounded in action at Battle of Resaca, GA May 15, 1864. Pumpkin Vine Creek, Dallas, Kenesaw Mt., Chattahoochie River, Siege of Atlanta, Campaign of the Carolinas, Battle of Bentonville, Surrender of Johnston and his army, Grand Review May 24, Mustered out at Washington D.C. June 10, 1865. G.A.R. Post 168.

20th MI Infantry

John R. Greenman Enlisted in Co. D. 20th MI Inf. Ann Arbor. Age 24. Mustered Aug. 18, 1862. Wash. D.C., Sharpsburg, Battle of Fredericksburg, Mud March, Falmouth, KY, Siege of Vicksburg, Knoxville TN, Blue Springs, Ft. Saunders, Strawberry Plains, Battles of the Wilderness, Spotsylvania, Salient, Totopotomoy, Cold Harbor, Petersburg, Mine Explosion, Weldon RR, Hatcher's Run, Appomattox Campaign, first federal troops (with 2nd MI Inf. and 1st MI Sharpshooters) to enter Petersburg at end of the Civil War. They were in the Grand Review. Mustered out at DeLaney House, D.C. May 30, 1865. Kasson resident. Burdickville Postal Address. Died Feb. 26, 1906. Buried in Rose Hill Cemetery. G.A.R. Post 168. (Others in the 20th: Captain **Alexander Bush** married Jennie McCormick & lived in East Jordan while **William & Samuel Miller** lived in Cadillac. A 20th MI Inf. reunion photograph is held in reserve at the Burton Historical Collection of the Detroit Public Library.)

21st MI Infantry

Sgt. Henry Dohm Sr. Co. E. 21st MI Inf. Mustered Sept. 3, 1862. Age 24. Battles of Perryville, Murfreesboro, Stone River, Chickamauga, Mission Ridge, became a Sgt. May 7, 1864. formed into Engineer Corps. March to the Sea, Savannah, Battle of Bentonville, Surrender of Gen. Johnston, Richmond, Washington Grand Review. Out at Washington, D.C. June 8, 1865. Lived at Mapleton, MI & in Solon, Leelanau Twp. Traverse City McPherson G.A.R. Post 18. Listed buried in Ogdensburg Cemetery, Peninsula Twp. (May 7, 1838 – Dec. 24, 1920.)

Surrounding Leelanau:

William H. Nelson Hopital Steward Co. A. 21st MI Inf. Leelanau Township. (Joined at Corunna with John Yaner.) Joined regiment at Chattanooga. Feb. 1864 – April 1865. Commissioned Assist. Surgeon with re-organized 11th MI Infantry Aug. 1865. Out at Nashville, TN Sept. 16, 1865. Oakwood Cemetery. Several more area men were said to have also joined the 21st including possibly: Francis Barden, Samuel Mapes, Carisle Miller, Daniel E. Padden (later of T.C.), George W.B. Oviatt, David Peckens (Honor), John E. Roys, Melvin J. Scott (Oakwood Cem.), & William W. Whipple (later of Kalkaska). A photograph of this unit at Murfreesboro is held by the National Archives in Washington.

22nd MI Infantry

Leander (Leonard) Clark[187] /Clerk Enlisted in Co.H. 22nd MI Inf. Age 23. Glen Arbor Draftee. Mustered from Green Oak Aug. 22, 1862. Service: Ohio River Valley, action at Covington KY, "Battle of Cabbage Hill," Townsend's Bridge, Duty at Lexington KY, where exposed to the cold and storms at Camp Ella Bishop brought suffering and death upon the regiment. Scores of noble men lie in the cemetery at Lexington, who died needlessly in consequence of exposure. Regiment had further duty at Danville, Hickman Bridge, and Nashville. Clark Died of Disease at Lexington, KY April 14, 1863.

Band of the 19ᵗʰ Michigan Infantry (Michigan Archives)

(Courtesy Leelanau Historical Museum)

fifteen hundred in one drove that was sent here to chattanooga after the battle was fought by sherman and Hood between chattanooga and Atlanta I dont recollect the name of the place but sherman sent into chattanooga Horses and waggons that he captured from the rebels in droves and they looked as though they were starved and the prisoners looked hard for they had no coats nor shoes on not more than half of them and they all were raggad and dirty and they all looked more like Robbers than they did like soldiers and when they come in all they had in their Haversacks was sugar cane and Hickory nuts and they all appeard to be well satisfied that they were taken prisoners I will close Jerome squires and George Jackson and all the dundee boys come to chattanooga when I did but they only staid there two nights and they started for their rigiments and I have not heard from them since so no more write as soon as you get this for I would like to hear from you all my respects to yourself and wife and all the folks Direct to Chattanooga Tenn 23d Michigan Infantry
Wm Houghton

Surrounding Leelanau:

R.C. Shreeves Co. B. 22nd MI Inf. Lake Ann G.A.R. Post 423. Northern Benzie Co. (The 22nd MI featured 11 year old drummer Johnny L. Clem of Co. C. who became a General in later life.)

23rd MI Infantry

William Houghton Enlisted in Co. G. 23rd MI Inf. Age 44. Jackson. Mustered in Sept. 7, 1864. Pursuit of Hood into AL, Johnsonville, Battle of Nashville & Campaign, Battle of Franklin, Wash. D.C., Fort Fisher, Wilmington, Campaign of the Carolinas, Goldsboro, Raliegh, Bennett's House, Surrender of Johnston and his army, Greensboro, Out at Salisbury, NC July 28, 1865. A Civil War letter is held in reserve at the Bentley Historical Library of the University of Michigan. Written from Savannah Valley (NE of Chattanooga) November 22, 1864. He had been sent to herd thirty-three hundred heads of cattle that had been destined for Sherman's army at Atlanta, but further orders were needed to move the cattle. His special duty was to issue rations for the thirty-six guards. He comments on the destruction of property around Chattanooga, and the wretched condition of the prisoners and horses after the battle. He also mentions Benjamin Vandevener. (See page from his letter.)[188] He died April/May 28, 1886 and is buried in Rose Hill (Ziegler) Cemetery. G.A.R. Post 168.

Abraham Frank Packard Co. D. 23rd MI Inf. Age 22. Kasson Township. Enlisted Sept. 2, 1864. Atlanta Campaigns, Jonesboro, Pursuit of Hood into AL, Johnsonville, Battle of Nashville & Campaign, Battle of Franklin, Wash. D.C., Fort Fisher, Wilmington, Campaign of the Carolinas, Goldsboro, Raliegh, Bennett's House, Surrender of Johnston and his army, Greensboro, Out at Salisbury, NC June 28, 1865. Died April 5, 1892. (Abram Packard) Buried in Round Top (Friends) Cemetery. Kasson, MI.

Surrounding Leelanau:

Andrew S. Clark Co. C. 23rd MI Inf. Buried in Linwood/Neal Cemetery. Long Lake Twp. G.A.R. Post 423 named in his honor.

26th MI Infantry

See earlier chapter.

28th MI Infantry

Frederic M. Benham Co. B. 28th MI Inf. Age 20. Enlisted at Walton on March 27, 1865. Appomattox Campaign. Discharged Sept. 25, 1865. Lived on South Manitou Island.

Peter Wilson Glen Arbor Draftee, enlisted in the 28th MI Infantry but was listed deserted the next day? (May have been Abba Wilson in disguise? See Andrew Wilson 1st Ill. in Glen Arbor Twp.)

Photographer's wagon and tent at Cold Harbor, Virginia
(Library of Congress)

President Abraham Lincoln's Funeral Procession
(Courtesy Chicago Historical Society)

Forest Haven Soldiers: The Civil War Veterans of Sleeping Bear & Surrounding Leelanau

Glen Arbor / Empire / Northern Platte Twp. / Burdickville Area Veterans Who Had Served in Other States [189]

Erastus Ames Co./ Battery E. 1st PA Light Artillery (43rd Vol.) Mustered Sept. 4, 1861 Duty at Camp Barry & the defences of Washington D.C. Discharged on Surgeon's Certificate Jan. 15, 1862. Buried in the woods at Bland Cemetery, Empire Township off the County line. (June 6, 1840-May 7, 1926).

Bert Bancroft Otter Creek (Aral) area. Went as a photographer in the Civil War. [190]

Samuel Berry Co. E. 1st Calif. Cav. Engaged with Indians at Sand Creek, CO. Services in CO & KS. Empire Township. Died Jan. 23, 1907 Age 66y, 5m, 21d. Buried in Rose Hill Cemetery. G.A.R. Post 168.

Sgt. John Oliver Boizard Sgt. Major Ill. U.S. Mustering and Disbursing Office in Springfield, Ill. during the War. Before the Civil War, he served in the U.S. Army Subsistence Department at Ft. McRae FL, Ft. Leavenworth KS, Ft. Keary NB, & Ft. Ridgely MN. In the "Boizard Letters" he wrote of his visit to the tomb of President Lincoln in Springfield. "Last Sunday I went to Oak Ridge about 12 miles from town, and I saw the Vault of Mr. Lincoln. He lies there in a Metallic Coffin, and there is also a square Walnut Box outside, also the Son. The doors are stone and iron gratting inside. 4 persons are allowed at a time to look at the Boxes through the Iron Grating. The place is the most Beautiful I see. There are squad of Soldiers stationed there. The Sentinel walks in front of the Vault. They are about commencing the monument, and then they will remove him only a few rods where they now lie." [191] He also sent home a picture of General Grant. [192] (Listed age 48 from PA, wife Elenor M. from VA and 8yr.old daughter Marretta in the pre-war 1860 Census of Glen Arbor Township.) Listed as Corporal Boijard, Glen Arbor Township 1890 Fed. Census Civil War Veteran.

Ruel K. Boynton Co. M 15th New York Cav. & Co. M. 2nd NY. [193] Enrolled Dec. 14, 1863. Unit History: Wash. D.C., action at Hillsboro, WV, Petersburg, Franklin, Woodstock, Waynesboro, Lynchburg, Bunker Hill, Snicker's Ferry, Winchester, Cumberland, Appomattox Campaign, Five Forks, Surrender of Lee, Grand Review, KY, Consolidated with 6th into 2nd on June 17, 1865. Out at Louisville KY Aug. 9, 1865. (Glen Arbor Township 1890 Fed. Census Civil War Veteran & Empire Township 1894 Veterans Census of MI.) G.A.R. Post 168. Also as Reed B. (Seth Boynton Co.A. 15th MI Age 18. Died of disease, buried in National Cemetery, Jefferson Barracks, MO Sec.53 Grave # 940.) [194]

Ezra Bracdon 64th NY Inf. Co. A. [195] G.A.R. Post 168 Marker. Died Feb. 4, 1877 47 Years Old. (also listed under Ezra Bragdon /Brajdon/Bracoon/Braydon Co. A & Co. C 64 NY Inf.). Enrolled Aug. 19, 1863. Unit History: Minr Run Campaign, Rapidan, Battles of the Wilderness, Spotsylvania, Salient "Bloody Angle," Totopotomoy, Cold Harbor, Petersburg, Strawberry Plains, Hatcher's Run, Appomattox Campaign, Sutherland Station, Surrender of Lee, in Grand Review. (Glen Arbor Township 1890 Fed. Census Civil War Veteran as 64th New York. Transferred to Co. A Sept. 22, 1864. Mustered out July 14, 1865 near Washington). Farm was east of Miller Hill. Buried in Kelderhouse / Port Oneida Cemetery.

Orlo W. Burch Bat. M. 1 NY L.A. Unit History: Defences of Washington D.C., Woodstock, Shenandoah Valley Campaigns, Winchester, Battle of Cedar Mt., Battles of Bull Run, Antietam, Chancellorsville, Gettysburg, Atlanta Campaigns, Battle of Resaca, Pumpkin Vine Creek, Kenesaw & Lost Mt., March to the Sea, Carolinas, Bentonville, in Grand Review Washington D.C. Buried in Platte Township Cemetery. East of Otter Creek - Benzie County.

Henry C. Burgess Co. D. 23rd Ohio Inf. on Grave & 33rd Ohio in some records. 23rd Unit History: Organized in June, 1861 under Colonel William S. Rosecrans and E.P. Scammon. The members of this Regiment gained distinction in military and civilian life. W.S. Rosecrans became a noted General. Col. Rutherford B. Hayes and William S. McKinley went on to become U.S. Presidents. Stanley Mattews became a U.S. Senator. The Regiment served in West Virginia, fought at Blue Stone, South Mt., and Antietam under McClellan where they lost over 200 men in these engagements. In March of 1863 moved to Kanawha Valley joining Gen. Crook's VA & TN Railroad raids. Joined Hunter's march on Lynchburg, returned to Charleston, then Martinsburg. Sheridan's Shenandoah Valley Campaigns. Lost 150 men at the Battle of Winchester, fought at Opequan, Battle of Cedar Creek, Duty at Kernstown & returned to Martinsburg/Cumberland areas. Mustered out July 26, 1865. 33rd Ohio Co. D Age 20 Entered Feb. 27, 1864 Wounded July 27, 1864 in the Battle of Winchester, VA. Transferred to Veterans Reserve Corp Nov. 18,1864. Said to have been working as an Empire school janitor around 1926.[196] Buried in Maple Grove (Empire Union) Cemetery. Also listed as Henry H. (See Herman Burgess 86ᵗʰ NY Cleveland Township.)

John & Neil Campbell Glen Arbor Draftees. 1ˢᵗ Eng. Co. K. Artif. New York. Listed twins age 26 in the pre-war 1860 Census of Glen Arbor Township. Younger Brother George served briefly with the 10ᵗʰ MI Cavalry. (At one time John was identified with the 8ᵗʰ MI Cav. And Neil with the 13ᵗʰ MI Bat. under the name Newton by Historian Roy Steffens. However, the listed ages do not match up with the Census reports). Their family had previous ties to New York and Illinois and we find a match for Neil in the 1ˢᵗ NY Eng. Co. K. Artif. and several possible matches for John including Cpl. of 1ˢᵗ NY Lt. Art. Bt. L. [197]

Samuel D.H. (Hempton/Hampton) Daniels Co. F. 147th Indiana Inf. (also listed as Co. F. 19th Indiana Inf) 147th: Harper's Ferry WV, Shenandoah Valley, Charleston, Winchester, Stevens Depot, Jordon Sp., Summit Pt., Baltimore, 19th IN : Perryville, KY, TN, Battle of · Chickamauga, Orchard Knob, Rocky Faced Ridge, Pumpkin Vine Creek, Dallas, Kenesaw & Lost Mt., Jonesboro, Atlanta March to the Sea, Carolinas, Battle of Bentonville, Glen Arbor Township 1890 Fed. Census Civil War Veteran & 1894 Veterans Census of MI. Owned land near Good Harbor Creek, NE of Traverse Lake, is listed as being buried in an unidentified marker in the abandoned Glen Arbor Township Cemetery in the woods near M22-Forest Haven Road. Member G.A.R. Post 168. (See Wade B. (or H.) Daniels listed in 1ˢᵗ MI SS or in L.A.? - see G.A.R. Post 168.)

Henry Decker Listed age 35 from New York in the pre-war 1860 Census of Glen Arbor Township with 6 children, the oldest three born in Wisconsin. Listed in Glen Arbor Township 1894 Veteran's Census of Michigan. (Harley Decker was listed as a Fifer in the 26ᵗʰ MI Inf.)

Lewis Deman Co. K. (or H.) 9th N.Y. Inf. (or Indep. Bat. listing for Lewis Demott 9th H.A. Co.A & H). Listed as resident in Glen Arbor Township. 9th Inf. History: "Hawkins Zouaves" Big Bethel, James River, Ft.Clark, Roanoke Is., Camden, S.Mills, Battle of Antietam, Fredericksburg, Siege of Suffolk, Assigned to 3rd Inf., Morris Is., Ft. Wagoner, Ft.Sumpter, Folly Is., James R., Cold Harbor, Mine Explosion, Petersburg, Battle of Fair Oaks, Ft. Fisher, Duty in the Dept. of NC. G.A.R. Post 168.

**1st New York Battery
Richmond, VA
(Library of Congress)
See Edwin Brooks, Orlo Burch,
Thomas Lee, Lewis Steele,
Albert Powers, William Sykes,
Samuel McClelland & many others**

**9th New York Infantry
Manassas, VA
(Library of Congress)
- See Lewis Deman**

George V. Donner Co. B. 94th NY Inf. "Belle Jefferson Rifles" Unit History: Wash. D.C., Manassas, Battle of Cedar Mt., Groveton, Bull Run, Chantilly, South Mt., Antietam, Fredericksburg, Chancellorsville, Gettysburg, Rappahannock, Mine Run, Totopotomy, Cold Harbor, Petersburg, Weldon RR, Hatcher's Run, Five Forks, Surrender of Lee and his Army, Grand Review Wash. D.C. Lived in Glen Arbor Twp. Born in Canada & Died Jan. 15, 1917. (Glen Arbor Township 1890 Fed. Census Civil War Veteran & 1894 Veterans Census of MI.) Also listed in Kasson Township. G.A.R. Post 168. (See brother Lewis in Kasson Twp. listings.)

Sgt. John Dorrington Bvt. Cpt. (Darington) Co. C. 8th PA Res. Corp[198]. Entered April 17, 1861 at beginning of War. Washington D.C., Tennallytown MD, Camp Pierpont, Great Falls, Manassas, Falmouth, Fredericksburg, Seven Days before Richmond, Mechanicsville, Gaines Mill, Charles City Cross Roads, Glendale, Malvern Hill, Harrison's Landing, Gainesville, Groveton, Bull Run, Battle of South Mt., Battle of Antietam, Wounded in action and discharged on Surgeon's Cert. Oct. 7, 1862. Had store in the Burdickville area and then moved to a farm. He is written about in "Footprints Where Once They Walked," by Nan Helm. "Capt. Dorrington always wore the blue uniform of the soldier, with its pretty brass buttons. It was the day of 'the beards' and he wore a beard which was of a golden coppery color. He was (tall and) handsome and (had a) distinguished appearance." [199] G.A.R. Post 168.

David Dunn Co. B. 13th NY Art. & Co. I. 6th NY H.A.[200]& 5th. (June 27, 1865). Defenses of Washington D.C., Shenandoah Valley, Rappahannock, Groveton, Bull Run, Chancellorsville, Knoxville TN, Battle of Resaca, Pumpkin Vine Creek/Dallas, Kenesaw & Lost Mt., Atlanta Campaign, Petersburg VA. Mustered out Aug. 24, 1865 at Washington, D.C. G.A.R. Post 168. (Men often stayed at the Dunn farm on their way to the Civil War.[201]See 10th MI Cavalry Cpt. William H. Dunn and John Dunn of Co. I. Also a James Dunn served in the Chicago Mercantile Bat. Ill. Lt. Artil.).

Moses G. Getchell 1st Ill. L.A. Bat. I. Mustered Feb. 1862. Listed Deserted. Unit History: Battle of Shiloh, Corinth, Grant's Central MS Campaign, "Tallahatchie March", Wall Hill, Siege of Vicksburg, Jackson , Chattanooga TN, Mission Ridge, Knoxville, Scottsboro AL, Battle of Nashville & Related Campaigns. Resident of Glen Arbor. (See George Getchell of Glen Arbor in the 10th MI Cav.)

Edwin Gould (Edward G.) Co. A. 8th Vermont. Inf. Unit History: Ship Isl, New Orleans, W/ Steamer "Cotton," Port Hudson, LA, Franklin, Tunica Bend, Snicker's Gap, Shenandoah Valley, Battle of Opequan, Winchester, Cedar Creek, Summit Point, Wash. D.C. Grand Review. Buried in Maple Grove (Empire Union) Cemetery. Listed in Empire Township 1894 Veterans Census of MI. G.A.R. Post 168. (See Augustus Gould 26th MI Inf.)

Hiram Hallett Listed in Empire Township 1894 Veteran's Census of Michigan. (Could be Hebron Hallet or Hiram Hallock listed in the 10th MI Cavalry?)

Daniel Hamilton Co. A 1st Battalion Ohio Sharpshooters Unit History: Attached to Birge's Western Sharpshooters, 14th Missouri Inf., later to 66th Illinois Inf. as Co.G. - Battle of Mt. Zion, St. Louis, Ft. Donelson, Battle of Shiloh, Corinth, Booneville, Battle of Iuka, White House, Hatchie River, Trans. to Ill. 66th Nov. 2, 1862. - Camp Davies, Tuscumbia Bridge, Danville, Pulaski, Battle of Resaca, Pumkin Vine Creek, Dallas, Kenesaw Mt., Decatur, Atlanta, Jonesboro, Carolinas, Bentonville, Grand Review. Glen Arbor Township 1890 Fed. Census Civil War Veteran.

BROTHER RALPH
CANADA

Dear Brother

It is with great pleasure that I at this time pick up my pen and as you have great interest in Account I will [tell] about the war as ordered by these [   ] guns. Our Brigade formation was already experienced. When I wrote you before I spoke of Columbus being our next Battlefield but turned out to be a [   ] preparations were made for our Positions. When we were bound to take it that fort and the Enemy seeing that we were bound to take it that presented a Play of [   ] think the object in that was [   ] that them 8 hours to leave it not they would storm the fort. When Popp was up the [   ] had already got in our Boys went into [   ] and Gen Popp is come immediately to his assistance that he was about to make an attack on New Madrid and had not force enough to accomplish it so as we could not get [go] there by water. But Popp and [   ] to the quantity and [   ] were the Artillery and men [   ] travelled night and day untill we reached Gen. Popp. We immediately commenced his command making them upward of 40,000 men consisting up in the war. I had often heard of war and fighting but never did it a great [   ] night as when these men were drawn up in a line of Battle as [   ] and would evacuate [   ] came to a halt. Then we rested all day and night expecting in the morning to go into business. The enemy appeared to be getting alarmed and by all appearances they were going to make a transparent stand New Madrid being on the Mississippi, is guarded a very strong position [   ] for the Bon [   ] run. The Boys could a Gun Boats came down from Cairo (Illinois) but on account of [   ] No it kept our Boats from coming down. We rested and waited for these to make an advance on the Enemy during the night and in the morning the work would begin. According to orders we advanced and made our night [   ] up entrenchments also planting [5] seige guns of [64] lb each. Got everything complete at daybreak in the morning when the Boys could to sight they opened on the Rebel. At the first we returned with throwing shell and ball in every direction. Nothing could be seen of Madrid but smoke and the roaring of Artillery. They had some 30

guns to our 4 but our Boys planted well. You don't know anything about war until you have a hand in it. If we were to be well secured by about [   ] is all around us. You have to [   ] of Balls faithing all around us. We could hear the Rebels say when their ball came too close to [   ]. The Yankees [   ] well. Just taking the Boys when coming into close action, there is no flinch to them. The fire was kept up all day, never ceased until dark. Our Boys stood the [   ] well but although at a great sacrifice of [   ]. The Fort could be taken, the Enemy must not hold it a day longer. Our Boys [   ] kept at it all night. By 6 oclock the Enemy got frightened and commenced to evacuate. By the break of day we thought they were reinforcing but morning broke and the Enemy had left all their Boyages, cooking utensils outside or in the Fort. They left in a mighty hurry leaving their artillery all in the Fort and all their Boyages, cooking utensils [   ] and that gave the [   ] full possession of the Fort I tell you this was about to a close. Secesh is about played out. They went into this thing that we could not raise the men that we have done but all I [   ] we are going down South now. Before 6 months we will be in New Orleans. They thought when they went into this thing that we could not raise the men that we have done but all I [   ] we are going down South now. Before 6 months we will be in New Orleans. They thought when they went into this thing that we could not raise the men that we have done but the Government. The United States is going to be more permanent than it ever has been before. When once the Rebellion is suppressed nation ever seeks to interfere they have me against them. We will be proud when this difficulty is settled will come and see you all one of my Brothers Slaters I tell them I can't be with them my love is for them. You will see by this letter that we are progressing in order now. The day we had the Battle I never saw a prettier day in [   ] now. The day we had the Battle I never saw a prettier day in [   ] now. The day we had the Battle I never saw a prettier day in me on account of being a Soldier but Soldiers life has not made me any different from what I was if a person has seen me he will see me on account of being a Soldier but Soldiers life has not made a very [   ]. But I will close this short letter, remember your Brother John has the same interest for you all as we use to have in old times. Let me [   ] I well wish I had them to come as a cash supply the inhabitants here are perfect cannibals they don't know anything a dirty ragged and know nothing set. Must close. My fear is bad and 1000 miles from home.

Remain yours as ever

Sincere Brother
John Hein
15th Regt Ills Vol

Address Cairo Ills.

(FORT)

Dunn's farm on east shore of Glen Lake

Dunn's Farm
(Courtesy Empire Area Heritage Group)

From John Helm's Civil War Collection
(Courtesy Nan Helm)

6th New York Artillery
Brandy Station, VA
(Library of Congress)
- See David Dunn

Sgt. Nathaniel King
2nd Wisconsin Cavalry
(Courtesy Leelanau Historical Museum)

John Helm Co. F. 16th Ill. Inf.[202] from Missouri, (was born in Canada in 1837),[203] Entered service on May 24, 1861. Unit: New Madrid, Ft. Pillow, Corinth, Columbia, Repulse of Forest's Attack, Nashville, AL, Atlanta Campaign, Rocky Faced Ridge, Pumpkin Vine Creek, Dallas, Kenesaw & Lost Mt., Battle of Jonesboro, March to the Sea, Mustered out June 19, 1864 and then served as Chief Clerk in the Quartermaster Department of General Stanley's corps. for another year. (Carolinas, Battle of Bentonville, in Grand Review?). In the fall of 1865 he started a general merchandise business in Glen Haven and later was a resident in Empire Township 1894 Veteran's Census/ Supervisor & Postmaster of <u>Burdickville</u>. G.A.R. Post 168. Died Jan. 26, 1910. Buried in Chicago. Correspondence letters are held in the archives of the Leelanau Historical Museum. (See examples.)

Sgt. George H. Hill Co. E. 11th Kansas Inf.[204] 1st Sgt. Originally from Maryland, enlisted Aug. 20, 1862. Age 47 from Topeka, Shawanee County. Unit: Old Ft. Wayne Maysville, Cane Hill, Boston Mts., Reed's Mt., Battle of Prairie Grove, Van Buren, Springfield & duties in MO, Regiment designated to 11th KS Cavalry - Operations against Quantrell's Raiders into Kansas, against Indians in Nebraska, against Price in MO & KS, Lexington, Little & Big Blue, Cold Water, Mine Cr., Osage R., Ft. Larned, against Indians, Dakota Ter., Ft. Halleck, Colorado. Glen Arbor Township 1890 Fed. Census Civil War Veteran. G.A.R. Post 168

George W. Kerr Recorded as a Civil War Veteran.[205] March 3, 1834 – April 20, 1908. Platte Twp. Cemetery, Benzie Co. Otter Creek area. Unmarked as a veteran.

Sgt. Nathaniel C. King Sgt. Co. A. 2nd Wisconsin Cavalry at Fond du Lac. Enlisted Oct. 16, 1861 and promoted to Commissary Sgt. 1st. Batt. Dec. 10, 1861.[206] Unit History: Organized in Milwaukee, WS. Duty in various locations in Dept. of Missouri, Cassville, action at Yellville, AK, Helena, Battle of Praire Grove, AK, Memphis, TN, Coldwater, Vicksburg and Jackson, MS, Yazoo City, Pearl River, Red Bone Church, Port Gibson, Woodville, Franklin Creek, Grenada, MS, Alexandria, LA, Hempstead and Austin, TX. He established a summer resort by lumberman Richard Tobin's land near the Glen Lake Narrows. Photograph featured in "Remembering Empire Through Pictures - Some Other Day." He was active in Fourth of July celebrations, being listed the reader of the Declaration of Independence at such events.[207] Also served in Co. S. Died Oct. 1890 72 Yrs. 10 mths. 11 Days. Buried in Maple Grove (Empire Union) Cemetery. G.A.R. Post 168.

Randall La Core Listed in Empire Township 1894 Veteran's Census of Michigan. (See Henry Marvin/Marion La Core 7th MI Inf.)

Lt. Chas V. Lackor Sgt. - 2nd Lt. Co. D. 8th NY Heavy Artillery - Unit History: Defenses of Baltimore, Rapidan Campaign, Spotsylvania Court House, Fredericksburg Road, Wounded in action June 3, 1864 at Cold Harbor, VA Discharged for Disability Oct. 6, 1864. (Also listed under Charles Lacker Sergt. Co. D and as Charles W.). Was Commissioned 2nd Lieutenant July 16, 1864 with rank from June 30, 1863. Listed in Empire Township 1894 Veterans Census of MI. Died May 2, 1901 Age 65 Years. Buried in Maple Grove (Empire Union) Cemetery. Book on the 8th N.Y. Artillery: "Full Measure of Devotion" by Wilbur Dunn, Newfane, NY & information from John Ladwig Niagra Co. Historical Society. Lockport, NY. (See Gilbert Lackor 26th MI of Traverse City.)

John Litzua Co. I. 1st Ill. Artillery Bugler from Glen Arbor, MI. Unit History: Battle of Shiloh, Corinth, Grant's Central MS Campaign, "Tallahatchie March", Wall Hill, Siege of Vicksburg, Jackson , Chattanooga TN, Mission Ridge, Knoxville, Scottsboro AL, Battle of Nashville & Related Campaigns. He was born in Russia in 1836 and lived at Aral (Otter Creek). He also had land in the field south of the D.H. Day farm and later lived in Charlevoix, MI. Member of Baxter G.A.R. Post 119 Charlevoix.

Cpl. James McCormick (also sometimes listed under James Cummings) Cor'p. Co. C. 19th Wis. Inf. Unit History: Norfolk, VA, Edenton Rd., Yorktown, New Berne operations, Fort Darling, Battle of Drury's Bluff, assaults on Petersburg, Richmond, Battle of Fair Oaks.Frederickbrg. Listed in Empire Township 1894 Veteran's Census of MI. Still an area resident around 1926.[208] 1841-1929. Buried in Maple Grove (Empire Union) Cemetery. G.A.R. Post 168. (See Thomas Mc. in 26th MI)

Lansing C. Miller Co. K. 4th Wis. Cavalry Unit History: Service near Baltimore, sailed on Steamer "Constitution" for Ship Island, Fort St Phillip, New Orleans, Vicksburg, Port Hudson,Battle of Baton Rouge and engaged against guerrillas in that area, Brookhaven, AL, GA, march to San Antonio, TX duty along Rio Grande. Discharged 1866. Glen Arbor Township 1890 Fed. Census Civil War Veteran & 1894 Veterans Census of MI. Buried in Maple Grove (Empire Union) Cemetery. GAR Post 168.

Leroy Morgan Co. K. 52nd IL Inf. Unit History: KY, Pittsburg Landing, Battles of Shiloh, Pulaski, Resaca, Dallas, Atlanta, Jonesboro, March to the Sea, Campaign of the Carolinas, Bentonville, Goldsboro, Surrender of Johnston, Grand Review Washington, D.C. May 24, 1865. Discharged at Chicago, IL. Born Aug. 26, 1839 – Nov. 10, 1912. Platte Twp. Cemetery, Benzie Co. Otter Creek area. Unmarked as a veteran.

Frank Payment Co. I.&C. 76th / 147th/ 91st NY Inf. Age 28. (from Buffalo), Entered Aug. 7, 1863. Transferred to 147th Jan. 28, 1865.[209] Service: On line of Rappahannock, Bristoe, Mine Run, Rapidan to James River Campaigns, Battles of the Wilderness, Laurel Hill, Spotsylvania & Ct. House, Salient, North Anna River, Totopotomoy, Cold Harbor, Petersburg, Weldon RR, Poplar Springs Church, Hatcher's Run, Appomattox Campaign, Five Forks, Appomattox Court House, Surrender of Lee, Washington D.C. Grand Review, Transferred to 91st NY. Born in Canada in 1842 or grave lists1844-1930 Buried in Rose Hill (Ziegler) Cemetery. G.A.R. Post 168. Buried near Wife Louisa (Bow) & Son William Sr. (See photograph pg. 159.)

Cpl. Adoneron J. Pratt / Adonison Pratt Co. F. 106th NY Inf.[210] Grave reads Cpl. 106th NJ Inf.? Age 21. August 27, 1862. Defenses of New Creek, VA. Greenland Gap. Captured in Action & Parolled April 29, 1863 at Fairmont, VA. Battle of Winchester, Rappahannock, Rapidan, Battles of the Wilderness, Spotsylvania & Ct. Hs., Salient "Bloody Angle," Cold Harbor, Petersburg, Monocacy MD, Shenandoah Valley, Winchester, Cedar Creek, Promoted Corporal March 1, 1865, Appomattox Campaigns, Mustered out at Washington D.C. June 22, 1865. Empire Addr. (From Vermont) Nov. 8, 1841 – Aug. 31, 1915. Almira Cemetery w/ newer marker. G.A.R. Post 423 & 168. (See Zimri Pratt 15th MI Inf., Drum Major William H. Pratt in 26th MI Inf., & H.B. Pratt 1st NY Cav. was in Traverse City McPherson G.A.R. Post 18. Also a Benjamin Pratt was listed age 50 in the 1880 Census of Empire).

Anson W. Randall (Randar Anson) Glen Arbor Township 1890 Fed. Census Civil War Veteran & Listed in Glen Arbor Township 1894 Veteran's Census of Michigan. Buried in Oakwood Cemetery. Traverse City. Listings match in 1st or 18th MI or Co. E. 10th MI Inf.? or Cav.? (See Charles and Gilbert Randall 10th MI Cavalry and George Randall 26th MI Inf. listed in Last Full Measure of Devotion section.)

136

The Grand Review
(Library of Congress)

N.B. Sheridan, Chas. Fisher, Jake Van Buskirk & Chas. Sheridan.

(Courtesy Glen Arbor History Group)

Newton B. Sheridan &
Ribbon of William E. Sheridan
(Courtesy Bertha Werbinski)

14th New York Artillery
Signal Tower Headquarters
Petersburg, VA
(Library of Congress)
- See Newton Sheridan &
Stephen McQueer

FIFTH ANNUAL

RE-UNION

24th

N. Y. Inf'y.

1ST BRIGADE
1ST DIVISION
1ST CORPS

PULASKI, N.Y.

JUNE 28, 1893.

Isaac Ranier (Raynor) Co. A 22nd Wis. Inf. Unit Service: Nicholasville, Danville KY, Thompson's Station against Gen. Bragg, Little Harpeth captured by Gen. Forest & Exchanged, Nashville TN, Battle of Resaca, Pumpkin Vine Creek, Dallas, Kenesaw & Lost Mt., Siege of Atlanta, Carolinas, Bentonville, Wash. D.C. Grand Review. In later life Captained sailing vessels on the Great Lakes and also lived in Mesick, MI. Glen Arbor Township 1890 Fed. Census Civil War Veteran & 1894 Veterans Census of MI under Isaac Ramow. Died April 29, 1925. Age 85. Internment at Glen Haven.

Dr. Charles R. Reed, M.D. Co. E. 15th IL Inf. Unit History: Springfield MO, Ft. Donelson, Pittsburg Landing, Battles of Shiloh, Corinth, Hatchie River, Grant's Central MS Campaign, Siege of Vicksburg, Meridan Campaign, Champion's Hill, Atlanta Campaign, Consolidated w/14th IL as 15th Battalion Inf. Campaign of the Carolinas, Grand Review, Out at Fort Levenworth, KS. Died at age 60. Platte Twp. Cemetery Benzie Co. Otter Creek area. Grave is unmarked as a veteran.

Henry Rehder 2nd PA Heavy Artillery Co. L. Joined Jan. 15, 1864 in a unit that had already been in: Harper's Ferry, Dranesville, Battles of Manassas, Mechanicsville, Gains Mill, Savage Station, Charles City, Glendale, Groveton, Bull Run, South Mt., Antietam, Fredericksburg, Wash. D.C., Battle of Gettysburg, Mine Run Campaign, Battle of the Wilderness, Laurel Hill, Spotsylvania, Pamunkey, Totopotomoy. Reformed June,1864.(112th Regt.) Cold Harbor, Petersburg, Ft. Gilmer, Chaffin's Farm, New Mkt Hts, Ft. Harrison, Laurel Hill, Bermuda Front, Petersburg, City Pt., VA 1866. Mustered out June 29, 1866. Died Nov. 9, 1877. Age 45. Also listed as Rehner/Radar. Buried in Kelderhouse / Port Oneida Cemetery.

Nathan Sargent Listed in Empire Township 1894 Veteran's Census of Michigan.

Cpl. John J. Shepard Co. C. 186th NY Inf.[211] Age 32. Enrolled Sept. 6, 1864. Siege of Petersburg, Hatcher's Run, Appomattox Campaign, Cpl. April 20, 1865, in Grand Review, Washington, D.C. Mustered out June 2, 1865 near Alexandria, VA. G.A.R. Post 168. Born in NY in 1833. Lived in Glen Haven in 1888. (See C.D. Shepard Bat.M. 2nd NY H.A. in Misc. Leelanau County.)

Newton B. Sheridan Co. K. 14th New York Heavy Artillery Joined Dec. 10, 1863 age 23 at Albion and listed Deserted? Aug. 11, 1864 due to the fatal illness of his wife.[212] Then said to have joined 23rd NY Heavy Artillery.[213] Service near Petersburg and Weldon RailRoad. (Glen Arbor Township 1890 Fed. Census Civil War Veteran & 1894 Veterans Census of MI). "Knube" was a Cooper (Barrel-maker.)[214] N.L.? Sheridan reported to have killed a large deer at Glen Arbor in 1894.[215] Buried in Kelderhouse / Port Oneida Cemetery.

William E. Sheridan Enrolled in Co. B. 24th NY Inf. & Co. A. 16th NY Heavy Artillery[216] Age 44. 5'10" Blue eyes. Enrolled Nov. 9, 1861. Discharged for Disability June 16, 1862.[217] Aug. 8, 1863. Enlisted for 34th New York Battery, Transferred to Co.A. 16th Heavy Artillery Sept. 28, 1863. Fortress Monroe, Engaged by White House while laying telegraph lines, Gloucester Pt., Siege of Petersburg & Richmond, Discharged for Disability at Willetts Point, New York Harbor on Dec. 1, 1864. (Also listing under 20th NY.) Glen Arbor Township 1890 Fed. Census Civil War Veteran. G.A.R. Post 168.

Frank J. Smith Listed in Glen Arbor Township 1894 Veteran's Census of Michigan. (See Manitou listings.)

9th New York Heavy Artillary, Company M, Washington D.C.   U.S. Civil War
Photo from the National Archives & Records Administration, Washington D.C.

John Tobin

Old, wooden crosses have long since rotted away leaving many Civil War Veteran's graves unmarked.
Identified from the old Glen Arbor Township Cemetery. (Grand Traverse Pioneer & Historical Society, *Archived Photograph by Al Barnes*)

Philander P. Smith Enlisted in Co. A. 24th Wis.Inf.[218] in August of 1864 - June 1865. Army of the Cumberland under Buell, Rosecrans and Thomas.[219] Unit Service: Battle of Perryville KY, Stone's River, Chickamauga, Chatanooga, Mission Ridge, Knoxville TN, Atlanta Campaign, Battle of Resaca, Pumpkin Vine Creek, Dallas, New Hope Church, Kenesaw Mt., Battle of Jonesboro, AL, Franklin, Nashville TN. (also listed as Philander L. in Glen Arbor Township 1890 Fed. Census Civil War Veteran). Listed in 1894 Veterans Census of MI. P.P. Smith served as Glen Haven Post Master and is listed as being buried in an unidentified marker by his wife in the old Glen Arbor Township Cemetery in the woods near M22-Forest Haven Rd. G.A.R. Post 168

Orville Thompson listing under 29th OH Cavalry Entered Sept. 25, 1861. Then under Co. D. 29th Ohio Inf. then Co. M. 9th NY Heavy Artillery - Unit History: 22nd NY Battery assigned as Co. M. NY H.A. Feb. 5, 1863. Defenses of Washington D.C. (See photo. of Co. M. or F.) Rapidan / Shenandoah Campaign, also listed with 2nd Regiment West Virginia Cavalry. Discharged Nov. 25, 1863 at Point Pleasant, W.V. on Surgeon's Certificate of Disability. Grave lists Co. M. 9th NY H.A. Buried in Maple Grove (Empire Union) Cemetery. (See Henry Thompson G.A.R. Post 399 Bingham Township.)

John or William Tobin Perhaps served in Wisconsin. Originally from Canada like the Father, Richard. (Photograph from "Some Other Day (Remembering Empire)" shows John with either a G.A.R. medal or his Life Saving medal). There was a William H. Tobin enlisted in Co. E. 48th WS Inf. at Oshkosh.

Jessie O. Tuttle Listed as a Glen Arbor Veteran. Later listed in Suttonsbay Township. Buried in Bingham Cemetery. Died in 1884. Age 49. (Unmarked as a veteran. Grave has no vet. flag staff marker.)

John J. Van Wormer 90th NY Inf. Co. H. & C. Age 23 joined Sept. 15, 1864 On Muster for Co. I. Transferred to Co. C. Nov. 28, 1864. Unit History: Duty at Key West Fla., Beaufort SC, action at Franklin, Assault on Port Hudson, Defenses of New Orleans, Red River Campaign, Morganza, Shenandoah Valley Campaign, Battle of Winchester, Stephenson's Depot & Kernstown, Wash. D.C. Grand Review, Savannah & Hawkinsville GA. Mustered out June 3, 1865. Died Aug., 1878 Age 42 or 43. Buried in the Kelderhouse / Port Oneida Cemetery.

Dr. William H. Walker 14th Wis. Inf. Major Surgeon General Entered Oct. 30, 1861 (with Nathaniel King) at Fond du Lac. Battle of Shiloh, Corinth, Iuka, MS, Resigned his position after these terrible bloody battles on April 19, 1862.[220] Glen Arbor Township 1890 Fed. Census Civil War Veteran. Dr. Walker created a large cranberry marsh amoung the woods South of Glen Arbor. It was once the second largest cranberry marsh in Michigan.[221] One story reported that Dr. Walker died in Milwaukee in 1898 though Wisconsin has no record of his burial.[222] He is also listed as being buried in the private Walker Cemetery in Glen Arbor Township in 1900, about a mile South of Glen Arbor along Northwood Rd. shore of Glen Lake. (Near 1997 homestead of Robert Sutherland). "He was buried on a high point of land by his cranberry marsh and a large marker stands (stood) over his grave."[223] (Lydon Walker 54th OH is buried in Fife Lake Cemetery.)

Ruell R. Welch Co. C. 127th Ill. Inf.[224] Mustered Sept. 5, 1862 Duty guarding Prisoners at Camp Douglas, Tallahatchie March, Sherman's Yazoo Expedition, Chickasaw Bayou & Bluff, Ft. Hindman AK, Young's Pt. LA, Deer Creek, Haine's Bluff, Jackson MS, Assaults on Vicksburg. Discharged for wounds June 20, 1863. Also listed as Renel R. Welch. Burdickville Postal Address. Listed as being buried in an unidentified? marker in the old Glen Arbor Township Cemetery in the woods near M22-Forest Haven Rd. Sleeping Bear Dunes National Lakeshore. (A marker was once there, but is now gone.)[225] Member of G.A.R. Post 168. (See Edward Welch 15th MI Inf.)

Andrew Wilson Bat. I. 1st Ill. L.A. Feb. 10, 1862-Feb. 10, 1865. Service: Battle of Shiloh, Corinth, Grant's Central MS Campaign, "Tallahatchie March", Wall Hill, Siege of Vicksburg, Jackson , Big Black River, Chattanooga TN, Mission Ridge, Knoxville, Scottsboro AL, Battle of Nashville & Related Campaigns. Resident of Glen Arbor. (See Peter Wilson 28th MI).

Additional Civil War Draftees listed from Glen Arbor who may have served in other States, used an assumed name, were excused, or had a substitute: Nicholas Barnes, William Briggs (or William Bickle? see 3rd MI Inf.), Eli Deening/Deering? (See 4th MI Inf.?), Charles Dumbrill, Warren E. Evarts, William Frizelle, Jacob Hartung/Harting, Martin Hoft, James/John H. Kelderhouse, Augustus Kemner, Willis P. Miller/Wells B. Miller? John Mitchell, Daniel H. Moore, John Nahascal, Job K. Perry, Julius Prause, Samuel Swartout, Victor F. Thurston, Andrew Towner, Simeon Townsend, Frank Valley, Vaclav Vileta (Port Onieda area. Selected to serve (possibly 15th MI) no record.), Augustus Vege/Veyle, Daniel Way, George West, and Andrew J. Wisner.[226]

Manitou County

At one time, part of our area made up a county called Manitou. In the late 1800's the Legislature disorganized the County (consisting of the Islands in East Lake Michigan) and attached the Fox Islands and North & South Manitou to Leelanau County. Some of the men listed from this area included, South Manitou Township:

Jeremiah Becker Co. E. 127th Ill. Inf. Unit: AK, Vicksburg, Resaca, Atlanta, Jonesboro, Bentonville, in Grand Review. Listed as Glen Arbor area veteran pensioned for Liver and Dropsy. Had land at North Unity and on South Manitou Island in 1882. Later listed in Leland. Born in New York, buried in Oakwood Cemetery. Traverse City McPherson G.A.R. Post 18. (See John Becker G.A.R. Post 168.)

George F. Lovejoy 2nd Missouri Cavalry (Major Merrill Horse) Unit Service: Dept. of MO, AK, TN, Atlanta, GA.

Thomas Price Co. A. 1st Missouri Engineers. 1862-1865. New Madrid Canal, Ft. Pillow, Corinth, Vicksburg, Memphis, Nashville, Jonesboro, Carolinas, Bentonville, in Grand Review.

Jacob R. (or W.) Smith or Sgt. William W. Smith of Buffalo, NY. Records list: Co. K. 5th NY Light Artillery Enlisted Aug. 26, 1862. Battle of Antietam, Falmouth, Battles of Fredericksburg, Chancellorsville, Gettysburg, Bristoe Campaign, Rappahannock, Mine Run, Rapidan, Battle of the Wilderness, Laurel Hill, Spotsylvania, Early's attack on Wash. D.C. and was later listed as killed in action July 18, 1864. (However William Smith was listed as owning a Boarding House in 1875 and was listed in Glen Arbor Township 1890 Fed. Civil War Veteran Census from South Manitou Island.)

See also summaries on: **Fredrick Haines & Paul Half 1st MI, George Haas/Hass 5th MI, George N. Sites 15th MI. Manrod Buckler 26th MI, & Frederic Benham 28th MI.**

Several from **Fox & Beaver Islands** including:

Galilee Township: **Edward Lastlee**

Chandler Township: **Benj. Fisher** (possible matches in 16th or 23rd MI) &

John Floyd (Enlisted in Indiana, wounded in the Battle of the Wilderness. Buried on Beaver Island).

Also: **Thomas Bedford** (Died July 5, 1889 in Eaton County) and **Alexander Wentworth** Co. F. 5th MN Inf. who were both involved in the assassination of Mormon Leader James J. Strang.[227]

Early photograph of North Manitou
(Courtesy U.S. Park Service, Sleeping Bear Dunes
  National Lakeshore)

South Manitou Light
(Courtesy Robert Overmyer
  Ann Arbor, MI)

Guns at Fort McAllister
Savannah, Georgia
(Library of Congress)

General Sherman by Artillery
(Library of Congress)

Forest Haven Soldiers: The Civil War Veterans of Sleeping Bear & Surrounding Leelanau

Maple City / Cedar / Cleveland Twp. Area Veterans Who Had Served in Other States [228] (Many of these veterans founded the Leelanau County Agricultural Society.)

<u>Cleveland Township</u>:

Herman J. Burgess Co. F. 86th NY Inf. Unit History: Wash. D.C., Pope's Campaign in Northern VA, Manassas Gap, Battle of Fredericksburg, Chancellorsville, Gettysburg, Rappahannock, Mine Run, Rapidan, Battle of the Wilderness, Spotsylvania, Salient "Bloody Angle," Totopotomoy, Cold Harbor, Petersburg, Weldon RR, Strawberry Plains, Hatcher's Run, Appomattox Campaign, Grand Review. Buried in Oakwood Cemetery.
(See Jacob Burgess 7th MI Cav. & Henry Burgess 23rd OH.)

Jacob H. Kliner Bat. D. 3rd NY L.A. Unit history: Washington D.C. New Berne NC, Campaign of the Carolinas, SW Creek, Battle of Kingston, Goldsboro, Bennett's House, Surrender of Johnston, Duty in NC.

Peter Loucks 12th CT Inf. Unit History: Ship Island MS, Ft. St. Phillip & Jackson, the first regiment to land New Orleans LA & subsequent expeditions, La Fourche, Action with Steamer "Cotton," Brashear City, in Western LA, Port Hudson, Sabin Pass (Texas) Expedition, Carrollton, Wash.D.C., Snicker's Gap, Sheridan's Shenandoah Valley Campaign, Battles of Opequan, Winchester, Cedar Creek, Summit Point, in Grand Review, out at Savannah, GA. Listed in Cleveland Township 1894 Veteran's Census of Michigan. G.A.R. Post 168.

Daniel B. Scott Co. B. 12th Ill. Inf.[229] Enlisted April 21 and Mustered in May 2, 1861. Garrison's. Out Aug. 1, 1861. Listed as a Glen Arbor Draftee. Commissioned? Listed with 1st MI Colored Inf. Co. E. July 25, 1864 - Aug. 28, 1865? with John Holland 1st MI Col. & Capt. Patrick McLaughlin 16th/1st-102nd MI Col. Inf. (see Andrew & John Scott of the 15th MI Inf.). Listed in Cleveland Township 1894 Veteran's Census of Michigan. G.A.R. Post 168.

1888 Maple City County Fair
(Courtesy Leelanau Historical Museum)

Maple City I.O.O.F. Organization believed to have included: Mr. Weston, A.E. Densmore, Abner S. Fritz, George Davis,
Clarence Trumbull, Sam Holsted, Rev. C.W. Williams, Stan R. Burke, H.C. Van Slyck, F.X. Herbert, Treff Herbert, John Van
Ostrand, John Trumbull, Miles A. Densmore, Dr. Roswell Burke, Fred Jens, A.E. Bellinger, and/or possibly Mr. Sheridan, Jim
Auton, & Adam DeVinger? ~ 1890. (Courtesy Leelanau Historical Museum)

Kasson Township: (Named after Kasson Freeman as suggested by the first town supervisor Jonathan Dewing,[230]While Maple City owes its start to William Parks & J.T. Sturtevant.)[231]

Ora W. Babcock 193rd Reg.NY Inf. Enrolled Feb. 2,1865. Age 48 (Listed 42) Shenandoah Valley & Harper's Ferry WV. Discharged for disability at Elmira June 26, 1865. Died July 1, 1888. Age 71. Buried at Round Top (Friends) Cemetery.

John Becker Co. B. 64th NY Inf.[232] Age 24. Served Aug. 20, 1864. Strawberry Plains, Hatcher's Run, Appomattox Campaign, White Oak Rd, Sutherland Station, Petersburg, Sailer's Cr., High Bridge & Farmville, Surrender of Lee, Wash. D.C., Grand Review. Out July 14, 1865 near Washington D.C. Had a farm by William Kellogg (15th MI) Listed in Bingham Township 1894 Veteran's Census of Michigan. G.A.R. Post 168. (See listing for Jeremiah Becker in Glen Arbor.)

Dr. Roswell W. J. (or O.) Burke Listed Co.A. 28th Reg. 1st IN Cavalry. Age 21. Listed also as Richard Co.H. 11th Ind. H.A. Mustered Aug. 20, 1861. Unit History: Maryland, sailed on Steamer "Constitution" for Ship Island, Ft. Phillip & Jackson, with 1st regiment to land at New Orleans LA, Battle of Baton Rouge & various skirmishes, Action with Steamer "Cotton," operations in Western LA, Port Hudson, Dept. of Gulf. Out Sept. 12, 1864 at Indianapolis IN. Lived in Maple City & Empire. (Once listed under 1st/11th IN H.A.)[233] Listed in Kasson Township 1894 Veteran's Census of Michigan. Possible listed death on Oct. 29, 1915? Buried in Kasson Cemetery. G.A.R. Post 168.[234]

Sgt. Frank B. Chatsey Co. K. 63rd OH Inf.[235] Age 25. Entered Aug. 21, 1862. Battle of Iuka, Corinth, Grant's Central MS Campaign, Parker's Cross Roads, Tuscumbia, Memphis TN, Prospect TN, Decatur AL, Atlanta Campaign, Battle of Resaca, Pumpkin Vine Creek, Dallas, Allatoona Hills, Kenesaw Mt., Chattahoochie River, Battle of Atlanta, Jonesboro, Campaign of the Carolinas, Rivers Bridge, Battle of Bentonville, Raliegh, Surrender of Johnston, Wash. D.C. Grand Review, Louisville KY. Out July 8, 1865. Listed in Kasson Township 1894 Veteran's Census of Michigan. Died 1910. Buried in Rose Hill (Ziegler) Cemetery. G.A.R. Post 168.

Lt. William H. Crowell Enlisted in Co. B. 125th OH Inf.[236] Born in Trumball Co. OH. Age 24. Aug. 31,1862. Camp Taylor, Louisville KY, Repulse of attack on Franklin, Promoted Quartermaster Sgt. May 12, 1863. Mid TN & Chickamauga Campaigns & Battle, Chattanooga, Knoxville & East TN, Atlanta Campaigns, Battle of Resaca, Pumpkin Vine Creek, Dallas, Kenesaw & Lost Mt., Battles of Jonesboro, Franklin, Nashville, Duty in AL, LA, & Texas. Became a Lieutenant. Mustered out in 1865. Listed in Kasson Township 1894 Veteran's Census of Michigan. Operated a Hotel & Saw Mill beside the Peg Factory in Maple City & served as Postmaster.[237] G.A.R. Post 168.

Lewis Donner (Louis) Co. B./K. 94th NY Inf. "Belle Jefferson Rifles" Unit History: Wash. D.C., Manassas, Battle of Cedar Mt., Groveton, Bull Run, Chantilly, South Mt., Antietam, Fredericksburg, Chancellorsville, Gettysburg, Rappahannock, Mine Run, Totopotomy, Cold Harbor, Petersburg, Weldon RR, Hatcher's Run, Five Forks, At some point was captured and sent to Andersonville Prison. Born Nov. 24, 1843 in NY. Died May 31, 1927.[238] Listed in Oakwood Cemetery. G.A.R. Post 168. (See George Donner in Glen Arbor Twp.)

S.C. Gearey Kasson Township. Ft. Smith, AK. Quartermaster's Dept. Indian fighting.[239]

147

U.S. Christian Commission (Library of Congress)

Joseph Price
1st Illinois Light Artillery
(Courtesy Kasson Heritage Group)

Lafayette W. Henderson 59th OH Inf.
(Courtesy U.S. Army Military History Institute
Carlisle Barracks, PA)

Dr. Roswell Burke
Served in Indiana
(Courtesy Leelanau Historical Museum)

Rev. Jasper B. Hall Kasson Township. Born in 1826. Served in the Army of the Potomic for the Christian Commission.[240] His farm was SE of Pollack Lake between Davis Lake.

Cpl. Nathaniel William Harrington Cpl. Co. B. Enlisted in the 12th U.S. Inf. July 13, 1861 in New York. (Herrington) He was wounded in the left leg at the battle of Gettysburg. He was also in the battles of the Wilderness and others before mustering out at Petersburg.[241] (There were several Harringtons in the 6th MI Cavalry.) Served as Sheriff & Justice of the Peace.[242] Listed in Kasson Township 1894 Veteran's Census of Michigan. Died of 'Cerebral Hemorrhage.' April 22, 1842 - Feb. 7, 1927. Listed in Solon Township Cemetery with his wife. (Buried in Oakwood Cemetery, Lot 75, Plat 2). G.A.R. Post 168. The last Commander of G.A.R. Post 168.[243]

Lafayette Henderson Co. H. & K. 59th OH Inf.[244] Age 18. Entered Aug. 19, 1862 Tranf. to K. Oct. 24, 1864. Unit: Louisville KY, Battle of Perryville, Nashville, Murfreesboro, Battle of Stone's River, Mid. TN Campaign, Battle of Chickamauga, Chattanooga, Knoxville, Atlanta Campaign, Battle of Resaca, Pumpkin Vine Creek, Dallas, Kenesaw Mt., Battle of Jonesboro, Lovejoy Station, Transf. to 23rd Army Corps. Tullahoma, Nashville TN. Listed in Kasson Township 1894 Veteran's Census of Michigan. Pensioned for injury to Right Thigh. G.A.R. Post 168. (Photograph in U.S. Army Military History Institute.)

Francis X. Herbert Buried in Kasson Cemetery, Feb.28,1843-June 6, 1925.

Robert H. Monroe M. D. Enlisted in Co. C. 29th Ind. Inf. in 1861. After his first battle he was appointed Hospital Steward and held that position until early 1863, when he was appointed Surgeon of his regiment and served out the rest of the war in the Western Department. He was born Jan. 5, 1822 and lived in Inland, Benzie County, Oviatt, Kasson Township,[245]& Almira area. Oakwood Cemetery. (James H. Monroe of Traverse City enlisted in 1861.)

John B. Nash Co. I. 42nd Ill. Inf.[246] Age 21. Entered Aug. 14, 1861. MO Campaigns, New Madrid, Island Number 10, Ft. Pillow, Corinth, Pursuit of Boonville, Memphis & Charlston RR, Columbia, Forest's Attack on Edgefield, Nashville, Battles of Stone's River, Chickamauga, Chattanooga, Knoxville, Stone's Mills, Dandridge, Atlanta Campaign, Battle of Resaca, Pumpkin Vine Creek, Dallas, Kenesaw Mt., Battle of Jonesboro, Lovejoy's Station. Out Sept. 16, 1864. Born in Hillsdale May 25, 1840. Farmer[247] in Kasson Township listing. Died Nov. 16, 1906. Buried in Nash/Pettengill (St. Rita's) Cemetery - Maple City, MI. (Large Family Marker.) G.A.R. Post 168. (William Nash served in 26th MI Inf.)

(Nathaniel) A. Palmer Buried in East Kasson Cemetery. Listed age 53 from New York in the Kasson post-war 1870 Census. Died March 3, 1883. G.A.R. Marker. (Walter Palmer had served in the 15th MI Inf. & Melville Palmer in the 26th MI Inf.).

Joseph P. Price Bat. I 1st Ill.[248] L.A. Mustered Feb. 2, 1862, Blue eyes. 5'4" Re-enlisted as a Veteran and served as a Blacksmith. Service: Battles of Shiloh & Corinth, where he was injured in his eye and ankle,[249] Grant's Central MS Campaign, "Tallahatchie March", Wall Hill, Siege of Vicksburg, Jackson , Chattanooga TN, Mission Ridge, Knoxville, Scottsboro AL, Battle of Nashville & Related Campaigns. Mustered out Feb. 10, 1865 at Eastport, MS. Listed Residence: Glen Arbor, MI. & Homesteaded a cabin in Kasson Township. Listed in Kasson Township 1894 Veteran's Census of Michigan. Was a Burdickville Blacksmith.[250] G.A.R. Post 168. Born in London, England Oct. 13, 1836. Second son of Joseph & Lydia. Died Nov. 7, 1914.[251] Buried in Rose Hill (Ziegler) Cemetery, Kasson Twp. off M-72. His son was also named Joseph Peter Price. His photograph is featured in "Remembering Yesterday" by the Kasson Heritage Group. (See Thomas Price of Manitou.)

Morris D. Spafford
2nd Ohio Cavalry
(Courtesy Albert K. Spafford)

James Stricklen
127th Illinois Infantry
(Courtesy Kasson Heritage Group)

Morris D. Spafford (Shepard) Co.A. 2nd Ohio Cavalry.[252] Enlisted at Akron, OH. Listed Age 19 / Then listed as age 37 on his Disability Discharge. Entered Aug. 16, 1861. Camp Dennison, Missouri Border, Independence MO, Fort Scott KS under Col. Chas. Doubleday, Discharged Mar. 25, 1862 on Surgeon's Certificate of Disability. (Listed as 5'11" Blue Eyes, Sandy Hair.) Was a Carpenter. Listed in Kasson Township 1894 Veteran's Census of Michigan. Grave lists Born April 15, 1825. Died Nov. 6, 1895. Green Briar / Almira Union Cemetery. G.A.R. Post 168. (See William Spafford 11th MI Inf.)

James S. Stricklin(d/g) / or Strickland Co.E. 127th Ill. Inf.[253] Entered Sept. 5, 1862. Guarding Prisoners at Camp Douglas, Tallahatchie March, Sherman's Yazoo Expedition, Chickasaw, Ft. Hindman, Deer Creek, Vicksburg, Missionary Ridge, Knoxville TN, Larkinsville AL. Out Feb. 3, 1864. Listed in Kasson Township 1894 Veteran's Census of Michigan. Died in November of 1894 with G.A.R. honors.[254] Pensioned for Hip injury. Buried in Greenbriar / Almira Union Cemetery. G.A.R. Post 168. Photo in "Remembering Yesterday" - Kasson Heritage Group.[255] (see Nathan Stricklin 14th OH.).

Nathan Stricklin Co. A. 14th OH Inf.[256] Age 23. Entered Aug. 28, 1861. Service: KY, Fishing Creek, Battle of Mill Springs, Nashville TN, Bear Creek AL, Corinth MS, Iuka, Tuscumbia, Action at Decatur, Battle of Perryville, Gallatin TN, Murfreesboro, Mid. TN Campaign, Battle of Chickamauga, Chattanooga, Atlanta Campaign, Rocky Faced Ridge, Battle of Resaca, Pumpkin Vine Creek, Allatoona & Pine Hills, Kenesaw & Lost Mt., Chattahoochie River, Battle of Jonesboro, March to the Sea, Savannah, Campaign of the Carolinas, Battle of Bentonville, Goldsboro, Raliegh, Bennett's House, Surrender of Johnston & his Army, Washington D.C. Grand Review, Louisville KY. Out July 11, 1865. Also listing under 6th OH. Was a Kasson Township Wagon-maker. Buried in Kasson Cemetery. G.A.R. Post 168. (see James Stricklin 127th Ill.).

Abraham Van Vuken Bat. I. 3rd NY L.A.[257] Unit History: Wash. D.C., New Berne NC, Ft. Macon, Goldsboro, White Oak River, Campaign of the Carolinas, Battle of Wise's Forks, Surrender of Johnston, Duty in Dept. of NC.

Charles H. Webb Co. G. 15th Iowa & 6th Cavalry[258] Age 32. Native of NY. Entered Nov. 25, 1861. Pittsburg Landing, Battle of Shiloh, Corinth, Grant's Central MS Campaign, Promoted to Cavalry Feb. 1, 1862. Sioux City Dakota, Ft. Randall operations against Sioux Indians, White Stone Hill, Ft. Sully, Bad Lands, Ft. Rice, Ft. Berthold & Yankton. Listed in Kasson Township 1894 Veteran's Census of Michigan. Died March 17, 1911. Buried in Kasson Cemetery. G.A.R. Post 168.

Solon Township:

David Bussey. Listed in Solon Township 1894 Veteran's Census of Michigan.

Sgt. Moses C. Cate Sgt. Co.D. 103rd Ohio[259] (Also listed 125th OH Inf.)[260] Age 33. Entered Aug. 31, 1862. Camp Taylor, Louisville KY, Nashville, Franklin, Mid. TN Campaigns, In December of 1862 his wife gave birth to a baby daughter and after a request for leave was refused, he and friend William Hannaford (who also had a baby daughter that was ill and subsequently died), went AWOL. Upon their return he was reduced to ranks and they were threatened with execution for desertion, but Cate was a personal friend of Governor Todd who threatened to refuse to furnish any more troops until Cate and Hannaford were pardoned. Both General Burnside and Col. Casement also assisted in their release and a pardon was eventually granted from President Lincoln.[261] Unit went on to Resaca, Kingston, Pumpkin Vine Creek, Dallas, Kenesaw Mt., Battle of Jonesboro, Lovejoy Station, Operations against Hood. He had again become 1st Sgt. Aug. 15, 1863 but Cate was often hospitalized for illness and again reduced to ranks. Unit was in Battle of Franklin, Battle of Nashville, in AL, TN (See opposite letter), New Orleans, Texas. Mustered out June 1865. The "History of Solon" being compiled by Carol Drezwiecki also includes several stories told by Cate about Knoxville in 1863, Fort Sanders, and about trading coffee for several bottles of canned fruit to help a sick friend. Traveled with the Hannafords and Dickerman's to Leelanau County, MI after the war. He served as first Supervisor[262] & a Postmaster of Solon Township. Also served as County Sheriff. Listed in Solon Township 1894 Veteran's Census of Michigan. Born April 7, 1833. Listed in Solon Township Cemetery. Buried in Oakwood. Died July 28, 1916. 87 Years, 11 Mos. 5 Days. G.A.R. Post 168.

Joseph W. Dickerman. Co. C. 13th New Hampshire Inf.[263] Age 25. Mustered Sept. 20, 1862. Served with Lt. Murray.[264] Washington D.C., Battle of Fredericksburg, Mud March, Suffolk, Dix's Peninsula Campaign, James River, Battle of Drewry's Bluff, Cold Harbor, Petersburg, Mine Explosion, Chaffin's Farm, Ft. Harrison, Battle of Fair Oaks, the first regiment to bring flag colors into Richmond VA, Manchester. Out June 21, 1865. Listed in Solon Township 1894 Veteran's Census of Michigan. Born Feb. 12, 1837 Died May 24, 1907. Due to complications of heart disease.[265] Solon Township Cemetery. G.A.R. Post 168 Adjutant. (Euphenia J. Dickerman listed in Woman's Relief Corps. Died 1929.)

Seth Griffin Co. G. 14th NY Inf. Unit History: Defenses of Washington D.C., Battle of Bull Run, VA Peninsula, Yorktown, Hanover Ct. Hs., Seven Days before Richmond, Battles of Mechanicsville, Gaines Mill, White Oak Swamp, Malvern Hill, Harrison's Landing, Battle of Antietam, Sharpsburg, Falmouth, Battle of Fredericksburg, Mud March, Battle of Chancellorsville. Transfers to 44th NY or 140th NY: Gettysburg, Mine Run, Wilderness, Spotsylvania, Salient, Totopotomoy, Petersburg, Appomattox Campaigns, Weldon RR, Five Forks. Also once listed with 98th NY. Born Feb. 12, 1837. Died Jan. 17, 1893. Aged 54 Yrs. Solon Township Cemetery.

Nathan P. Grover Co. D. 98th NY Inf. Unit History: VA Peninsula, Yorktown, Battle of Williamsburg, Battle of Seven Pines/Fair Oaks, Seven Days before Richmond, Carolinas, Beaufort, Battle of Drury's Bluff, Cold Harbor, Mine Explosion, in trenches before Petersburg, Chaffin's Farm, Fair Oaks, duty in NY during 1864 Presidential Election of Abraham Lincoln, duties Richmond, VA. Died Jan. 14, 1899. Age 63 Yrs. 10 Mos. Solon Township Cemetery. G.A.R. Post 168.

Sgt. Moses C. Cate, 103rd Ohio
(Courtesy Carol Drzewiecki)

Sgt. William F. Hannaford, 103rd Ohio
Went AWOL for funeral of daughter seated on left.
(Courtesy Carol Drzewiecki)

Charles A. Hannaford

Sgt. Charles A. Hannaford
(Courtesy Carol Drzewiecki)

Sgt. Charles A. Hannaford Co.I. 124th Ill. Inf.[266] (Also listed 103rd[267]/124th Ohio.) Enlisted Aug. 12, 1862. Mustered Sept. 10, 1862. Operations on MS Central RR, various LA, Battle of Thompson's Hill, Port Gibson, Raymond MS, Jackson, Champion's Hill, Siege of Vicksburg being under fire for eighty days,[268] Big Black, regiment awarded 'Excelsior Prize Banner' by General J.B. McPherson to Gen. Leggett. AK, Meridan Campaign, Benton, New Orleans, Canby's Campaign, Montgomery AL, Vicksburg. Out Aug. 15, 1865. Has served as Justice of the Peace & a Supervisor for Solon where he had given the township its name after his birthplace in Ohio. Listed in Solon Township 1894 Veteran's Census of Michigan. Died Dec. 19, 1907. Listed in Solon Township Cemetery. G.A.R. Post 168.

Sgt. William F. Hannaford Co. D. 103rd OH Inf. Age 24. Mustered Aug. 7, 1862. KY, TN, Monticello, had been reduced to ranks before being pardoned for leaving to see his infant daughter (see Moses Cate story), Atlanta Campaign, Battle of Resaca, Dallas, Pumpkin Vine Creek, Kenesaw & Lost Mt., Decatur, Jonesboro, Hood in AL, Battle of Franklin, Nashville, the Carolinas, Goldsboro, Raliegh, Surrender of Johnston. Out June 12, 1865.[269] Served as first Postmaster for Solon.

Sgt. Robert Hewitt Co. B. 193rd NY Inf. Shenandoah Valley & Harper's Ferry, West VA. Born in England, Died Jan. 10, 1891. 73 Yrs. 8 Mos. 2 Days. Buried in Solon Township Cemetery. G.A.R. Post 168. (& **Joseph Hewitt**? possible match for Co.C. 1st MI Eng. & Mech.? if birth date on grave should read 1832 rather than 1852?).

Lt. John Iiles Co. C. 124th OH Inf.[270] Unit History: KY, TN, Battle of Chickamauga, Chattanooga, Atlanta Campaign, Resaca, Dallas, Pumpkin Vine Creek, Kenesaw & Lost Mt., Jonesboro, Franklin, Nashville, AL, Strawberry Plains. Listed in Solon Twp. 1894 Veteran's Census of Michigan. Born in Ireland July 9, 1821.[271] Died Oct. 31, 1895. Age 74. Solon Twp. Cemetery.

Gordon B. (George/Gideon) Lewism Co. K. 95th Ill. Inf.[272] Unit History: MS Campaign, Siege of Vicksburg, Meridan & Red River Campaign, Battle of Pleasant Hill, Guntown, Brice's Creek/Cross Roads, Battle of Nashville, Atlanta Campaign, Kenesaw Mt., Jonesboro, Fort Blakely AL, Transf. to 47th Ill. Duties in Montgomery, AL.

Stephen McQueer (McGreer) Bat. A. 14th N.Y. H.A.[273] or L.A. Age 18. Entered Aug. 8, 1863. NY Harbor, Rapidan Campaign, Battles of the Wilderness, Spotsylvania & Ct. House, North Anna River, Pamunkey, Totopotomoy, Cold Harbor, Bethesda Church, Mine Explosion - Petersburg, Weldon RR, Poplar Springs Church, Hatcher's Run, Appomattox Campaign, Ford's Station, Washington D.C. Grand Review. Out At Harewood Hospital in Washington D.C. on June 19, 1865. Listed in Solon Township 1894 Veteran's Census of Michigan. Died July 31, 1912. 67 Yrs. 10 Mos. 19 Days. Buried in Solon Township Cemetery. G.A.R. Post 168.

Leonard Stevenson Listed in Solon Township 1894 Veteran's Census of Michigan, **& Lewis Stevenson** Bat. I. 1st Ill. L.A.[274] Battle of Shiloh, Corinth, "Tallahatchie March," Memphis, Vicksburg, Jackson, Chattanooga Campaigns, Re-enlisted. Scottsboro AL, Nashville. (Leonard was listed as deserted 3 months after he re-enlisted)?

G.A.R. Post 168 In Lower Centerville including: (See later listings.)

Louis N. Brabant Co. B. & D. 1st WS Cav./ Inf.[275] (also listing 5th WS)? Enlisted in Co. B. 1st WS Cavalry at Stevens Point. Cav. Unit History: Bloomfield MO, Guerrilla Campaigns, Greenville, West Plains, Mid.TN Campaigns, AL, Battle of Chickamauga, Missionary Ridge, East TN, Mossy Creek, Dandridge, Atlanta Campaign, Battle of Resaca, Kenesaw & Lost Mt., Louisville KY, Nashville TN, Chickasaw AL, Capture of Davis. G.A.R. Post 168 & G.A.R. Post 399. Died July 16, 1904 Age 61. Buried in Leland, MI (Beechwood Cemetery).

William J. Buckingham Co. H. 11th NY Cav.[276] (Scott's 900). Age 35. Joined Jan. 15, 1864. Defenses of Washington D.C., Blue Ridge Mt., Harper's Ferry, Baton Rouge LA, Northern MS, Brookhaven, Western TN, Out at Memphis, TN - June 4, 1865. Lived in Leland area. Listed in Leland Township 1894 Veteran's Census of Michigan. G.A.R. Post 168. Buried in Leland, MI (Beechwood Cemetery).

Jacob Jazdewski Co. B. 9th WS Inf.[277] (Jarschensky/Jerjefski/Zerferski) Enlisted Jan. 11, 1865 out Jan. 11, 1866. Unit History: KS, Indian Expeditions, Newtonia, Battle of Praire Grove, St. Louis MO, Burton, Camden, Jenkin's Ferry, Little Rock AK. Listed in Centerville Township 1894 Veteran's Census of Michigan. Died in 1914. Listed in Isadore (Holy Rosary/ Mt. Calvary) Cemetery. G.A.R. Post 168.

Joseph Vincent LaVanture Levanture/Levanthar Co. G. 41st Ill. Inf.[278] Mustered Aug. 5, 1861. Paducah KY, Columbus, Ft. Henry, Ft. Heiman, Ft. Donelson, Pittsburg Landing, Battle of Shiloh (left wing of Hornet's Nest), Corinth, march to Memphis, Lamar MS, Moscow TN, Coldwater, Vicksburg where he helped as a Nurse in Hospitals,[279] Jackson, Meridan & Red River Campaign, Battle of Pleasant Hill, Alexandria & Plantations, Lake Chicot AK, Tupelo, Harrisburg, & Oxford MS, Memphis, TN. Mustered out Aug. 20, 1864. Listed in Centerville Township 1894 Veteran's Census of Michigan. Pensioned for Kidney complications. Born in Canada Feb. 22, 1843. Died Dec. 24, 1916. St. Mary's Cemetery, Lake Leelanau.[280] G.A.R. Post 168.

G.A.R. Post 168 In Northern Almira or Long Lake Township:
(Additional veterans from these areas are listed further in the book.)

L.A. (Lovett/Loretto) Jenne Co. C. 186th NY Inf.[281] Age 27. Enrolled Aug. 27, 1864. Siege of Petersburg, Hatcher's Run, Appomattox Campaign, Grand Review, D.C. Mustered out June 2, 1865 at Alexandria,VA. Lived at Cedar Run, Long Lake Twp. G.A.R. Post 168.

Horace B. Johnson (Harrison R.Johnston) Co. B. (or D.) 53rd PA Inf.[282] April 4, 1864. Stevensburg, Rapidan, Battles of the Wilderness, Spotsylvania, Po River, Salient, Totopotomoy, Cold Harbor, Petersburg, Weldon RR, James River, Strawberry Plains, Hatcher's Run, Appomattox Campaign, Sutherland Station, Surrender of Lee, Grand Review, Washington D.C., Mustered out with Company June 30, 1865. Lived in Long Lake Twp. Buried in Benzonia. G.A.R. Post 168.

Joseph Lavanture 41st Ill.
G.A.R. Post 168
(Courtesy Sharon L. Miller)

Joseph LaVanture / Levanture 41st Ill. Inf.
on right with his son, Adolph (Alfonse/Dolph) Joseph
La Vanture holding Gabriel's Horn.
Josephine Levanture – Drow (Drew/Wasung) Collection
(Courtesy Carol Ann Drew Sanctorum)

Members of the 164th New York (See Ruben Stetson)
fish along Pope's Run near Sangster's Station, VA
(Courtesy Western Reserve Historical Society of Cleveland, OH)

Jermiah Mowers Co. G. 22nd NY Cavalry.[283] Age 17. Joined Feb. 13, 1864. Unit History: Battles of Wilderness, Spottsylvania Ct. Hs., Escorted ambulance trains to Fredericksburg, Cold Harbor, White Oak Swamp, Malvern Hill, Danville, Stony Creek, Sheridan's Shenandoah Valley Campaigns, Battle of Winchester, Woodstock, Battle of Cedar Creek, Kernston, Lacy's Springs, Waynesboro, & West VA duties. Confined to Ft. Deleware in May of 1865. Discharged Aug. 9, 1865. (B- Aug. 23, 1847. D- July 15, 1922) Green Briar / Almira Union Cemetery. Lake Ann G.A.R. Post 423 & Glen Lake Post 168.

Daniel G. Shorter Co. K. 38th OH Inf.[284] Age 19. Entered Sept. 1, 1861. Camp Hamilton KY, Battle of Mill Springs, Louisville KY, Corinth, Huntsville AL, Battle of Perryville KY, Nashville, Battle of Stone's River, Chickamauga Campaign, Atlanta Campaign, Battle of Resaca, Pumpkin Vine Cr./Dallas, Kenesaw/Lost Mts., Battle of Jonesboro, Mustered out Sept. 19, 1864. Died Jan. 29, 1915 Age 72y, 11m. 13d. Almira Twp. resident. G.A.R. Post 168.

Nathan W. Stephins Cpl. Co. H. 85th NY Inf.[285] Age 30. Enrolled Sept. 16, 1862. Suffolk VA, Franklin, Discharged for Disability April 23, 1863 at New Berne, NC. Listed in Green Briar / Almira Union Cemetery. G.A.R. Post 168.

Ruben E. Stetson Co. B. 164th NY Inf. Musician, Regt. Band. Unit: Suffolk VA, Dix's Peninsula Campaign, Rapidan, Spotsylvania Ct. Hs., North Anna River, Totopotomoy, Cold Harbor, Petersburg, Welden RR, James, Strawberry Plains, Hatcher's Run, Appomattox Campaign, Surrender of Lee and his Army, Grand Review at Washington D.C. (Part of the Corcoran Legion, they accidently left their flag behind at Fairfax Station when it was stolen during an assault by the Confederates from the quarters of Cpt. McAnally of the 155th NY who was holding it to give back to Colonel McMahon.)[286] Born Jan. 26, 1833 – Feb. 17, 1896. Lake Ann Cemetery (w/ newer marker, west of ~ 600 yr. old White Pine). Lake Ann G.A.R. Post 423 & Post 168.

Additional G.A.R. Post 168 Members:

R.H. Bishop U.S. Navy. Mississippi – Le Stenard.

Richard E. Deming Co. K. 1st WS Cavalry.[287] Entered Nov. 19, 1861.[288] Bloomfield MO, Guerrilla Campaigns, Greenville, West Plains, Mid.TN Campaigns, AL, Battle of Chickamauga, Missionary Ridge, East TN, Mossy Creek, Dandridge, Atlanta Campaign, Battle of Resaca, Kenesaw & Lost Mt., Louisville KY, Term expired and Mustered out Nov. 1, 1864. Unit went on to Nashville TN, Chickasaw AL, Capture of Jeff Davis. G.A.R. Post 168. (See Benjamin D. 4th MI)

George Dennis Co. B. 9th NY Cavalry. Unit History: Defenses of Washington D.C., Cedar Mt., Pope's Northern VA Campaign, Bull Run, Berryville, Brandy Station, Gettysburg, Rapidan, Mine Run Campaign, Battles of the Wilderness, Todd's Tavern, Spotsylvania where they were ordered to dismount by General Sheridan himself and attacked in heavy fighting,[289] James River, Yellow Tavern, Totopotomoy, Cold Harbor, Petersburg, Sheridan's Shenandoah Valley Campaign, Battle of Winchester, Woodstock Races, Cedar Creek, Appomattox Campaign, Surrender of Lee and his Army, Danville, Grand Review Washington D.C. G.A.R. Post 168.

James L. Green Co. H. 8th IN Inf.[290] Also listing under Co. A. 9th IN Inf. Mustered April 25, 1861 at Wayne Co. West VA Campaign, Clarksburg, Buckannon, Battle of Rich Mountain. Out Aug. 6, 1861. G.A.R. Post 168. & Kalkaska G.A.R. Post 313, Kingsley – Fife Lake.

William L. Green Co. H. 127th Reg. Vol. / 12th IN Cav.[291] Physician. January 12, 1864. Duty at Nashville TN, Big Cove Val. AL, Madison Co., Huntsville, Murfreesboro, Hillsboro, Vicksburg, Mobile. Discharged June 19, 1865. Listed in Leelanau Township 1894 Veteran's Census of Michigan. Elmwood area. Traverse City McPherson G.A.R. Post 18 & Post 168.

Robert Harritt New York Infantry.

Jerome Spaulding Co. H. 49th NY Inf.[292] Age 22. Defenses of Washington D.C., Wounded at Lee's Mills April 5, 1862. (Unit in 7 Days Battles). Discharged for wounds Oct. 11, 1862. Re-enlisted in Co. H. 8th NY L.A. Petersburg / Richmond Campaigns, Carolinas. Discharge for wounds July 28, 1865. G.A.R. Post 168 and G.A.R. Post 399. Lived in Kingsley, Grant Twp. Died Aug. 3, 1908 age 77. Listed in Oakwood Cemetery.

Anthony (Henry) Sychoff (Sythoff) Co. M. & Co. L. 5th NY Cavalry.[293] (1st Ira Harris Guard) Age 22. Enrolled from NY City. Mustered in Co. M. Transf. to Co.L. Operations in the Shenandoah Valley, Cedar Mt., Pope's Northern VA Campaigns, Groveton, Bull Run, Antietam, Discharged for Disability Oct. 8, 1862. G.A.R. Post 168.

Old Settlers Picnic ~ 1911
Believed to be Frank Payment - 76th NY, Jim Auton - MI L.A.,
William Beeman - 13th MI, Dr. Roswell Burke - 1st IN Cav.,
Moses C. Cate - 125th OH, John White - (of Ohio, perhaps served in 15th MI?),
& Abner Fritz - 1st MI Cav. (Courtesy Leelanau Historical Museum)

Murray G.A.R. Post # 168 of Maple City Glen Lake

This was originally formed at Empire, MI in 1883. Meetings were also held in Oviatt, Burdickville and Solon, though most were eventually at Maple City. The first Post Commander was John Dorsey of the 15th MI Infantry. Other Charter members were: Samuel Berry (1st Cal. Cav.) Post Adj't., George Cook (4th MI Inf.) Post Sgt. Mjr., Robert Day (11th MI), William Houghton (23rd MI) Post Quarter Master, Nathaniel C. King (2nd WS Cav.) Senior Vice Commander, David Knox (10 MI Cav.), H. Marvin LaCore (Navy-Portsmith) Post O.D., James McCormick (19th WS.) Post O.G., David McLaughlin (1st MI E&M), Robert H. Monroe (29th Ind.), Daniel Parker (15th MI), Joseph Price (1st IL), William E. Sheridan (16th NY H.A.) Post Chaplain, & George W. Stetson (10th MI Cav.) Post Jr.Vice Commander. In addition, George W. Slater was a Charter Petitioner. Grand Army of the Republic Post met "on or before the full moon of each month."

It was never made clear just who "Murray" actually was. The post was also referred to as the Murray Wagner Post 168, which may have referred to two individuals from the community. A possible connection is John T. Murray of Empire, MI who may have died around the time the post was formed and we find a match in Co. B. 158th NY Inf., or it may have been someone else who served in Michigan or another State.[294] Never the less, the name was important enough to be chosen by the mutual consent of the charter members.

From the Grand Army of the Republic, Department of Michigan: "On August 11th, 1883 in obedience to Special Order Department Headquarters, Comrade A.B. Carrier, Past A.A.G., proceeded to Empire, Mich., and there mustered in Murray Post, No. 168, J. Dorsey, Commander. Number of charter members, 15." At the Sixth Annual Encampment of the Department of Michigan G.A.R. held at Detroit, MI in January 1884 we see that M. LaCore is also representing the Post as a delegate and R.H. Monroe is listed as alternate. On Thursday, January 24th, the chief feature of the evening was a reception to Mrs. Geo. A. Custer, who was introduced by the chairman and was received with a tremendous volley of cheers and applause from the Michigan veterans. That spring, we find the Leelanau Enterprise mentioning Decoration Day being observed in Northport under the auspicious of the G.A.R. Post.

The seventh encampment was held in East Saginaw and by the time of the Eighth Annual Encampment held in Jackson in 1886 we find that M. LaCore was now Commander and the post was now reporting at Oviatt. That same Memorial Day the Post would record that they decorated 4 veteran's graves with 40 veterans and 1000 citizens involved in the ceremonies!

On Sept. 7, 1887 we find John Helm reporting from Burdickville as Post 168 Adjuct. that the Post was up to 47 members in good standing and the Headquarters were now at Maple City. An official Muster Roll of Murray Post 168 as of December 31, 1887 listed 46 members.

Aside from the internal reports, we find no more official reports in the Department of Michigan until 1897 at the Nineteenth Annual Encampment at Greenville where J.W. Dickerman is listed as a representative and Post 168 is then listed at Maple City. The post reported they decorated 18 graves during the 1896 Memorial Services with 1 member having died during the year and a concern that there were then 12 graves that were not

Murray G.A.R. Post correspondence included
Their original application, the Mustering list
From Empire, MI August 1, 1883, An 1887
Report signed by John Helm at Burdickville,
And an 1887 Muster Roll at Maple City.

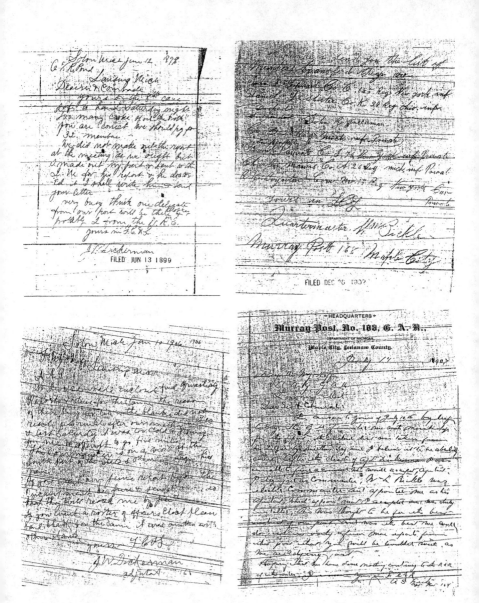

Murray G.A.R. Post correspondence included
Reports signed by J.W. Dickerman at Solon,
William Bickle at Maple City, and Abner Fritz.

properly marked. The orator on Memorial Day was L.H. Gage of Traverse City, MI. This same year we also see that Northport Post #399 decorated 7 graves with William Russel of Northport as orator. They noted 4 graves as not properly marked.

On June 12, 1898 J.W. Dickerman filed a report from Solon, MI where he mentioned that the Post was now at 32 members. Meanwhile, at the Twentieth Annual Encampment in 1898 we find Andrew Scott of Woolsey Post 399 listed as an Assistant Inspector. The next documentation found is not until December 26, 1902 where Quartermaster William Bickle writes about several membership transfers. By the time of the Twenty-fifth Annual Encampment in 1903 we see that Chester McIntyre of Post 168 is listed as an appointed Assistant Inspector. He is again listed for 1904 at Battle Creek.

The Twenty-seventh Annual Encampment of the Department of Michigan, Grand Army of the Republic was held June 20-21, 1905 at Traverse City, MI. It conveyed at 10 a.m. at the City Opera House. The encampment at Traverse City was practically opened on the evening prior to the official date, a reception having been tendered for that evening by the good people of the city and proved to be a foretaste of the good things which the large hearted people of Traverse City have planned for the enjoyment of their guests.

During the days which followed, there were excursions on the beautiful Traverse Bay, automobile rides about the city and along the beach, with carriage rides about the city and its environs. All of which evinced an unflagging determination on the part of the people of Traverse City to leave nothing undone which could in any way contribute to the pleasure or comfort of the representatives of the Grand Army of the Republic, convened in their city. It was written that no city of our State has opened its doors and hearts for the entertainment and comfort of the members of an encampment with more generous welcome and loyal devotion to the men who in the misty days of war, spared not themselves, if they might but contribute to the perpetuity of the Nation union.

Campfires were held during each evening of the encampments. No doubt this was a special time for all the area G.A.R. Posts especially McPherson Post 18 of Traverse City and we see listed that A.S. Fritz was Commander of Maple City G.A.R. Post 168 at this time. The official Delegate was M.C. Cate and the Past Commanders listed were H.A. Hannaford, N.W. Herrington, John Dago (Dechow), Wm. Bickle, and J.W. Dickerman.

The next year we find a letter dated January 10, 1906 from Adjutant J.W. Dickerman about Quarterly reports and for the Twenty-eighth Annual Encampment in Saginaw in 1906 we see that Abner S. Fritz is still Commander, Delegate is John Dago, Alternate is Louis Donner, and listed Past Commanders were Marvin La Core, A.S. Fritz, C.A. Hanneford, N.W. Herrington, Wm. Bickle, Chester McIntyre, and J.W. Dickerman. At Woolsey Post 399 we see that Wm. B. Green is Commander, Delegate is E.F. Rodgers, Alternate is John Thomas, and listed Past Commanders were Wm. H. Porter, I. Comstock, John Thomas, and John Scott.

For the Twenty-ninth Annual Encampment at Bay City in 1907 the positions for Post 168 remained similar (Harrington served as delegate & John Dago, listed as Dayo, as Alternate). Membership was at 25 veterans. Abner Fritz acting as Adjutant after the death of Adj. Dickerman completed a report dated July 14, 1907. William Bickle was then elected new Commander and Fritz remarks at the end of his report that "we are all dying fast."

The Thirtieth Encampment at Detroit would see Wm. L. Bickle listed as Commander of Post 168, Louis Donner as Delegate and D. McLaughlin as Alternate and the same listed Past Commanders. Membership was now at 18 veterans. The Woolsey Post 399 in Northport would again see Ishmeal Comstock as a Commander with Delegate Jacob B. Vanatter and Alternate James Mason. Past Commanders still being the same with 10 members in the Post.

The Thirty-first Encampment in Kalamazoo would list Bickle again as Commander and the same Past Commanders with no Delegates. Membership stood at 18 veterans. Post 399 again listed Commander Comstock with John Scott and John Thomas Delegate and Alternate and the same Past Commander listings. Membership stood at 10 veterans. The only change we see in the Thirty-second Encampment in Lansing is that W.H. Porter is now listed Commander for Post 399 and membership was at 8 veterans.

The Thirty-third Encampment in 1911 would report a large loss in Post 168. This was also one of its last official active years. Membership was now down to 9 veterans with Commander Bickle still listed, Delegate Abner Fritz and Alternate N.W. Harrington both listed. They were also included as Past Commanders. They also officially reported the death in Maple City on January 26, 1910 of John Helm who served in Co.F. 66th Ill. Infantry. Post 399 in Northport remained unchanged. For the Thirty-fourth Encampment we find Commander Bickle and Delegate Abner Fritz still listed. The same listings for Past Commanders and membership. Post 399 remained the same except John H. Thomas was listed as a Delegate, though a special mark was by his name.

The following years would see many smaller Posts joining up with the Traverse City McPherson Post 18. G.A.R. Post 168 is officially closed in 1913 with N.W. Harrington as the last Commander. A copy of the last report sent in by the Murray Post 168 of Maple City, MI was copied from the records in Lansing, MI Archives on June 9, 1968 by Roy H. Steffens.

To Wit,
Maple City, May 25, 1913
Assistant Adjutant general.
Dear Comrade:
Received reports and general order for Murray Post GAR Maple City No. 168. This is to inform you that we disbanded a month ago, the reason (was) our quartermaster is dead. Senior Vice and the Commander moved to Traverse City Oct. 4. Also, there are 3 or 4 more (who have) not attended the Post for 2 or 3 years, they are too old and used up. Commander Harrington said he would take all books and send them to you. I can not make out the orders for, I (have) no books. No Post, myself is the only one of Maple City G.A.R. left.
Wm. Bickle, former Adjutant of Murray Post GAR 168 (& Past Commander) Maple City, MI.

The Woosley Post 399 in Northport would still report at the Fortieth Annual Encampment in Saginaw in 1918. The Commander was still W.H. Porter with John Thomas and W.B. Green listed as Past Commanders and membership was down to 5 veterans. At the Forty-first Annual Encampment in 1919 Commander W.H. Porter and Past Commander John Thomas had a special mark by their name, indicating they may have passed away. Delegate was Thomas Haynes and W.B. Green was listed as a Past Commander. Membership was listed at 5 veterans though the Post finally closed up 2 years later.

(Courtesy Leelanau Historical Museum)

Murray G.A.R. Post 168 items of Moses C. Cate
(*Lowell Cate Collection* Courtesy Carol Drzewiecki)

Murray G.A.R. Post 168 of Glen Lake
(Courtesy Empire Area Museum)

Murray Post # 168 G.A.R. Membership Listings:

Gooding Adams Co. I. 1st MI Inf., William H. Amidon Sr. Co. B. 4th MI Cav. Cleveland(Kasson Cemetery), James U. Anton Bat.1st MI Art. & 9th Cav. (Buried in Rose Hill Cemetery)., William Bannon / (Brennon) Co. M. 10th MI Cavalry., John Becker Co. B. 64th NY Inf.(Bingham TS, Age 24, Served 8/20/1864-7/14/1865 Wash.D.C.), Samuel Berry Co. E. 1st Cal.(Buried in Rose Hill Cemetery)., William E.(or L.)Bickle Co. G. 3rd MI Inf Kasson TS.(Buried in Oakwood Cemetery), R.H. Bishop U.S. Navy, Ruel K. Boynton Co. M. 15th NY Cav. & 2nd NY Prov., Louis N. Brabant Co. B.&D. 1st Cav. & 5th WS Inf. (Also listed for Post 399)., William J. Buckingham Co. H. 11th NY Cav.(Leland area, Age 35.), Roswell W. (or O.) Burke Co. A. 1st Ind. H.A.(Kasson Cemetery), Sgt.Moses C. Cate Co. D. 125th OH Inf.(Solon TS.), Sgt. Frank B. Chatsey Co. K. 63rd OH Inf. (Rose Hill Cemetery)., George Cook Co. C. 4th MI Inf., J.F. Crain Co. C. 4th MI Inf. & 1st. (Wounded at Gettysburg), Sgt.William H. Crowell Co. B. 125th (or 123rd) OH Inf.(Age 24, 8/31/1862-Promoted5/12/1863)., John Dago Sr.Co. K./B. 26th MI Inf./Co. D. 14th Reg.Res. Cleveland TS.(Wounded at Spottsylvania), Samuel Daniels Co. F. 19th & 147th IN Inf., Wade B. Daniels Co.A 1st MI?SS, Robert S. Day Co. E. 11th MI Inf. (Empire resident, buried in Rose Hill Cemetery), Lewis Deman Co. K.(or H.) NY Inf.(Glen Arbor TS.), R.E. Deming Co. K. 1st WS Cav., George Dennis Co. B. 9th NY Cav., Miles A. Densmore Co. D. 13th MI Inf. (Buried in Maple City, Kasson Cemetery), Joseph W. Dickerman Co. 13 NH Inf., Justin B. (Doane) Donne Co. K. 19th MI Inf. (Wounded at Resaca,GA), George & Louis(Lewis)Donner Co. B/K 94th NY Inf.(Kasson TS.), Sgt. John Dorrington Co. C. 8th PA Res.(Entered 4/17/1861-Wounded in action, Surgeons Cert. 10/7/1862), John Dorsey see 15th MI Inf., David Dunn Co. I. 6th NY HA (& 13th NY Art. 6/27/1865-8/24/1865 at D.C.), Arnold Freeman Co. C. 5th U.S. Cavalry / 6th U.S. Colored Inf. (Listed in 6th Colored Inf. Co. C. in National Archives, unit served with Cavalry. Buried in East Kasson Evangelical Cemetery), Charles Franisco Co. A. 11th MI Inf., Abner S. Fritz Co. G. 1st MI Cav. (Bugler, disabled at Winchester, lived in Maple City, buried in Rose Hill Cemetery), James L. Green Co. H. 8th Ind. Inf. (Wayne Co. 4/25/1861-8/6/1861)., William L. Green Co. H. 127th Ind. Reg.or 128th(& 12th Ind. Cav. 1/12/1864-6/19/1865)., John R. Greenman Co. D. 20th MI Inf. (Rose Hill Cemetery)., Nathan P. Grover Co. D. 98th NY Inf., Fredrick Haines see 1st MI Inf., Robert Harritt NY Inf., Wensel/Vancella-Hyac/Highlick/Husick see 15th MI Inf., Samuel (Halsted/Hilsted) Holsted Co. C. 16th MI Inf. (Wounded in Action 1862)Centerville TS., Sgt. Charles A. Hannaford Co. I. 124th Ill. Inf.(Solon TS.), Nathaniel W. Harrington Co. B. 12th U.S. Inf. Kasson TS.(Buried in Oakwood Cemetery), John Helm Co. F. 16th Ill. Inf.(Empire TS.), Lafayette Henderson Co. H. & K. 59th OH Inf.(Kasson TS.), Sgt. Robert Hewitt Co. I. 92nd & 193rd NY Inf., Sgt. George H. Hill 11th KS Inf., William Houghton Co. G. 23rd MI Inf. (Rose Hill Cemetery)., Jacob (Jarschensky /Zerferski) Jazdewski Co. B. 9th WS Inf.(Centerville TS), Horace B. Johnson Co. B. 53rd PA Inf.(4/4/1864-6/30/1865), (Lovett/Loretto)L.A. Jenne Co. C. 186th NY Inf.(Age 27,Out 6/2/1865 Alex.VA 10 Months)., John Kehl (Kept)Co. A. 26th MI Inf. (Northport), William Freeman Kellog see 15th MI Inf., Alonzo Kenney Co. H. 11th MI Cav. (Kasson Cemetery), Sgt. Nathaniel C. King Co. A. 2nd WS Inf., Henry Kirchert see 15th MI Inf., David C. Knox see 10th MI Cav., Anthony Kucera see 15th MI Inf., John Kulenda see 15th MI Inf., Marvin(Marion) LaCore U.S. Navy., Joseph Laventure Co. G. Ill. Inf.(Centerville TS.), Peter Loucks 12th CT Inf.(Cleveland TS.), James McCormick 19th WS Inf. see summary, David McLaughlin Co. K. 1st MI Eng. & Mech. & 1st MI Inf. (Kasson Cemetery)., Stephen McGreer/McQueer Bat. A. 14th NY HA.(Solon TS.), Charles (Maus) Manns Co. A. 26th MI Inf. Centerville TS.(Wounded in action at Topopotomy Creek), Lansing C. Miller 4th WS Cav. see summary., Robert H.(or W.) Monroe Co. C. 29th Ind. Inf., Jeremiah Mowers Co. G. 22nd NY Cav.(Age 17, 2/13/1864-8/9/1865)., John B. Nash Co. I. 42nd Ill. Inf. (St. Rita's Cemetery-Maple City)., Oliver Neddo Co. F. 11th MI Cav. & 8th Cav. (Blacksmith ,Centerville TS), Daniel Parker see 15th MI Inf., Frank Payment Co. I. 76th NY Inf. (Rose Hill Cemetery)., Adonison J. Pratt Co. F. 106th NY Inf.(Age 21, 8/27/1862-Captured in action & parolled 4/29/1863 Fairm.VA, Out as Cpl.6/22/1865 at Wash.D.C.), Joseph P. Price Co. I. 1st Ill. Inf. (Kasson)see summary., Jonothan W. Russel see 10th MI Cav., Daniel Scott Co. B. 12th Ill.Inf. Age 26(5/2/1861-8/1/1861) and listed in 1st MI Colored Inf. Co.E.(7/25/1864-8/28/1865)., C.F.(or T.) Severance Co. E. 5th MI Cav., John J. Shepard Co. C. 186th NY Inf.(Age 32, 9/6/1864-6/2/1865Alex.VA)., Morris D. Shepard/Spafford Co. A. 2nd OH Cav. (Buried in Greenbriar Cemetery), William E. Sherdian 24th NY Inf. (see summary)., Daniel G. Shorter Co. K. 38th OH Inf.(Age 19, 9/1/1861-9/19/1864)., Philander P. Smith 24th WS(see summary)., Jerome Spaulding Co. H. 49th NY Inf. (Age 22, Wounded April 5, 1862 - Shiloh, Discharged for Wounds 11/11/1862, Re-enlisted in Co. H. 8th NY L.A. Discharged for Wounds July 28, 1865), Nathan W. Stephins Co. H. 85th NY Inf.(Age 30, 9/16/1862-Dis. for Disability 4/23/1863 New Berne,NC)., George W. Stetson see 10th MI Cav., Ruben E. Stetson Co. B. 164th NY Inf., James E.(or S.) Strickling Co. E. 126th Ill. Inf. Kasson TS.(Buried in Greenbriar Cemetery), Nathan Stricklin Co. A. 14th OH Inf. (Kasson Cemetery)., Anthony Sychoff (Sythoff) Co. L.&M. 5th MI Cav.(Age 22, Dis. for Disability 11/8/1862)., Charles B. Taylor Co. I. 5th MI Inf. (Wounded in action at Gettysburg July 1, 1863), John W. Van Nostrand see 15th MI Inf., Charles Webb Co. G. 15th Iowa & 6th Cav. (Kasson Cemetery)., Ruell R. Welch 127th Ill. Inf. see summary., & David Wright Co. K. MI Eng. & Mech.

167

Members of Woolsey Post, #399, Veterans of the Civil War. Top row: Ish Comstock, unknown, Fred Baumberger. Third row, 3rd from right: Payson Wolfe. 2nd row, 1st from left: Jake Vannetter. 2nd row, third from left: J.S. Middleton Front row, fourth from left: John Kehl; extreme right, John Thomas. ELDEN DAME COLLECTION

Woolsey G.A.R. Post 399 of Northport
(Courtesy Leelanau Historical Museum)

50th New York Engineers Commissary Department Petersburg, VA
(Library of Congress)
- See Ishmael Comstock (Northport G.A.R. 399) & Charles Comstock

Grand Army of the Republic G.A.R. Department of Michigan

Northport Woolsey Post # 399 Membership Roster included:[295]

James Arwonogefic (Arnowogzice/Aonegesic) Co. K. 1st MI Sharpshooters. Omena, went to Soldiers Home.

Gen./Col. Charles Barnes 9th PA Inf. & 6th PA Heavy Artillery (Wounded at Glendale & Bull Run, Brevet General). July 10, 1820 – July 12, 1896. Buried in Northport. (See Martin Barnes.)

Fredrick Baumbarger / Baumberger Co. E. 11th NY Inf.(Leelanau TS.). 1844-1911 Northport Cemetery near veteran **Robert T. Baumbarger.**

Wilhelm Bockstalher / Bockstaller (Bookstahles) Co. K. 3rd NY H.A.&L.A. Leland TS. (Buried in Good Harbor Lutheran Cemetery, Centerville).

Cpl. Simon /Samuel P. Boston/Borton Co. E. 64th NJ Inf. Aug. 1864 -Aug. 1865. (Suttons Bay / Centerville Twp.). ^ Gunshot foot wound.

Louis N. Brabant Co. B. 1st WS Cavalry.

John Bramer 15th MI Inf.

Kerr (Cornelius) Budd Co. A 15th MI Inf. (Leelanau TS.).

Thomas Chapman Navy USS Terror / Vermont. Omena, MI.

Sgt. Edgar S. Charter Co. E. 10th MI Cav. Leelanau TS. & 19th MI Cav. Died in 1911.

Edgar E. (or F.) **Chase** Co. E. 3rd MN Inf. [296] Had been a Sailor. Was captured by the Confederates as a spy, and was saved by hanging and helped to escape by a friendly guard. Owned large homestead known as the "Ranch."[297] Wounded in Battle of Murfreesboro by a Sabre cut. Born in Ohio Jan. 1, 1832 - Died Jan. 11, 1911. Buried in Oakwood Cemetery. Had also been in Post 168. (See Ira & Oscar Chase 10th MI Cavalry.)

Ishmael Comstock Co. D. 50th NY Eng. 1843 – 1929. Northport Cemetery.

Sgt. Fredrick Cook Co. A. 26th MI Inf. (Buried at Leland).

Noel Coutourier Co. H. Headquarters Troop. Died Nov. 24, 1903. Age 68. St. Mary's Cem. Lake Leelanau.

George E. Dame Co. I. 134th Ill. Inf. / Co. A. 147th Ill. Northport Cemetery.

Robert F. (or A.) De Golier/Golin Co. E. 58th PA Inf. Leelanau Twp./Northport, Pensioned for Liver. Had been in Post 168. Moved to Colorado in 1895.(Others from area went to Gladstone, North Dakota.). Said to be buried back in Northport?

Philip Easternight Co. A. 15th MI Inf. (Leelanau Twp.).

Alphonso Emeroy Co. G. 37th Ill. Inf. Leelanau Twp. (Wounded in left arm at Pea Ridge). Northport Cem.

Alexander Fall Co. D. 2nd St. Louis Militia.

William B. Green Co. D. 128th Ind. Inf. (Leelanau Twp./Northport), Farmer & Horse Doctor.

Thomas Haynes Bat. H. 1st MI L.A.

David Hollinger Co. K. 26th Inf. (Buried at Leland).

John Howell Co. B. 15th MI Inf.(Leelanau TS.).

Dr. Stephen James Hutchinson Co. K. 105th Ohio Inf. Leelanau Township, Northport Cemetery. A transcipt of Dr. Hutchinson's Civil War letters are in the archives of the Leelanau Historical Museum. They tell of his battles (Chaplin Heights, Milton, Hoover Gap, Chickamauga, etc.) and how, after the Battle of Lookout Mt. TN, he lay on the ground outside the hospital and prayed under the stars for peace. (also listed in 1st NY L.A.) July 3, 1830 – Aug. 11, 1911. (Also recorded as died of Pnemonia June 1901?) Northport Cemetery. (George Hutchinson of Ohio had served about three months in the 8th NY Cavalry at the age of 12.)

2nd Lt. George J. Kaebs Co. F. 169th OH.

John Kehl Co. A. 26th Inf.Leelanau TS. (From France). Also in G.A.R. Post 168.

Byron O. Leslie Co. B. 169th OH Nat.G. (Leelanau Twp.), Carpenter. Died in 1901. Northport Cemetery. See Elmwood Twp.

Col. / Capt./ Sgt. Daniel S. Leslie Co. F. 41st OH Inf. (Wounded at Shiloh), Was a veteran of the **Mexican War.** Had twelve children. Northport Cemetery. Died of Dropsy in the summer of 1901

James Mason US Navy "Juliet?" (Leland Twp.) Feb. 28, 1846 – Feb. 6, 1916. St. Mary's Lake Leelanau Cemetery, See 1st MI L.A. / (Marion)

Joshua S. Middleton Co. A. 26th MI Inf.Leelanau Twp. (Wounded at the Battle of the Wilderness).

Encampment of Leelanau County Civil War Veterans.
(Courtesy Leelanau Historical Museum)

Civil War Veterans of the Grand Traverse Region
(Grand Traverse Pioneer & Historical Society)

Woolsey Post # 399 Continued:

William P. Newton Co. K. 1st MI Sharpshooters (Indian).

Napoleon Paulus Co. B. 15th MI Inf. Leland Twp.(Wounded April 12, 1865).

William H. Porter Co. D. 12th WS Inf. Musician. (Leelanau Twp.). Northport Cemetery. Had been a Post Commander.

Albert W. Powers Co. G. 1st NY Light Artillery. Musician. Had once been listed as killed in the Battle of Shiloh. 1847-1918. Petersen Cem./Northport Cemetery Voice family lot. (J.F. Powers of the 68th OH was in the Traverse McPherson G.A.R. Post 18 and soldier John Powers, Father-in-law to Rev. Geo. Smith, was a War of 1812 Veteran buried in the Northport Cemetery.)

Joseph Prickett / Percket Co. L. 3rd MI Cav.Leelanau Twp. (Indian).

Sgt. Edward F. Rodgers Co. D. 1st MI Sharpshooters (Leelanau Twp.) Died Nov. 1, 1906.

Aron Sargarnargeeton Co. K. 1st MI Sharpshooters.

Andrew & John Scott Co. F. 15th MI Inf. (Leelanau Twp.).

Frank Shaubut Co. E. 9th MN Inf. (Indian).

Jerome Spaulding Co. H. 49th NY Inf. & 8th Artillery (Wounded in Battle). Also G.A.R. Post 168.

Edmund J. Stebbins Co. K./F. 104th NY Inf. [298] (Leelanau Twp.), Had farm off Co.Rd. 631. Northport Cem.

Edmund P. Taylor Co. D. 10th Ill. Cav.[299]or IN (Leelanau Twp.). Listed as a 32 year old from Pennsylvania in the pre-war 1860 Census of Leelanau Township with 5 children. Died Dec. 7, 1901. Age 72. Northport Cemetery. (See photograph.)

John H. Thomas Co. I. 1st MI Sharpshooters Wounded in Battle of Wilderness[300] (Leelanau Twp.).

Henry D. (or A.) Thompson Co. D. 29th OH Inf. (Bingham Twp.). (See Orville Thompson Glen Arbor/Empire area.)

Jacob R. (B. VanNatter) Vannetta/er Co. H. PA Vol. 46th PA Inf.(Leelanau Twp.), Northport Cemetery. Lived into the 1930's and was the last surviving member of the Post.

Sgt. Edward P. Van Valkenberg Co. E. 10th MI Cav. / I. 1st MI Eng.?

Simeon Williams Co. G. 78th & 102 NY Inf. of Omena (Wounded in action at Chancellorsville & others).[301] Also was in Traverse City McPherson G.A.R. Post 18. 1844-1925 Oakwood Cemetery. (See Chas. Williams of Leelanau Twp.)

Payson Wolfe Co. K. 1st MI Sharpshooters (Buried by Petoskey, MI).

Additional Area Veterans Listed in Veteran Census, Cemetery Listings, or associated at one time with Leelanau County Townships or Surrounding Areas that served outside of Michigan:[302]

Bingam: (Area founded by C.S. Darrow. Though Twp. formally chartered after the War, draftees were still listed under this as a Twp.).

John (Jonathan) M. Akers Co.A./I. 47th OH Inf. Buried in Oakwood Cemetery.

Frederick (Luplon) Luplow Co. F. 65th Ill. Inf. (Wounded Forearm). Oakwood Cemetery.

S.H.Roosa.

Charles D. Shepard Bat.M. 2nd NY H.A. (See John J. Shepard in G.A.R. Post 168, also Byron S. in 8th MI Cav., Fred M. in 110th NY Wagoner)

Emmet Whitney

Draftees who may have served in another State, used an assumed name, were excused, or had a substitute: Cashmere Deerwood, John Smith, William Sweet.[303]

also see Suttons Bay: Bingham Township Cemetery listings.

Old Settlers are pictured in this rare photograph taken in Northport. Those identified are: sitting next to the post on the left side, Mrs. George N. Smith. In front of Mrs. Smith, Hoyt Spencer. Right of post, sitting on edge of porch: E. Stebbins, Wm. McMacken, John P. Howell. From right to left, ladies on right side of post: Mrs. Otis White, Mrs. Voice, Mrs. J. Howell, Mrs. Stebbins. Back row, right of post from left to right: Charles Kennedy, Otis White, John Scott, two unidentified, Capt. Peter Nelson, R.A. Campbell, Mrs. Wilson. EDDINSMORE COLLECTION

Insert of several Civil War Veterans with Northport area settlers
from "A History of LeelanauTownship" (Courtesy Leelanau Historical Museum)

Fred Baumberger. FAYE DINSMORE COLLECTION

Edmond P. Taylor. COURTESY LORI GRIFFIN

Insert of: Fred Baumberger
11ᵗʰ NY Infantry,
"A History of Leelanau Township"
(Courtesy Leelanau Historical Museum)

Insert of: Edmond P. Taylor
10ᵗʰ IL Cavalry, from "A History
of LeelanauTownship" (Courtesy
Leelanau Historical Museum)

Stephen James Hutchinson,M.D.,Northport,Michigan

In 1866, the doctor wrote his old regiment as follows:
"Comrades of the Grand Old 105th Regiment,Ohio, for the
years during the war when we joined hands, heads, and hearts
to champion the cause of Union and Freedom in this Republic,
as further still of freedom and union for the whole world;Co-
smic union for the whole world as the key to the millenium
for which we must all pray."
   "During that time which tried mens' souls we proved to all
rebels, to all who held to the sentiment of secession and the
practice of rebellion, the philosophical and principle that
unity is strength and their arithmetical or mathematical exiom
that the whole is greater than a part and inversely that a part
is less than the whole, This we sum up as the actual solution
of this great problem - the weakness of secession and dis-union
as compared with the solidarity and safety of the union. Divide-
ed we fall, united we stand. We as unionists, fighting for the
integrity of our common country, helped to save this Great Republic as a model object lesson and great exemplar for the whole
world and for all time to come; cementing it into a great and
indissoluable nation. Consolidated and cemented as its birth-
right. "Freedom and Union Forever" was our battle cry, and nobly
ringing down through the ages; while into our lives we illustrate
and proved the positive side of the truism."

                    "United We Stand"

                    S.J.Hutchinson,M.D.
                    Volunteer Soldier from Columbia
                    University,Physicians and Surgeons,
                    New York City, 1866

Dr. Stephen J. Hutchinson 105ᵗʰ Ohio Volunteer Infantry
(Transcripts by Martin A. Melkild, in the Leelanau Historical Museum)

MR. AND MRS. JOHN R. FOUCH.

(Insert from the Traverse Region
Historic & Descriptive 602-603)

*Samuel and Margaret McClelland in a pre-Civil War
photograph. COURTESY MARY RUSSELL*

Insert of: **Samuel McClelland &
Wife 1st NY L.A.** from "A
History of LeelanauTownship"
(Courtesy Leelanau Historical Museum)

UNCLE DAN WHIPPLE.

(Insert from Sprague's History 797)

Centerville:

Samuel Anderson Co.E. 143rd OH

Phillip Egler (Egeler) Listed at age 11 in the pre-war 1860 Census of Leelanau Township and reported in the "Grand Traverse Herald" as enlisting late in the war.

Charles F. Egler (Egeler) also listed as a Draftee.

Charles A. Lee Bat. C./G. 1st NY L.A.(Listed age 20 in the pre-war 1860 Census of Centerville Twp.).

Thomas Lee Co.G. 1st NY L.A. .(Listed Farmer age 50 in the pre-war 1860 Census of Centerville Twp.).

Sgt. Benjamin Minsker Co. D. 76th PA Inf. Oct. 28, 1861 – July 18, 1865 Lived in Good Harbor, Pensioned for Gunshot wound left heel. 1846 – 1934. Buried in Beechwood Cemetery, Leland Twp.

Joseph (James) L. Manseau U.S. Navy "Potomac," (Listed from Wisconsin in the pre-war 1860 Census with the Antoine Manseau family.) Later lived in Manistee, MI.[304]

Dick Schomberg of Good Harbor, attended 1892 G.A.R. encampment with Sid Rodgers in Washington.

Leonard (Livert) Soper Co.M. 3rd WS Cavalry.

Sidney Rodgers of Good Harbor, attended 1892 G.A.R. encampment with Dick Schomberg in Washington.[305]

Centerville Draftees who may have served in another State, used an assumed name, were excused, or had a substitute: S. Anderson (See Gustaff 10th MI Cav.), Carter Bardenhagues, Walter W. Barton, John (Baser) Boser (Was also under Elmwood Township), Sidney Brooks, Almer M. DeBelloy, John Degemoolk, John Hodnek, Mathias Keller, John D. Kilroy, Edward Kimorer, Exavier Larague (LaRue?), Francis Leroy (See Charles 3rd MI Inf.), Maurice Nolan, Ralph Pyvas, Matthias Steige, Leonard F. Swift.[306]

Elmwood:

Porter Belknap NY Militia.

Charles A. Cole 103rd OH (Wounded in Battle of Resaca.) T.C. G.A.R. Post 18. Oakwood Cemetery.

H.B. Connine Co.C. 13th IN Infantry in Oakwood Cemetery.

Maj. John Dalzell Co. B. 5th OH Vol. Cav. McLaughlin's Squadron. G.A.R. Post 18.Oakwood Cemetery.

John R. Fouch (Foutch/Vogt) 169th OH[307] Served at the age of 19 with several of his cousins by the name of Overmyer who were related ancestors of the Author of this book. Cousin Joseph Fought was Gen. Custer's Bugler in the 5th U.S. Cavalry. (See Byron Leslie & John Thacker.)

Frank Hoxie 106th NY, Wm. Hoxie.

Fred Moses Jewett 21st Maine. Co.F. July 24, 1845 – Oct. 7, 1912. Oakwood Cemetery.

Addison E. Kilpatrick 58th PA, Traverse City McPherson G.A.R. Post 18.

Vincent Meahann (Neason)17th WS. (Also Co.C. 17th MO/MI/Inf.?) Died Oct. 29, 1906 Age 73 Oakwood Cem.

Capt. John B. Muller.

James L. Murray Bat. E. 1st Ill. L.A. 1842-May 6, 1904. Traverse City McPherson G.A.R. Post 18.

Lyman B. Snow Co. A. 7th MN. 1825-1913 Oakwood Cemetery.

John B. Thacker Co. B. 169th OH. Fouch Cemetery. (See John Fouch & Byron Leslie.)

Wallace W. Walker 2nd OH Artillery. (See Dr. William Walker of Glen Arbor.)

Howard (Harlan)P. Weller 2nd OH Artillery.,

Wallace W. Weller.

(Uncle) **Daniel Whipple** 1st Iowa Regiment & listed Co.B. 124th Ill. Inf. Also served in **War of 1812** (Died in 1908 at the age of 108 years old).,[308] Oakwood Cemetery G.A.R. Lot.

Frank Whitney Co. D. 67th OH. Born in 1847.

Elmwood Draftees who may have served in another State, used an assumed name, were excused, or had a substitute: Benjamin Brown, Herman Hulbert, Elias McCoy, Frederick Noak.[309]

The Grand Traverse Herald.

MORGAN BATES, Editor and Proprietor.

TRAVERSE CITY:

FRIDAY MORNING, AUGUST 15, 1862.

A Patriotic Supervisor.

Timber Seizures—Decision of the Supreme Court.

The Federal Licenses Due on the First of August.

LETTER FROM LIEUT. McCLELLAND.

Citizens Forbidden to go out of the United States.

WASHINGTON, Aug. 8.

From McClellan's Army.

THE NEW POLICY OF THE WAR.

WAR BULLETIN.

WASHINGTON, August 8, 1862.

EDWIN M. STANTON,
Secretary of War.

WAR DEPARTMENT.

Secretary of War.

WASHINGTON, August 11.

Leelanau:

(See information on General **Custer** & General **Grierson** listed prior to the 6th MI Cavalry.)

Martin V. Barnes (Brown) Co.G.&E.1st NY L.A. (Listed as a 19 year old School Teacher in the pre-war 1860 Census of Leelanau Township), Eventually moved to Petoskey.

John J. Blanchard Co. G. 21st OH Inf. & 1st OH L.A. Born in NY, lived in Omena. G.A.R. Post 18.

Charles Comstock 50th NY Eng. (See Ishmael Post 399.)

Alex B. Dahlmer U.S. Navy "City of New York."

Thomas Davidson Co.C. 45th U.S. Vet. Inf. (Northport Cemetery).

Willard Heath. 10th NY L.A./ 19th NY L.A. Mar.15, 1834-Aug. 1910 Age 76 Oakwood Cemetery.

Frank May Bat. C. 1st NY L.A.

Capt. Samuel A. Mc Clelland Bat. G. 1st NY L.A. (Wounded at Malvern Hill). Letter featured in August of 1862 Grand Traverse Herald of action before Savage Station, Fair Oaks, and Melvern Hill from June.

Thomas E.H. McLean Co.F. 137th OH. 1833 – 1903. Omena Cemetery.

William H. McLean 76th PA Inf.

Jesse Morgan U.S. Federal Army of the Potomac. (Listed as a 30 year old Farmer from Vermont in the pre-war 1860 Census of Leelanau Township with 2 young children.) Died of camp fever during the campaign at Old Town Landing, AK in 1864. (See Morgan's in 10th MI Cav. & 15th MI Inf.)

Theodor Nelson Co. C. 45th U.S. Vet. Inf. Northport Cemetery. (See William Nelson 11th MI Inf.)

Aaron B. Page Co. G. 1st NY L.A. & also under Chicago Lt. Inf. Enlisted Sept. 20, 1861. (Listed as a 30 year old School Teacher in the pre-war 1860 Census of Leelanau Township with a young son. See Daniel 2nd CT H.A.)

Joseph Ritter.

Daniel B. Roberts.

Sgt. Ferris Rose Co. L. 2nd NY Mounted Raiders (Wounded in action).

Peter Shawandasse in Onominee Indian Cemetery. Said to have served in 3rd Regt. Cav. **War of 1812.**

Louis Shawandasse in Onominee Indian Cemetery. Civil War Vet. SS? Had been taken prisoner & released.

Lewis Steele Co.G. 1st NY L.A. Died June 16, 1886. Age 49. Northport Cemetery.

William E. Sykes Co.G. 1st NY L.A. Sheriff. (Listed as a 44 year old Hotel Keeper from New York in the pre-war 1860 Census of Leelanau Township with 2 children.) Northport. Died from wounds at Spotsylvania.

Chas. Williams (See Simeon Williams in G.A.R. Post 399 listing).

Leelanau Twp. Draftees who may have served in another State, used aa assumed name, were excused, or had a substitute: Almon J. Beers, H.L. (Hong)Hoag, Francis Leroy, Daniel McTaggart, William Putt, Eli Tolluse, Allen Wilbur[310]

Leland:

Henry Alpers.

Claus Kahrs Co. D. 69th Missouri Militia Home Guards. East Leland Cemetery.

Heinrich / Henry Steffens Co. B. Benton Co.Missouri Vol. Home Guards. April 2, 1840 – Oct. 31, 1890. East Leland Cemetery.

Claus Warner (Clouve Warren) U.S. Navy Missouri Vol. "Red Rover & Ozark." 1845 – 1930. Suttons Bay Twp / St. Michael's Cemetery.

Suttonsbay: (named after H.C. Sutton) –

John Bennets Navy "Neptune."

Hiram M. Gillman Co. D. 1st NY Dragoons (& Leland Twp.).

Sgt. George J. Leeney (Leaney)Co. E. 10th NY Artillery.

John Litney Co. D. 3rd WS Cav. (Buried in Oakwood Cemetery).

Solomon H. Trude Co. C. 35th NY Vol. Inf. Discharged for Disability. Traverse City McPherson G.A.R. Post 18. (Aug. 27, 1838 – Jan. 4, 1908. Buried in Bingham Cemetery).

Jesse O. Tuttle (Buried in Bingham Cemetery).

Smith A. Whitfield.

Daniel Whipple
(Grand Traverse Pioneer & Historical Society)
Featured in "Heritage of Grand Traverse Bay:
The City and Its People" by Donna S. Bollinger

Leelanau Enterprise.

J. O. NELSON, Pub. LELAND, LEELANAU CO., MICHIGAN, THURSDAY, JULY 11, 1889. VOL. XII.—NO. 35.

THE ENTERPRISE,

OFFICIAL PAPER FOR LEELANAU COUNTY.

Published every Thursday at
LELAND, MICHIGAN.

Terms, $1.00 per Year.

BUSINESS CARDS.

DR. G. A. HAMMOND, Dentist, Traverse City, Michigan. Office at his old room over Ashton and Kneeland's Office.

M. A. KNEELAND—Attorney at Law and Solicitor in Chancery, Notary Public, Collections. Conveyancing, Insurance, Loans.
Suttons Bay, Mich.

PRATT & DAVIS—Attorneys at Law. Will attend the circuit courts in the several counties of the 10th Traverse region. Office cor. Front and Union sts, Traverse City, Mich.

W. O. GREENE, Surveyor, will give prompt attention to all orders in that line of business.
Omena, Leelanau Co., Mich., April 27th 1883.

W. M. GILL—Dealer in dry goods, groceries, boots and shoes, furniture, pure drugs and medicines. Northport.

FRANK JOHNSON—Blacksmith, carriage and wagon maker, Northport, Mich.

J. L. ASHTON—Attorney at Law; Visalized title for the painless extraction of teeth, entirely painless; satisfaction guaranteed. Office in Moffatt's Building, Traverse City, Michigan.

J. SUTTLER, surveyor, land looker and all other estimation. All business attended to promptly.
Frankfort, Mich.

J. A. WHITNEY, Attorney at law, and solicitor in Chancery. All legal work attended to with dispatch.
Frankfort, Mich.

VM. P. KEARNS, L. L. B., Attorney and Counselor Wills, Deeds, Mortgages, Contracts and Leases drawn. Collections made. Titles perfected.
LELAND, MICH.

WARNER HOUSE,
—OF—
Leland, Mich.

Claus M. Warner, Proprietor.

Good board with rooms by the day or week at reasonable rates. Also, single meals at any time. Our house is pleasantly situated, fine lawn for swing croquet; and those wishing to enjoy fishing will be furnished with boats, fishing tackle, &c.

Cummings House
LELAND, MICH.
B. B. ELLIS, PROPRIETOR.

Pleasantly located on the shore of Carp Lake. A place where summer tourists can enjoy the finest fishing in northern Michigan. Boats and fishing tackle to let.

Union Hotel
Suttons Bay Mich.
J. C. ANDERSON Prop'r.

This House is delightfully situated fronting the Bay are it enjoys the cool breezes at all times. Located in the midst of the fine drawn-trout fishing region in Northern Michigan.

Clarendon House,
LELAND, Mich.

ROBERT BROWN Proprietor.

Good accommodations are afforded at this house, and boarders by the day or week are solicited.

E. W. HASTINGS,
GENERAL MUSIC DEALER.

Palace
Estey } Organs.
Kimball

ONLY $60. $75. $85 to $150.
E. W. HASTINGS,
Traverse City.

Provemont House
This house is pleasantly located at "The Narrows" of Carp lake—the most

THE FIRST
National Bank
—OF—
Traverse City, Mich.

Paid in capital $50,000. Authorized capital $200,000.

LOANS AND COLLECTIONS MADE AND A GENERAL BANKING BUSINESS TRANSACTED. A MODERATE INTEREST ALLOWED ON TIME DEPOSITS.

DIRECTORS

Jno. G. eele, Jno. T. Beadle, W. S. Johnson, Hon. D. C. Leach, E. J. Morgan, Frank Hamilton, C. A. Hammond.

Leelanau Locals.

—Beautiful weather for haying.

—Fishing in Carp Lake is No. 1.

—Mr. Quaife, of Chicago, is at the Warner House.

—Everything passed off quietly on the 4th at Leland.

—We had a pleasant call from Mr. Larue, of Empire on Monday last.

—Dr. Sifton, of Suttons Bay has been in town for the last two days.

—Mr. Brezina and Miss Mary Zeitz, of Traverse City, was in town this week.

—The teachers institute of Leelanau County will be held at Maple City commencing August 5th.

—Mrs. J. E. Lewis, of St. Louis is at the Warner House, en-route to the North Manitou Island.

Mr. Densmore, school superintendent and Mr. Savage, teacher, of Northport, were in town on Sunday.

—We noticed on board the Charlevoix this morning, S. S. Burke, manager of the Northern Michigan Line.

—Steamer City of Charlevoix, called here this morning with six passengers and some merchandise for our merchants.

—Schooner Bauer, took her hold full of wood for Grobben & Gill, and a deck load of bark, for W. S. Johnson & Co. Milwaukee.

—Dr. Herdman, of Ann Arbor arrived at this place yesterday. He is on professional business. He expects to leave for home to-day.

—The dance held at Brow's hall on the evening of the Fourth was a grand success. Music was furnished by the Paulus Sisters which was very fine.

—The Toledo and Northern Michigan R. R. authorities say that great multitudes of people are going north. This is on account of the very warm weather.

On Thursday evening as the party was going along very quietly at A. & O. Brow's hall, some of the boys indulged in throwing firecrackers in through windows. After being warned several times to leave the premises, and not seeming to recognize the warning, one of them delib-

County Correspondence.

Good Harbor,
July 7th 1889.

Rather damp haying weather.

Fine cord weather the first part of the week.

The J. V. Jones a part cargo of Tan bark.

Our merchants are offering $4.50 for tanbark.

Born to Mr. and Jacob Hansen, a little girl, much joy to the parents.

J. J. Kilwy's Champion Mower was the first in the field this season.

Our teacher, Miss Bragdon expects to spend the 4th with her folks at Glen Arbor.

Miss Schomberg of Milwaukee is visiting at her brother, Henry Schomberg.

The Hattie B. Perue was loaded with hardwood lumber by the L. L. Co. for Chicago markets.

Two of our people made a flying trip to Empire last week and Oh! how they fell in love with the place.

Two farmers from the North Manitou called at Good Harbor, looking for young stock that does not chew its cud.

J. J. Kilwy will give these 18 and 20 year old kids 5 lb of stick candy if they will return the tools they found in his mower box and not say a word about it.

Bingham.

C. Melosky will set "em up" it is a boy.

Ed Beck is building a new house. So is H. F. McFall.

Dan Baker has his new house enclosed and has moved in.

John Larkins bought another four hundred dollar team last week.

Ed Ashton, of Traverse City, had a splendid run after fish Saturday last.

Ed. Weese had seventeen sheep killed by dogs recently. Kill the dogs.

J. Larkins is landing on an average of about two vessels a week with lumber.

The night run at Larkins Mill has stopped and the mill will run daytime the balance of the year.

John Ansor our Hotel keeper, is building a new boat house and two new boats, for the accomodation of his guests, fishing is good in Carp Lake.

We think there should be more copies of the ENTERPRISE taken here than there is. The way to build up a new county, is to patronize home institutions.

Capt. Hankstead with the jolly Julia Driscoe, took a jolly crowd of fifty eight a few evenings since down to the Narrows and all report a

Northport.

Cherries are ripening.

Trolling is played out.

Dennis Hoxie went home for the 4th.

Misses Myrta and Gertie Ross are at Omena.

Deacon McMackin is not a success as a sprinter.

Miss Cynthia Keyes spent the 4th with friends here.

It is possible that the town hall will be built this year.

Chas. Savage and A. E. Densmore were here last Saturday.

Dick Thomas has added a span of colts to his livery outfit.

A. B. Fenton and family are boarding with H. R. Hitchcock.

The Camp of Sons of Veterans is constantly receiving recruits.

Geo. Brown wants to bet that he can beat "Sebe" Dame running.

Will Thomas has not parted company with his rheumatism altogether.

Haying is in full blast, and the crop promises to be an unusual good one.

Miss Gertie Blacken came down from the Mission to spend the 4th at home.

A. B. Fenton and family attended the opening of the Fountain Point House.

Miss Alice Nelson is entertaining her friend Miss Anna Coulter of Williamsburg.

Miss Eaton and Miss Carrie Belknap, of Grand Rapids, are summering at E. E. Chase's.

Byron Woolsey and Jack Howell settled their cow difficulty without letting it come to a trial.

A trio of fisherman brought 90 speckled trout and half a bushel of bull heads, to town last Saturday.

The notice for prospective business change in the ENTERPRISE of last week, was a surprise to most folks.

Mrs. W. H. Porter has returned from the visit to Ludington. She was accompanied by her daughter Mrs. M. D. Leslie.

Mrs. Nelson who has been spending some time with her aunt Mrs. W. H. Porter, will soon return to her home on Washington Island.

D. S. Leslie has purchased a farm near Missionary Ridge Tenn., and will move his family there as soon as the weather gets a little cooler.

A little more filling in around the M. E. Church and some shade trees around the school house would improve the appearance of the hill.

There is a scarcity of dwelling houses in Northport, every house in town is occupied, and many contain two and three families. This certainly indicates a prosperous town.

A swarm of bees belonging to W. B. Green left their live the other day and took up their residence, in the woods near Ed Charter's place. Ed says there was no bees after him when he won the race.

Mrs. Golden, of Old Mission is visiting at the home of Capt. J. U. Emory. There is also a young boy visiting there, and Mr. and Mrs. Emory both like him so well they think they will keep him. Capt. Emory was called here on Saturday by the serious illness of Mrs. Emory. At last accounts she was improving and is now thought to be out of danger.

The Fourth of July celebration in Maple Grove was a pronounced success and was attended by about all of Northport and Omena, and a large part of Leland. Refreshments of the ham sandwich and ice cream were served from the G. A. R. booth and music, soul stirring and patriotic, was discoursed by the brass band. One interesting feature of the day was a donation of $27 to the band's uniform fund. It was not really a donation either, as the boys earned the money. The G. A. R. Post took in about $80, and the dancing floor also yielded a fair harvest. The ball game was rather tender, but the foot racing took the cake. The most exciting race was the one for old men, in which the starters were William McMackin, Ed Charter and Sebe Dame. All got away well together with heads and tails up, early in the race McMackin cast a shoe and was distanced while Charter had a safe lead. Dame hurt his chances of winning by spending too much time in a frantic effort to clutch Charter's coat tails in a vain endeavor to hold him back.

It is fast becoming a leading business of this country, and that together with wine making requires years of practice. Mr. Speer, of New Jersey one of the largest producers in the East, commenced years ago in a small way to make wine from currants, blackberries and other fruits. He soon turned his attention to grape raising and planted large vineyards of the Portugal wines from which his famous Port Grape Wine and unfermented Grape Juice is made which chemists and Physicians use as rivals the world for its beneficial effects on weakly or aged persons.

Brace Up.

If you are feeling depressed, your appetite is poor, you are bothered with Headache, you are fidgety, nervous and generally out of sorts, and want to brace up. Brace up, but not with stimulants, spring medicines, or bitters, which have for their basis very cheap, bad whisky, and which stimulate you for an hour, and then leave you in worse condition than before. What you want is an alternative that will purify your blood, start healthy action of Liver and Kidneys, restore your vitality, and give renewed health and strength. Such a medicine you will find in Electric Bitters, and only 50 cents a bottle at drug store of L. J. Grubbens, Leland, H. & J. Dexter, Suttons Bay and Wm. Gill, Northport.

Agents Wanted For The Book

JOHNSTOWN

Northern Almira or Long Lake Township, Benzie Co. Veterans who served in other States.

John J. Atkinson Co. I. 9th NY Cav. Mar. 2, 1841-Jan. 13, 1913. Cedar Run, Linwood/Neal Cemetery. Lot 10-A Unmarked Veteran. Lake Ann, Andrew Clark G.A.R. Post 423.

T.P. Barber Co. B. 3rd OH Cavalry. Lake Ann, Andrew Clark G.A.R. Post 423.

Thomas Brooks 1833-1900 Green Briar (Almira Union) Cemetery. (See Brooks 10th MI Cav. & Inf.)

Orien C. Case (Chase) Gunboat "Sirene" Past Commander of Lake Ann Post 423. Was from Elk Rapids. 1844-Feb. 5, 1909 Linwood/Neal Cemetery, Unmarked as Veteran.

Calvin Conklin listed in Long Lake in 1894 Veterans Census.

Thomas Cooper U.S. Navy "Vindicator" Lake Ann, Andrew Clark G.A.R. Post 423.

Wm. (Wiley) A. Corbit Co. H. 152nd Ohio Died July 4, 1903 Age 68 Linwood/Neal Cemetery.

Robert Crawford Co. G. 4th PA Cavalry. Lake Ann, Andrew Clark G.A.R. Post 423.

A.S. Dobson Co.D.124th Ill./Co.G.34th&55th IN Inf.Long Lake.Died July 14, 1922 Age 80. Oakwood Cem.

Strata Elijah Co. H. 6th NJ H.A. Long Lake Twp. Traverse City McPherson G.A.R. Post 18.

William Elmer Co. K. 157th NY Vol. Inf. Unit at Chancellorsville, Battle of Gettysburg, Carolinas, Trans. to 54th NY: Duty in SC. Buried in Almira Union / Green Briar Cemetery.

Josiah Gray Co. E. 106th NY Inf. Killed in action. Family in Long Lake area.

Ed S. Harvey Veterans Marker in Green Briar (Almira Union) Cemetery.

Edwin Collins Lake Co. F. Vermont Inf. Post 423. G.A.R. Marker in Lake Ann Cemetery.

Elihu Linkletter Co. A. 179th NY Suffered gunshot wound. Lake Ann, Andrew Clark G.A.R. Post 423.

Wm (Lucian W.) Lyon Co. F. 31st Maine Inf. Interlochen. Died Aug. 7, 1906 Age 69. Linwood/Neal Cem.

(James) Wareen Neal Co. H. 16th Ill. Cav. 1849-May 23, 1934 Age 80. Linwood/Neal Cemetery.

W.C. Neale Co. F. 41st. Ill. Inf. Unit was in Battle of Shiloh, TN, Siege of Vicksburg, Consol. W/ 53rd Ill.: Campaign of the Carolinas, Buried in Almira Union / Green Briar Cemetery.

John W. Nedry 1814-1890 G.A.R. Marker Almira Union / Green Briar Cemetery.

D. O. (or C.) Page Co. C. / B? 2nd Conn. Heavy Artillery & 19th CT Cav. Died July 1896 Age 57. Linwood/Neal Cemetery.

Washington Paul Co. I. 9th IN Inf. Lake Ann, Andrew Clark G.A.R. Post 423 Commander.

David Plennon Co. C. 21st OH Inf. Lake Ann, Andrew Clark G.A.R. Post 423.

C. Roxbury 6th OH Cavalry. Lake Ann, Andrew Clark G.A.R. Post 423.

Oliver N. Segar Co.H. 10th NY Inf./Co.B. 8th NY H.A.Almira Twp.1843-1911 Lake Ann G.A.R. Post 423.

W. H. Sherman Co. J. 111th NY Inf. Lake Ann, Andrew Clark G.A.R. Post 423.

Collins C. Shilling Co. G. 21st OH 1843-1898 Cedar Run, Long Lake Oakwood Cemetery.

R.C. Shreeves Lake Ann, Andrew Clark G.A.R. Post 423.

Phillip F. Simmons Co. K. 11th IN Inf. Long Lake Twp.

George A. Sinclair Co. E. 29th OH Inf. Lake Ann, Andrew Clark G.A.R. Post 423

Isiah Skiver (Skiner) 9th IN Inf. Cedar Run, Long Lake. May 19, 1840-Feb. 10, 1923 Linwood/Neal Cem.

Joab Somers Co.L. 1st Iowa Vol. Cav. May 4, 1830-Feb. 2, 1913. Lake Ann Cemetery.

William Bruce Stewardt Co.A. 1st NY L.A. Oviatt, Benzie Co.1844-1910 Oakwood Cem. (John Stewart in Hannah Rifles, Harrison was in 5th MI Cav., William C. in 152nd NY.)

H.W. Stowe Co. B. 105th Ohio Vol. Inf. Post 423. Buried in Almira Union / Green Briar Cemetery.

John W. Tucker 1842-1905 Co. D. 7th NH Inf. Veterans Marker in Green Briar (Almira Union) Cem.

Charles Thomas Co. C. 144th NY Inf. Lake Ann, 1846-1934 Oakwood Cem. (See John in 1st MI SS.)

George Vallean Co. D. 7th OH Inf. Unit Battles of Winchester, Antietam, Chancellorsville, Gettysburg, New York Draft Riots, Chattanooga, Mission Ridge, Atlanta Campaigns, Trans. to 5th OH: March to the Sea, Carolinas. Buried in Almira Union / Green Briar Cemetery. (see Richard Valleau 10th MI Cav.).

Samuel Ward Co. D. 23rd OH Inf. b. Oct. 20, 1835 – d. Mar. 8, 1915 Veterans Marker in Green Briar (Almira Union) Cemetery.

James Wilson Long Lake Twp. 1894 Veterans Census.

Aligag Worner 53rd Ill. Inf. Lake Ann, Andrew Clark Post 423.

Elias Wyckoff Co. H. 161st NY Inf. Grayling Post 240, T.C. Post 18, Long Lake 1894. Oakwood Cemetery.

Misc. Surrounding Leelanau County (Partial Listings: Men possibly associated at times with Leelanau County, Alphabetical):[311]

A., B. & C.) Jordan Barr 15th & 16th MI Inf. Died in 1939 in MI Vet. Home. **John Boser/Baser**, Capt. **Silvester Beckwith** 1812-1891 Linwood cem.?, **George Cowen** Co. I. 54th Mass. Colored Inf. in Joyfield Cemetery, Benzie Co., **Calvin A. Carpenter** (Benzie Co.), **Mark W. Curtis** – T.C. McPherson G.A.R. **D., E. & F.) Lt. Henry Z. Eaton** Co.B. 7th OH Inf., Possibly **John Ellis** 23rd Ill.? in Almira., **Ernst?** right arm amputated April 13, 1865 from a battle before the surrender of Lee.[312] **James Fisher** 1822-1905 (Brother of John) served at the age of 41 in the 5th WS Vol. Inf. (pioneer **John E. Fisher** had served at the age of 21 from 1838-1841 on the Indian frontiers up-state NY. 8th U.S. Inf. Co. F.)

G., H. & I.) Jacob Maizen Hammer 26th MI, **Ed Hauly** possible matches under Hawly in 5th MI Cav. or 12th MI Inf. Almira Union Green Briar, **Herman Hilbert, Lorenzo P. Holden** Co. B. 15th MI Mackinaw City., **David Imes** Co. K. 5th U.S. Colored Troops in Joyfield Cemetery, Benzie Co.

J., K. & L.) Mrs. Leon Johnson of Empire was a slave until the age of 12, **Harry Lince** Co.K. 110th NY Inf. **M., N. & O.) Marshall McLouth** 26th MI, **Anton Meereis?** 1844-1908 (Solon)., **William Miner** Co.G. 35th WS Inf. was once listed with Leelanau County in error.

P., Q. & R.) Emile Rouget Co. B. 44th Ill. Age 38. Traverse City, Joined in Chicago Aug. 18, 1861., **S., T. & U.) Orriang Salisbury?** (Solon), **C. Saurins** Lake Ann G.A.R. Post 423, **Frank Scott** U.S. Reserves, **Simeon Townsend**, Capt. **J.H. Turrill** killed on the Battlefield of Antietam (of Elk Rapids), **V., W. X. Y. & Z.) George West, Henry Ziegler** Co.A. 82nd Ohio born ~ 1812. ....**and many, many others.**

Possible additional connections in the U.S. Navy included: **William Baxter, N.J. Brooks, Edward Campbell, Jacob Decker, George W. Dougherty, Earle S. Dunn, Thomas Fitch** (U.S.S. Grand Gulf), **David Gance** (MS Squadron/Pore/Choctaw), **John Goldsmith** (Able Seaman/Gulf Squadron/Sabine), **William Goldsmith, Hiram Hawkins, John Lutzinkisgan** (MS Squadron/Ozaski), **Joseph Manseau, Jas. Mason** (Porters/Juliete), **Alonzo and Charles Moore, Moses Nash, Thomas Porter, Orlando Pratt, John Reed, Andrew Rose, Alonzo Slater, Charles Wilcox,** and **Thomas Wright.**

Civil War records are notoriously incomplete and inaccurate. In part due to the lack of educational opportunities during that time period. There are also many more unmarked Civil War veteran's graves in Leelanau County including Glen Arbor, at least 7 in Northport, and Peshawbestown Cemeteries. This work is dedicated in part to the worthy Veterans that were **NOT** listed here. There were many, many men from our area who died in action and were not easily traced or who traveled elsewhere after the War and were not listed in any Michigan Census. My apology to those that were missed in this book. To add information for future editions, please write to the Author or send information copies to The Leelanau Historical Museum in Leland (203 E. Cedar St. 49654) or the Empire Area Museum (LaCore St. 49630). Please send these organizations copies of your family histories and photographs to be preserved. The State Archives in Lansing and the U.S. Army Military History Institute in Pennsylvania can also preserve your **original** military photographs in climate controlled conditions.

It is my sincere hope that interest from this book may help generate additional County Veterans Monuments, (including Old Settlers Park)., to honor ALL the veterans who served from Leelanau Co.

The prayer of St. Patrick's Breastplate was said to have been traditionally part of prayers in March (St. Patrick's Day) and around fall Harvest Bonfires at Halloween (old Celtic Traditions). It is listed here as a final tribute to the memory of our early pioneers.

I Bind myself to this day, the strong virtue of the Trinity, the Three in One, and One in Three. The Faith of the Trinity in Unity, The Creator of the Elements. I Bind myself of the great love... all good deeds done unto the Lord. I Bind myself to this day. The power of Heaven, The light of the sun, The whiteness of snow, The force of fire, The flashing of lightening, The swiftness of wind, The depth of sea, The stability of earth, The hardness of rocks... I Bind myself this day. The Power of God to guide me, The Might of God to uphold me, The Wisdom of God to teach me, The Eye of God to watch over me, The Ear of God to hear me, The Word of God to give me speech, The Hand of God to protect me, The Way of God to lie before me, The Shield of God to shelter me, The Host of God to defend me... Christ be with me, Christ within me, Christ behind me, Christ before me, Christ beside me, Christ to win me, Christ to comfort and restore me, Christ beneath me, Christ above me, Christ in quiet, Christ in danger, Christ in hearts of all that love me, Christ in mouth of friend and stranger. I Bind myself to the strong virtues of Christ. Of whom all nature has creation: Eternal Father, Spirit, Word. Praise to the Lord salvation, ... Salvation is of Christ the Lord.

Lyric Poem of the Civil War period by Mrs. W.L. Lyster of Detroit, MI - Michigan Pioneer & Historical Collections 1907 Vol. 35 pg. 155.

State Song : Michigan My Michigan

Home of my heart, I sing to thee!
Michigan, My Michigan,
Thy lake-bound shores I long to see,
Michigan, My Michigan,
FromSaginaw's tall whispering pines,
To Lake Superior's farthest mines,
Fair in the light of memory shines,
Michigan, My Michigan,

Thou gav'st thy sons without a sigh,
Michigan, My Michigan,
And sent thy bravest forth to die,
Michigan, My Michigan,
Beneath a hostile southern sky,
They bore thy banner proud and high, Ready to fight, but never fly,
Michigan, My Michigan,

From Yorktown on to Richmond's wall,
Michigan, My Michigan,
They bravely fight, as bravely fall,
Michigan, My Michigan,
To Williamsburgh we point with pride--
Our Fifth and Second, side by side,
There stemmed and stayed the battle's tide,
Michigan, My Michigan,

When worn with watching traitor foes,
Michigan, My Michigan,
The welcome night brought sweet repose,
Michigan, My Michigan,
The soldier, weary from the fight,
Sleeps sound, nor fears the rebels might,
For "Michigan's on guard to-night!"
Michigan, My Michigan,

Afar on Shiloh's fatal plain,
Michigan, My Michigan,
Again behold thy heroes slain,
Michigan, My Michigan,
"Their strong arms crunble in the dust,
And their bright swords have gathered rust,
Their memory is our sacred trust,"
Michigan, My Michigan,

And often in the coming years,
Michigan, My Michigan,
Some widowed mother'll dry her tears,
Michigan, My Michigan,
And turning with a thrill of pride,
Say to the children at her side,
At Antietam your Father died,
For Michigan, Our Michigan

With General Grant's Victorious name,
Michigan, My Michigan,
Thy sons still onward march to fame,
Michigan, My Michigan,
And foremost in the fight we see,
Where e'er the bravest dare to be,
The sabres of thy cavalry,
Michigan, My Michigan,

Dark rolled the Rappahannock's flood,
Michigan, My Michigan,
The tide was crimsoned with thy blood,
Michigan, My Michigan,
Although for us the day was lost,
Still it shall be our proudest boast:
At Fredericksburg our Seventh crossed!
Michigan, My Michigan,

And when the happy time shall come,
Michigan, My Michigan,
That brings thy war-worn heroes home,
Michigan, My Michigan,
What welcome from their own proud shore,
What honors at their feet, we'll pour,
What tears for those who'll come no more,
Michigan, My Michigan,

A grateful country claims them now,
Michigan, My Michigan,
and deathless laurel binds each brow,
Michigan, My Michigan,
And History the tale will tell,
Of how they fought and how they fell,
For that dear land they loved so well,
Michigan, My Michigan,

Grand Rapids resident makes cemetery his own special project

By BILL O'BRIEN
Record-Eagle staff writer

GLEN ARBOR — For years Leonard Overmyer III has been coming to the little cemetery off M-22 south of Glen Arbor, not to pay homage to ancestors buried there but to keep alive his ties to northern Michigan.

The 1982 Glen Lake grad, who now lives in Grand Rapids, travels every spring from his family farm near Copemish to rake and clear the old graveyard, sometimes placing flowers and flags at the headstones.

"I've been coming out to this place for 20 years," he said. "It was just kind of a tradition."

Overmyer first visited the old Glen Arbor Township cemetery when he was a teen-ager. His father showed him the graveyard one day during a hunting trip. It was overgrown with brush and covered with fallen trees.

"We cleaned it out," he said. "Since then, it's pretty much stayed the same."

Record-Eagle/Bill O'Brien

Former Glen Arbor resident Leonard Overmyer and his 2-year-old son Nathaniel share a tradition started by Leonard's father.

See **CEMETERY**, Page 2B ▶

Cemetery is
his pet project

◀ Continued from Page 1B

The cemetery is off Forest Haven Road, within the boundaries of the Sleeping Bear Dunes National Lakeshore. There hasn't been a burial there in decades. It was primarily used in the late 1800s and early this century for the white settlers of the Glen Arbor area.

Overmyer's attachment to the cemetery stems from his love of history and his hobby as an astute historical and genealogical researcher.

He looked up names listed on the gravestones and learned that two men buried there served in the Civil War.

One was Edmund Trumbull of the 14th Michigan Infantry, who served at the beginning of the war from Pittsburg Landing to Corinth, Farmington and operations in Alabama and Tennessee.

The other was Daniel Parker of the 15th Michigan Infantry. He served late in the war, and was part of Gen. William T. Sherman's march from Atlanta to the sea and participated in the Grand Review in Washington D.C., on May 24, 1865, making him part of the country's first Memorial Day observation.

Overmyer compiled one-page summaries of the service records of the two soldiers, had them laminated and attached them to flags at their gravestones so visitors can learn more about the men who are buried there.

"You always think that's somebody's dad or somebody's son out there," he said. "I think it makes you respect it a little more."

Overmyer has also done extensive genealogical research on his own family, tracing his roots to Bavaria in 1680.

His ancestors fought in the Revolutionary War and the French and Indian War. His grandfather is a World War II veteran, and his father served early in Vietnam War. While Overmyer didn't serve in the military, he has a deep respect for his family's military service, and he serves as a chaplain in the Sons of American Legion post in Eaton Rapids and is a member of the Sons of Amvets post in Mesick.

Overmyer is an engineer, and his wife Jill is an instructor at Grand Valley State University. They are still regular visitors to northern Michigan and hope they can someday move back to the area.

Until then, they'll stay close through their friends and family and the small graveyard where Overmyer makes his yearly pilgrimage. He hopes others in the immediate area also will keep an eye on the cemetery.

When he came this spring, he that saw several trees around the graveyard had been spray-painted with grafitti. None of the graves were desecrated, but Overmyer is concerned that a place of reverence and history could become a target for vandals.

MEMORIAL DAY

George M. Vickers

Like stars that sink into the west,
So one by one we seek our rest;
The column's brave and steady tread
With banners streaming overhead,
Will still keep step, as in the past,
Until the rear guard comes at last.

Ah, yes, like stars we take our flight,
And whisper, one by one, "Good night;"
Yet in the light of God's bright day,
Triumphant, each again will say,
"Hail, comrade, here has life begun,
The battle's fought, the victory's won!" [313]

---

[1] Al Barnes, *Supper In The Evening*, as referenced from M.L. Leach, (Philadelphia, PA: Dorrance & Company, 1967),14.

[2] Brig. Gen.Geo. H. Brown and the Michigan Legislature, *Michigan Soldiers and Sailors of the Record Of Service of Michigan Volunteers in the CivilWar 1861-1865* (Lansing, MI,1915).

[3] Bruce Catton, *Waiting for the Morning Train*, (Garden City, NY: Double Day & Company, Inc. 1972), 189-190.

[4] Al Barnes, *Vinegar Pie and Other Tales, of the Grand Traverse Region*, (Detroit, MI: Harlo – Detroit, 1971),105.

[5] George S. May, *Pictorial History of Michigan: The Early Years*, (Grand Rapids, MI: William B. Eeardmans Publishing Company, 1967),146.

[6] Elvin L. Sprague and Mrs. George N. Smith, *Sprague's History of Grand Traverse and Leelanaw Counties Michigan* (MI: B.F. Bowen Publisher, 1903), 333.

[7] Ethel Rowan Fasquelle, *When Michigan Was Young*, (Grand Rapids, MI: WM. B. Eerdmans Publishing Company, 1950), 141.

[8] Edmund M. Littell, *100 Years In Leelanau*, (Leland, MI: The Print Shop, 1965), 43.

[9] D. Taghon, *Remembering Empire Through Pictures*, (Empire, MI: Empire Township Historical Group, 1978). Passim.

[10] Julia Terry Dickinson, *The Story Of Leelanau*, (Omena, MI: Solle's Bookshop, 1951), 44.

[11] Steve Harold, *Shipwrecks Of The Sleeping Bear*, (Traverse City, MI: Pioneer Study Center, 1984), 1.

[12] Dickinson, 12.

[13] Catton, *Morning Train*, 15.

[14] Littell,, 11-12.

[15] Robert Dwight Rader, *Beautiful Glen Arbor Township, Facts, Fantasy & Fotos,* (Leelanau County, MI: Glen Arbor History Group, Village Press, 1977), 8-9.

[16] Ferna Frehse Walls, *Empire History Notes III*, (Empire, MI: Empire Township Heritage Group, July, 1979), 17.

[17] Sprague, 334.

[18] Littell, 34.

[19] Fasquelle, 134-139.

. [20] Dickinson, 9.

[21] Henry Schoolcraft, *Leelanau or The Lost Daughter*, An Odjibwa Tale; Larry Wakefield, *Postcard History, Early History of Leelanau County*, (Leland, MI: Leelanau Historical Society, 1992), 4.

[22] Dickinson, 8.

[23] Wakefield, 4.

[24] Ibid.

[25] Littell, 4.

[26] Sprague, 335.

[27] Littell, 12.

[28] Sprague, 335.

[29] *The Traverse Region Historical & Descriptive*, (Chicago, IL: H.R. Page & Co. 1884), 227.

[30] *Traverse Region...*, 354.

[31] Frank S. Fradd, *Empire History Notes II*, (Empire, MI: Empire Township Heritage Group, July, 1977), 18.

[32] Sprague, 337.

[33] *History of Leelanau Township* ed. L. Wakefield (Chelsa, MI: Book Crafters, Inc. 1982 Friends of the Leelanau Township Library), 29.

[34] St. Philip Neri Catholic Church, *St. Philip Neri Centennial Mass*, (Empire, MI: Oct. 22, 1995).

[35] Dickinson, 38.

[36] Sprague, 337.

[37] Grand Traverse Area Genealogical Society, *Kinship Tales*: Aug. 1988 from Grand Traverse Herald Nov. 12, 1896 p.5.

[38] Sprague, 349; & *Traverse Region*, 246; Bud Fisher 1973 Family Histories, Tawas City, MI.

[39] Walter Romig, *Michigan Place Names*, (Grosse Pointe, MI: Walter Romig- Publisher, 1972), 225.

[40] Charles F. Johnson, *A History of Old Settlements from Leelanau County*, (Grand Rapids, MI: 1993),19.

[41] Barnes, *Vinegar Pie and Other Tales*, 104-105.

[42] Radar, 79.

[43] S.E. Wait and W.S. Anderson, *Old Settlers*, (Traverse City, MI: S.E. Wait, 1918), 69-70.

[44] Littell, 58, based on Bohemian writing by Joseph Krubner in 1909.

[45] Robert Ellis Schrader, *Early Traverse City "Little Bohemia" Historical and Descriptive*, (Los Angeles, CA: Dockweiler Station, 1985), 183.

[46] *Traverse Region...*, 227; Dr. M.L. Leach, *A History of the Grand Traverse Region*, (Traverse City, MI: Grand Traverse Herald, 1883), 70-71.

[47] Sprague, 349.

[48] Passim, U.S. Census; Sprague; *Traverse Region*; Taghon; Radar.

[49] Radar, passim.

[50] Barnes, *Vinegar Pie and Other Tales*, 106.

[51] *Traverse Region*, passim.)

[52] Littell, 8.

[53] *Traverse Region...*, 230.

[54] Littell, 7.

[55] Dickinson, 15.

[56] See M.E.C. Bates and M.K.Buck, *Along Traverse Shores*, (Traverse City, MI: 1891).

[57] Barnes, *Supper in the Evening*, 7.

[58] Ibid. 8.

[59] Ulysses S. Grant, *Personal Memoirs of U.S. Grant*, Vol.I, 1885 (New York: Charles L. Webster & Company, 1886), 355-356.

[60] Michael Shaara, *The Killer Angels*, (New York: Ballantine Books, 1974), 21.

[61] *Grand Rapids Evening Press*, 20 June 1913, p.8. (Carl Bajema Collection, Grand Rapids Public Library).

[62] Grant, *Personal Memoirs..*, Vol.II, 572.

[63] Dr. Howard Peckham, *Chronological List of Battles Of The Civil War, Showing the Particular Michigan Units Involved*, Michigan Civil War Centennial Observance Commission, (Ann Arbor, MI: Clements Library, ~1961/1965), passim.

[64] Shelby Foote, *The Civil War: A Narrative, Red River to Appomattox*, (New York: Random House, 1974), 751-753; Jack K. Overmyer, *A Stupendous Effort: the 87th Indiana in the War of the Rebellion*, (Bloomington and Indianapolis, IN: Indiana University Press, 1997), 162-163.

[65] Albert Bigelow Paine, *Mark Twain's Notebook*, 1st. ed., (New York: Harper & Brothers Publishers, The Mark Twain Company, 1935), 174-190.

[66] Based on information from US Army Center of Military History, 1099 14th St. NW, Washington D.C. 20005-3402, and the Statistical Summaries of the U.S. Civil War Center, Louisiana State University, in Baton Rouge, LA 70803.

[67] Barnes, *Supper In The Evening*, 13.

[68] Lt. C. Stewart Peterson, *The Last Civil War Veteran In Each State*, (Baltimore, MD: 1951).

[69] Passim sources include: *Michigan Soldiers and Sailors of the Record Of Service of Michigan Volunteers in the CivilWar 1861-1865* Brig. Gen.Geo. H. Brown and the Michigan Legislature, Lansing, MI,1915; *Official Records of the Union and Confederate Armies* 1889 Washington Archives; *Michigan in the War* by John Robertson, Adj. General, (Lansing, MI: W.S. George & Co. State Printers and Binders, 1882), 354-359,716-729; Library of Congress; National Archives & Records Administration; Roy H. Steffens Military Records 1968 GTP&HS, (Original Roy H. Steffens sources included: Adjutant General Report Illinois, Report of Adjutant General Indiana, Adjutant General Report Iowa, Adjutant General Report Kansas, Michigan Volunteers 1861-1864, Adjutant General Report New Hamshire, Adjutant Generals Report New York, Muster Rolls New York State, Roster of Ohio Soldiers 1861-1865, History of Pennsylvania Volunteers, Wisconsin Volunteers 1861-1865.); Elvin L. Sprague and Mrs. George N. Smith, *Sprague's History of Grand Traverse and Leelanaw Counties Michigan* (MI: B.F. Bowen Publisher, 1903), 227-249; Preston M. Smith, *Partial Listing Of The Civil War Veterans From Leelanau County, Michigan*, (Omena, MI: January 1961); *Michigan Soldiers in the Civil War* by Frederick D. Williams 1960/1994 Bureau of Michigan History - Michigan Department of State; *The Traverse Region Historical & Descriptive* 1884 Chicago: H.R. Page & Co.; Don L. Harvey's *Michigan in the Civil War* WWW St.Clair, MI; State Library of Michigan, Michigan State Archives; Newspaper Archives of the Grand Traverse Herald; Ryerson Historical Room of the Grand Rapids Public Library; June 1894 Veterans Census of Michigan; Holdings of the Grand Valley State University Library; Leland Museum & Library, Leelanau Historical Society, *History of Leelanau Township* ed. L. Wakefield Chelsa, MI: Book Crafters, Inc. 1982 Friends of the Leelanau Township Library; Holdings of the: Northport Library; Empire Library; Traverse Area District Library; Burton Historical Collection of the Detroit Public Library; Osterlin Library of Northwestern Michigan College; Various other State Archives; *Remembering Yesterday* collected by Kasson Heritage Group 1976; *Remembering Empire Through Pictures* by Empire Township Historical Group 1978 D. Taghon; *Kinship Tales*: Grand Traverse Area Genealogical Society; Western Michigan University Historical Collection; Michigan Civil War Centennial Observance Commission, Graves Registration Committee Mrs. Donald T. Owen, State Chairman and Preston Smith, County Chairman; Bently Historical Library at University of Michigan; Clarke Library of Central Michigan University; Michigan State University Historical Collections; Grand Traverse Herald; Leelanau Enterprise; "The War, for those in the Traverse area," by Evelyn Tolley Buckingham (Brevard, NC: 1991); and *Frederick Dyer's Compendium of the War of the Rebellion* 1908 Torch Press / 1994 Republished Broadfoot Publishing, Morningside Press Wilmington, NC.

[70] William H. Powell, *Officers of the Army and Navy (Volunteer) Who served in the Civil War*, (Philadelphia, PA: 1893).

[71] W.W. Dickinson, "Camp Report of the Tenth Mich. Cavalry, Knoxville, TN, Feb. 22, 1865," *Grand Rapids Eagle*, 07 March 1865, p.2.

[72] John William Nichoson, *1865 Letters 10th MI Cavalry*, (Ann Arbor, MI: Bentley Historical Library, 1865).

[73] Reverand Henry Cherry, *Personal Letters June 25, 1865*, (Kalamazooo, MI: Western Michigan University Historical Collections, 1865).

[74] Primarily from: Brig. Gen.Geo.H.Brown and the Michigan Legislature, *Michigan Volunteers in the CivilWar 1861-1865*, (Lansing, MI,1915); John Robertson, Adj. General, *Michigan in the War*, (Lansing,

MI: W.S. George & Co. State Printers and Binders, 1882), 354-359,716-729; General L.S. Trowbridge, *A Brief History of the Tenth Michigan Cavalry*, (Detroit, MI; Friesema Bros. Printing Co. 1905), selected pictures.; *Official Records of the Union and Confederate Armies* 1889 Washington Archives; and other Passim sources, Ibid.

[75] *Grand Rapids Daily Eagle*, 13 May 1864, (Carl Bajema Collection, Grand Rapids Public Library).

[76] 1999 Saugatuck Interviews with Lou & Elizabeth Plummer, her mother Mrs. Esther Eddy Age 103 who was a daughter in-law to a Civil War veteran, Everard Thomas and Mrs. Mertile Stremler who lived across from Mjr. Will Dunn in Ganges in their youth, Barb Crandell, & other area Historians.

[77] Bill Kemperman and Elizabeth Plummer, Letters and Visits with members of the Saugatuck Historical Society, in 1999.

[78] Ibid; *Michigan Volunteers*, Vol. 40

[79] Rev. Leander Curtis, *Grand Traverse Herald*, (Traverse City, MI: December 16, 1864).

[80] *Empire History Notes V*, (Empire, MI: Empire Heritage Group, July 1982), 4.; Cici Morse, Great Granddaughter of Enslee Benoni Larue/LaRue, personal letter to Author, (Stockton,CA: 1999).

[81] Dr. M.L. Leach, *A History of the Grand Traverse Region*, (Traverse City, MI: 1883).

[82] U.S. Kasson Township Census of 1870; E.L. Hayes, *1881 Township Map*, (Philadelphia, PA: C.O. Titus, 27 South Sixth St.,1881), Empire Area Museum.

[83] Everard Thomas Age 87 of Saugatuck, MI who lived across from Capt. Dunn in Ganges, MI in his youth, from his Personal Collections of William H. Dunn.

[84] Passim sources; *Michigan Volunteers*, Vol. 15.

[85] Passim sources; *Michigan Volunteers*, Vol. 15; Michigan Pioneer and Historical Society, *Historical Collection, Collection and Researches*, Vol. XXXI, (Lansing, MI: 1901), 102; National Archives, *The Draft Book 1864*, #15 4th District Michigan, Vol. 2. (Washington, D.C. 1864) 134.

[86] *Grand Traverse Herald*, September 1864.

[87] John S. Dorsey, (Grandson of John Dorsey from youngest son, Volney) Personal letter to Author, (Empire, MI: June 24, 1999).

[88] Ibid.

[89] Gertrude Dorsey Coppens, *Empire History Notes 1*, (Empire, MI: Empire Heritage Group, July, 1973).

[90] Empire Area Heritage Group, *Some Other Day (Remembering Empire)*, (Empire, MI: 1974), 8.

[91] Obituary copy from John S. Dorsey, Empire, MI Thursday, April 16, 1903).

[92] *Grand Traverse Herald*, Sept, 17, 1891 Obituary written by William H. Crowell, Miles A. Densmore, Sam Holsted, and J.W. Dickerman of G.A.R. Post 168.

[93] National Archives, *The Draft Book 1864*, #15 4th District Michigan, Vol. 2. (Washington, D.C. 1864) 134; Letter from Donald Pratt June 19, 1999.

[94] *Traverse Region...*, 233.

[95] Passim; *Michigan Volunteers, Grand Traverse Herald*.

[96] Morgan Bates, ed. *Grand Traverse Herald*, (Traverse City, MI: Sept. 5, 1862).

[97] Chas. A. Gunn, Feb. 4, 1863 Alexandria, VA Civil War Letter donated by Eleanor Wilson & Joyce Beck, (Clarke Historical Library, Central Michigan University).

[98] Passim; *Michigan In The War*, 296.

[99] Preston M. Smith, *Some Letters and A Short Diary of Joshua Middleton*, (Leland, MI: Leelanau Historical Museum Collections, 1864-1865).

[100] Grant, *Personal Memoirs...*, 204.

[101] Bruce Catton, *A Stillness at Appomattox*, (New York: DoubleDay, 1953), 127.

[102] Smith, *...Middleton*, Ibid.

[103] Ibid.

[104] Passim sources; *Michigan In The War; Official Records; Michigan Volunteers*, Vol. 26.

[105] Ibid.

[106] *Some Other Day*, 4.

[107] Donald F. Dechow, *Our Family*, (Elkhart, IN: Heirloom Publishing, Co. 1995), 41.

[108] Eula Martin, *Summary Of John Dago's Civil War Service*, (National Archives, Washington, D.C. 1981), as referenced in *Our Family*, 41-43.

[109] Dechow, *Our Family*, Ibid; John Dago Civil War Letter from 1864; Fred & Rose Dechow Info.

[110] Kasson Heritage Group, *Remembering Yesterday*, (Maple City, MI: Kasson Heritage Group, 1976),30-31.

[111] Dechow, *Our Family*, passim.

[112] Passim sources; *Official Records; Michigan Volunteers*, Vol. 26.

[113] *History of Leelanau Township*, ed. L. Wakefield, (Leland & Chelsea, MI: Friends of the Leelanau Township, Book Crafters, Inc. 1982), 65-66.

[114] *Traverse Region...*, 233.

[115] Beatrice Bowen, *History of Leelanau Township*, ed. L. Wakefield, (Leland & Chelsea, MI: Friends of the Leelanau Township, Book Crafters, Inc. 1982), 61.

[116] *History of Leelanau Township*, 50.

[117] Byron Woolsey, *A Reminiscence*, (Leland, MI: Leelanau Historical Museum Collections, 1873; Charlotte Giltner, *Early Death Records of Leelanau Co., Michigan*, (Leland, MI: Leelanau Historical Museum Collections, Book I, Pg.1-64, 1867-1887).

[118] *Traverse Region...*, 234.

[119] Philip Payment, *Empire History Notes 1*, (Empire, MI: Empire Heritage Group, July, 1973) 6.

[120] Passim sources; *Official Records; Michigan Volunteers*, Vol. 26.

[121] Laura Lindley, *Our First Families*, (Michigan, 1954), 38.

[122] Bowen, Ibid.

[123] *Traverse Region...*, 234.

[124] Jacque Palmer, *Palmer Family with Leelanau County Connections*, (Leelanau Historical Museum, J. Palmer, B. Macksey Printer, June 1998).

[125] Bowen, Ibid.

[126] Byron Woolsey, *Reminiscent Sketch Book*; Bowen, Ibid.

[127] Passim sources; *Official Records; Michigan Volunteers*, Vol. 26.

[128] *Grand Traverse Herald*, May, 1865.

[129] *Grand Traverse Herald*, April, 1864.

[130] Michigan Volunteers; Francis Hall, *Obituary Transcripts Michigan Veterans 1898-1939*, (Ryerson Historical Room, Grand Rapids, MI: Public Library).

[131] Laurence M. Hauptman, *Between the Fires: American Indians in the Civil War*, (New York, NY: The Free Press, 1995), passim 126-138; *Official Records; Michigan Volunteers*, Vol. 44.

[132] Passim sources; *Michigan In The War;Official Records; Michigan Volunteers*, Vol. 44

[133] Hauptman, Ibid.

[134] Passim sources; *Michigan In The War;Official Records; Michigan Volunteers*, Vol. 44.

[135] Passim sources; *Official Records; Michigan Volunteers*, Vol. 44.

[136] Minnie Dubbs Milbrook, *Twice Told Tales of Michigan and Her Soldiers in the Civil War*, F. Clever Bald, Chairman., (Lansing, MI: Michigan Civil War Centennial Committee, 1961), 48.

[137] Raymond J. Herek, *These Men Have Seen Hard Service: The First Michigan Sharpshooters in the Civil War*, (Wayne State University Press, MI: 1998), 61; *Official Records; Michigan Volunteers*, Vol. 44.

[138] Ibid.

[139] Ibid.

[140] Bowen, *History of Leelanau Township*, 61-62; passim sources.

[141] Bowen, *History of Leelanau Township*, 62; passim sources.

[142] Bowen, *History of Leelanau Township*, 61; passim sources.

[143] Bowen, *History of Leelanau Township*, 62; passim sources

[144] Herek, Ibid.

[145] Bowen, Ibid.

[146] Ibid.

[147] Ken Stormer, Obituaries and letter of family information to Author. (Lake Ann, MI:1999).

[148] Harek, Ibid.

[149] *History of Leelanau Township*, 51.

[150] Passim sources; *Official Records; Michigan Volunteers*, Vol. 44.

[151] Harek, Ibid.

[152] Passim sources; *Michigan Volunteers.*

[153] Charles Moore, *History of Michigan*, (Chicago: The Lewis Publishing Company, 1915), 429-431.

[154] Mattew C. Switlik, "Loomis' Battery First Michigan Light Artillery 1859-1865," (Wayne State University, MI 1975), 14.

[155] Evening News Association, *Men of Progress*, (Detroit, MI: Press of John F. Eby & Co. 1900), 24.

[156] May, 139.

[157] Passim sources; Roy H. Steffens, *Grand Traverse Pioneer & Historical Group Collections.*

[158] Lawrence Wakefield, *All Our Yesterdays*, (Traverse City, MI: Village Press, 1977), 52-53.

[159] Hayes, Ibid.

[160] *Traverse Region...*, 235.

[161] *Traverse Region...*, 238.

[162] Dickinson, 36.

[163] Kasson Heritage..., 22-23; Passim sources.

[164] Frederick D. Williams, *Michigan Soldiers in the Civil War* (Lansing, MI: Bureau of Michigan History - Michigan Department of State, 1960/1994), 12.

[165] Passim sources; *Michigan Voluteers*, Vol. 4.

[166] Luther S. Trowbridge, *Archives Letter #338, July 7, 1863*, (Ann Arbor, MI: Bentley Historical Library, University of Michigan, 1863).

[167] Moore, 434.

[168] Edward G. Longacre, *Custer and His Wolverines, The Michigan Cavalry Brigade, 1861-1865*, (PA: Combined Publishing, 1997), passim.

[169] Moore, 429.

[170] Sylvia Kruger, *German Settlement / Burials on South Manitou Island, Michigan*, (Lansing, MI: Michigan Dept. of State, Board of Education, 1982), 16-20.

[171] *Grand Traverse Herald*, March 1865.

[172] Marre J. Eckerle, *Michigan Civil War Prisoners Buried In Andersonville National Cemetery, Michigan Heritage Magazine*, (Kalamazoo, MI: Dr. Ethel W. Williams, Ed. Vol. VI No. 1, 1964) 11.

[173] Ibid.

[174] Ibid.; Leonard G. Overmyer III, *Family Pride: Generations of Service to God & Country Since 1751, Obermayer – Overmyer*, (Copemish, MI: 1997).

[175] Edward G. Longacre, *Custer and His Wolverines, The Michigan Cavalry Brigade 1861-1865*, (Conshohocken, PA: Combined Publishing, 1997), 294.

[176] *Empire History Notes VI*, (Empire, MI: Empire Heritage Group, July 1983), 6.

[177] Frank S. Fradd, *Empire History Notes II*, (Empire, MI: Empire Heritage Group, July, 1977), 4.

[178] Stormer, *Marvin LaCore Obituary*, passim.

[179] Harold Rohr and Dave Taghon, *Harold Rohr Remembers Empire...in the good old days*, (Empire, MI: Empire Heritage Group, 1997), 2.

[180] F.W. Herves, *History of the Tenth Regiment*, (Detroit, MI: John Slater's Book and Job Printing Establishment, 1884), 138.

[181] Alfred H. Van Vliet and W.B. Thompson, *27th Annual reunion Eleventh Michigan Volunteer Cavalry*, (Benton Harbor, MI: 1912), 3-20.

[182] Frederick D. Williams, *Michigan Soldiers in the Civil War*, 3rd ed. (Lansing, MI: Bureau of Michigan History, Michigan Department of State, 1994), 62.

[183] T. Rich, *History of the Michigan Organizations at Chickamauga, Chattanooga, and Missionary Ridge 1863*, (MI Legislature 1899), passim.

[184] Leelanau Enterprise, Vol. XVI No. 31, Thursday May 18, 1893

[185] Paula (Price) Radont, Great Granddaughter of Edmund Trumbull, Joseph Price and Great, Great Niece to William Kellogg, Family information, Letter to Author, (Jackson, MI: 1999).

[186] Passim, *Michigan Volunteers 1861-1865*, Record of 16th MI Inf. Vol. 16, p. 106; Record of 1st MI Col. Inf. Vol. 46, p.3.

[187] Passim sources; Steffens, Ibid.

[188] Ida C. Brown, *Michigan Men in the Civil War*, Bulletin No. 9. ed. Dr. Richard M. Doolen, (Lansing, MI: Michigan Historical Collection / Bentley Library), 1959; William Houghton, *Civil War*

Letter from Savannah Valley Nov. 22, 1864, (Ann Arbor, MI: Bentley Historical Library, University of Michigan, 1864).

[189] See passim sources.

[190] Ferna Frehse Walls, *Empire History NotesIII, The Settlement of Aral*, (Empire, MI: Empire Heritage Group, July, 1979), 17.

[191] Julia Terry Dickinson and Dorothy Joan Bolton, *The Boizard Letters: Letters from a Pioneer Homestead*, (Empire, MI: Empire Heritage Group, 1993), 50.

[192] Ibid. 59.

[193] *Muster Rolls New York State* Vol. 7 p. 394; *Adjutant General's Report New York* p. 492.

[194] *Michigan Voluteers*, Vol. 15.

[195] *Adjutant Generals Report New York*, Vol. 27 p.219.

[196] Rohr and Taghon, 2.

[197] *The Roster of Union Soldiers 1861-1865 New York*, Janet B. Hewett, ed. (Wilmington, NC: Broadfoot Publishing Company, 1997), 315-316.

[198] *History of Pennsylvania Volunteers*, Vol. 1, p.768

[199] Nan Helm, *Footprints Where Once They Walked*, (Glen Lake, MI: Printing ~1959-1977?), 3.

[200] *Adjutant Generals Report New York*, p. 840; Steffens Ibid.

[201] *Empire History Notes VI*, (Empire, MI: Empire Heritage Group, July, 1983), 19.

[202] *Adjutant Generals Report Illinois*, Vol. 2, p.20

[203] *Traverse Region...*, 248.

[204] *Adjutant General's Report Kansas*, p.442; Steffens ibid.

[205] Steffins, Ibid.

[206] *Roster of Wisconsin Volunteers*, p.54.

[207] Empire Area Heritage Group, *Empire Village Leader - Journal Centennial Edition*, (Traverse City Record-Eagle June 30, 1995), 2.

[208] Rohr and Taghon, 2.

[209] *Traverse Region...*, 235; *Adjutant Generals Report New York*, Vol. 15, p.130

[210] *Muster Rolls New York State*, Vol. 4, p.29

[211] *Adjutant Generals Report New York*, Vol. 42, p.377

[212] Bertha Werbinski & Mike Sheridan, Sheridan Great Grandchildren, Correspondence with Author, (Glen Arbor/Traverse City, MI: 1999).

[213] Radar, 39.

[214] R.L. Polk, *Michigan State (Polk) Gazeteer*, (MI, R.L. Polk & Co. 1875). Passim.

[215] Charles Fisher, *Leelanau Enterprise*, Vol. XVIII No.8, Thursday Dec. 6, 1894.

[216] *Adjutant Generals Report New York*, p.828; Steffens Ibid.

[217] Discharge Papers of William Sheridan 1862, 1864.

[218] *Wisconsin Volunteers 1861-1865*, p.938; Steffens Ibid; Smith Ibid.

[219] *Traverse Region...*, 248.

[220] *Roster of Wisconsin Volunteers*, p. 770.

[221] Dickinson and Bolton, *The Boizard Letters*, 114-115.

[222] Radar, 26.

[223] Barnes, *Vinegar Pie and Other Tales*, 105.

[224] *Adjutant Generals Report Illinois*, Vol. 6, p.498

[225] Donald and Ray Welch, Personal letter to Author, June 24, 1999.

[226] Preston M. Smith, *A Partial Listing of the Civil War Veterans from Leelanau County, Michigan*, (Omena, MI: January 1961), passim.

[227] Roger Van Noord, *Assassination Of A Michigan King, The Life of James Jesse Strang*, (Ann Arbor, MI: The University of Michigan Press, 199?), 267-274.

[228] See passim sources.

[229] *Adjutant Generals Report Illinois*, Vol. 1, p.399.

[230] *Traverse Region...*, 236.

[231] Littell, 71.

[232] *Adjutant Generals Report New York*, Vol. 27, p.209

[233] See passim sources.

[234] Kasson Heritage...,27; Passim sources.

[235] *Roster Of Ohio Soldiers 1861-66*, Vol. 5, p.419

[236] *Roster Of Ohio Soldiers 1861-66*, Vol. 8, p.423

[237] *Traverse Region...*, 249.

[238] Evelyn Tolley Buckingham, *"The War" for those in the Traverse area*, (Brevard, NC: TB Enterprises, 1991).

[239] *Traverse Region...*, 237.

[240] *Traverse Region...*, 238.

[241] *Traverse Region...*, 237.

[242] Kasson Heritage...,41; Passim sources.

[243] Roy H. Steffins, Last Post 168 GAR Report May 25, 1913, Michigan Archives June 9, 1968.

[244] *Roster Of Ohio Soldiers 1861-66*, Vol. 6, p.232

[245] *Traverse Region...*, 236.

[246] *Traverse Region...*, 237; *Adjutant Generals Report Illinois*, Vol. 3, p.234

[247] Kasson Heritage...,40; Passim sources.

[248] *Adjutant Generals Report Illinois*, Vol. 8, p.641

[249] Kasson Heritage..., 9; Passim sources.

[250] Johnson, 24.

[251] Paula (Price) Radont, Ibid.

[252] *Roster Of Ohio Soldiers 1861-66*, Vol. 5, p.60

[253] *Adjutant Generals Report Illinois*, Vol. 6, p.502

[254] A.S. Fritz, *Leelanau Enterprise*, Vol. XVIII, Thursday Nov. 15, 1894.

[255] Kasson Heritage Group, 16.

[256] *Roster Of Ohio Soldiers 1861-66*, Vol. 2, p.417

[257] Steffens, Ibid.

[258] *Adjutant General's Report Iowa 1865*, Vol. 1, p.569

[259] *Traverse Region...*, 237.

[260] *Roster Of Ohio Soldiers 1861-66*, Vol. 7, p.522

[261] Carol Drzewiecki, *History of Solon*, (Cedar, MI: 1999-2001) #954; Letter held by Arthur L. Miller; Order Book of the 103rd Ohio Regiment, *Gov. Todd Letters, Col. Casement & court martial reply Feb. 6, 1863*, (Ohio State Archives and Historical Society Library, Columbus, OH. 11-12,71; Western Reserve Historical Library, Cleveland, OH; Library of Congress, National Archives, Washington, D.C.)

[262] Romig, 522.

[263] *Adjutant Generals Report New Hampshire*, p. 665

[264] Catton, *Appomattox*, 333.

[265] *Grant Traverse Evening Record*, (May 25, 1907); Drezewicki, *History of Solon*, # 112, ibid.

[266] *Adjutant Generals Report Illinois*, Vol. 6, p.440

[267] *Traverse Region...*, 237.

[268] Sprague 522-523; Drzewiecki, *History of Solon*, # 33, ibid.

[269] *Official Roster of the Soldiers of the State of Ohio in the War of the Rebellion, 1861-1866*; Vol. VII, 522.

[270] *Roster Of Ohio Soldiers 1861-66*, Vol. 8, p.396

[271] *Leelanau Enterprise*, Nov. 7, 1895.

[272] *Report Of Adjutant General Illinois*; Steffens Ibid.

[273] *Adjutant Generals Report New York*, p.636; Steffens Ibid.

[274] *Adjutant Generals Report Illinois*, Vol. 8, p.641

[275] *Wisconsin Volunteers 1861-1865*, p. 100

[276] *Adjutant Generals Report New York*, Vol. 3, p.704

[277] *Wisconsin Volunteers 1861-1865*, p. 503

[278] *Illinois Adjutant General's Report*, Vol. 3, p.188

[279] U.S. Department of the Interior, *War Department Records, Bureau Of Pensions*, Washington D.C. 1894 from the National Archives and Records Service 1861-1865.

[280] Passim sources; Carol Ann (Drew) Sanctorum & Joseph M. LaVanture, Additional information from various family correspondence with Author in 1999.

[281] *Adjutant Generals Report New York*, Vol. 42, p.737

[282] *History of Pennsylvania Volunteers*, Vol. 2, p.111

[283] *Adjutant Generals Report New York*, Vol. 5, p.628

[284] *Roster Of Ohio Soldiers 1861-66*, Vol. 4, p.80

[285] *Adjutant Generals Report New York*, Vol. 30; Steffens Ibid.

[286] Captain John McAnally, *How The 164th New York Lost Its Colors*, from *Under Both Flags, A Panorama of the Great Civil War*, (C.R. Graham, Veteran Publishing Company, 1896), 302-303.

[287] *Wisconsin Volunteers 1861-1865*, p. 244

[288] *Roster of Wisconsin Volunteers*, p. 37.

[289] Catton, *Appomattox*. 95-98.

[290] *Report of Adjutant General Indiana 1861-66*, Vol. 4, p.35

[291] *Report of Adjutant General Indiana 1861-66*, Vol. 7, p.246

[292] *Adjutant Generals Report New York*; Steffens Ibid; Smith Ibid.

[293] *Adjutant Generals Report New York*, Vol. 2, p.320; Steffens Ibid.

[294] (There were also men named both Murray and Wagner in the 15th MI and 26th MI Infantry that were both killed in action. Though the first Murray was killed before the men from Glen Lake joined the 15th MI and none of the original charter members were from the 26th MI.; There were two families listed in the pre-war 1860 Census of Leelanau Township: John Murray, Farmer age 23, and George Murray, Sailor age 22, that may have later served in the war; There was a boat tragedy in the area during the late 1800's that involved people by the name of Murray; There was also a James L. Murray (Bat. E. 1st Ill. L.A.) over in Elmwood Township; It may also have been a later member of the community).

[295] See passim sources; Michigan Archives; Steffens ibid.

[296] *Traverse Region...*, 234-235.

[297] *History of Leelanau Township*, 250.

[298] *Traverse Region...*, 234

[299] *Traverse Region...*, 234

[300] *Traverse Region...*, 234

[301] *Traverse Region...*, 234-235.

[302] See passim sources; U.S. Census; Michigan Archives, Steffens Ibid; Smith Ibid.

[303] Preston Smith, Ibid.

[304] Joseph Littell, *Leland – An Historical Sketch - Antoine Manseau*, (Indianapolis Printing Company, Feb. 1920), 26.

[305] *Leelanau Enterprise*, (No.50 Vol. XV Thursday Sept. 29, 1892) 3?

[306] Preston Smith, Ibid.

[307] *Traverse Region...*, 602.

[308] Sprague, 797; Donna Stiffler Bollinger, Heritage Of Grand Traverse Bay: The City and Its People, (Traverse City, MI: Village Press, 1975), 80.

[309] Preston Smith, Ibid.

[310] Preston Smith, Ibid.

[311] See passim sources; U.S. Census; Michigan Archives.

[312] Lindley, 39.

[313] George M. Vickers, from *Under Both Flags, A Panorama of the Great Civil War*, (C.R. Graham, Veteran Publishing Company, 1896), 127.

Forest Haven Soldiers: The Civil War Veterans of Sleeping Bear & Surrounding Leelanau

Placing Flags on Memorial Weekend 1994 in the old Glen Arbor Cemetery
(Photo by Jill R. Overmyer)

Forest Haven Soldiers: The Civil War Veterans of Sleeping Bear & Surrounding Leelanau by Leonard G. Overmyer III.

Growing up hearing about the histories of our family inspired a desire to research more about the events that took place in our past. This led to a compilation of family history that dated back to the time of the French & Indian and Revolutionary War, (Captain John George Obermayer / Overmyer of Northumberland and Union Co. Pennsylvania). The experience I gained gathering family history I now like to put to use as time allows on special projects for my community. "Forest Haven Soldiers" is the result of a special desire to record this type of information about these very brave souls and to remember that **what we are in the present, is a result of who we were in the past.** - Leonard G. Overmyer III

THE
GIFT *of a* HOME

Dorothy Hamilton

Illustrated by
Edwin B. Wallace

Herald Press
Scottdale, Pennsylvania
1974

Library of Congress Cataloging in Publication Data

Hamilton, Dorothy, 1906-
    The gift of a home.

    SUMMARY: Tim's family adopts a new and more expensive life-style and
gradually begins to fall apart.
    [1. Family problems — Fiction] I. Wallace, Edwin B., illus. II. Title.
PZ7.H18136Gi   [Fic]   73-13989
ISBN 0-8361-1727-1

THE GIFT OF A HOME
Copyright © 1974 by Herald Press, Scottdale, Pa. 15683
Library of Congress Catalog Card Number: 73-13989
International Standard Book Number: 0-8361-1727-1
All rights reserved.
Printed in the United States of America
Designed by Alice B. Shetler